AUG 19

D1029576

TEXAS FLOOD

TEXAS FLOOD

THE INSIDE STORY OF

STEVIE RAY VAUGHAN

Alan Paul and Andy Aledort

ST. MARTIN'S PRESS ⚏ NEW YORK

First published in the United States by St. Martin's Press,
an imprint of St. Martin's Publishing Group

TEXAS FLOOD. Copyright © 2019 by Alan Paul and Andy Aledort. Foreword copyright
© 2019 by Chris Layton. Afterword copyright © 2019 by Tommy Shannon. All rights
reserved. Printed in the United States of America. For information, address St. Martin's
Publishing Group, 120 Broadway, New York, NY 10271.

www.stmartins.com

Designed by Ellen Cipriano

LIBRARY OF CONGRESS CATALOGING-IN-PUBLICATION DATA

Names: Paul, Alan, 1966– author. | Aledort, Andy, author.
Title: Texas flood : the inside story of Stevie Ray Vaughan / Alan Paul and
　Andy Aledort.
Description: First edition. | New York : St. Martin's Press, 2019. | Includes
　index.
Identifiers: LCCN 2018055443| ISBN 9781250142832 (hardcover) |
　ISBN 9781250142849 (ebook)
Subjects: LCSH: Vaughan, Stevie Ray. | Guitarists—United States—Biography. |
　Blues musicians—United States—Biography.
Classification: LCC ML419.V25 P39 2019 | DDC 787.87/166092 [B]—dc23
LC record available at https://lccn.loc.gov/2018055443

Our books may be purchased in bulk for promotional, educational, or business use.
Please contact your local bookseller or the Macmillan Corporate and Premium Sales
Department at 1-800-221-7945, extension 5442, or by email at
MacmillanSpecialMarkets@macmillan.com.

First Edition: August 2019

10　9　8　7　6　5　4　3　2　1

*To our wives and kids, who share us with the music
and support us every day in every way.*

Rebecca, Jacob, Eli, and Anna
—*Alan Paul*

Tracey, Rory, and Wyatt
—*Andy Aledort*

CONTENTS

FOREWORD

Twelve years on the clock doesn't seem like a long time at this point in my life, but playing with Stevie Ray Vaughan during that span of time provided me the greatest education I ever could have received, both as a musician and as a person learning to navigate life's many challenges.

The intent of what we were doing never changed from the time I joined Stevie in 1978 until his tragic death in 1990, whether we were jamming in dive bars as a duo, or the years on the road in a van with Double Trouble, to eventually touring arenas around the world. Everything we did as a group was based around Stevie's fierce dedication to always giving it his all. The single-minded devotion we all shared helped to guide us through all of the low points and the dark days.

Stevie was a sheer force of desire, seemingly incapable of giving anything less than 100 percent every time he picked up the guitar. His intent was exactly the same whether he was alone in the back of the bus, sitting with the two of us in a hotel room, onstage at Carnegie Hall, or in front of 115,000 people at the Chicago Blues Festival. The statement was, "Don't do it unless you are going to do it with everything you've got." That was apparent from the very first time I ever saw him play. He always seemed to be emotionally and spiritually in the music *right now,* which fascinated me. It's what attracted me to him and made me know that I wanted to play with him, period.

I had never played blues before, and Stevie actually liked that. He said, "There are a lot of things about you I really admire. Maybe I've got something I can give to you, too." I told him I had a feeling that great things could happen if we could work together, not knowing anything other than that. The thought of it all was exciting.

Stevie reached people profoundly because of the feeling and the emotion that he communicated. It was something that was truly mystical and baffling; he hooked the listeners and pulled them close. This was something that Tommy and I, and later Reese, understood without discussion.

Stevie's untimely death was tragic for me and for many others. Dying in the prime of his life put a stamp in time that can't exist any other way. Something precious and rare was lost, and there's an enduring curiosity about what might have been. I, too, can only wonder what the future would have held.

Being involved in the writing of *Texas Flood* gave me a lot of insight into my own history and the life that we all shared together. I hope this book will give you a deeper understanding of who Stevie was as a person, as an artist, and as a friend.

—Chris Layton, Double Trouble drummer
Austin, Texas

AUTHORS' NOTE

Unless otherwise noted, all quotes in this book came from interviews conducted by one or both of us. The only exception are the quotes from Cutter Brandenburg, which were adapted from his memoir, *You Can't Stop a Comet*, with permission from his son Robert.

Texas Flood represents three decades of work for two writers and musicians who have dedicated our lives to understanding and spreading the gospel of the music we love, music which has been at the very center of our lives. As important as Stevie Ray Vaughan has been to each of us, we came to his music from slightly different routes.

ALAN PAUL

I didn't "get" Stevie Ray Vaughan when I first heard him because I was a young, dumb blues snob, and, like all snobs I was oblivious. I thought Stevie was too loud, too rocked up, and, frankly, too white to be legitimate. But a funny thing happened as I began meeting and interviewing my blues heroes: one by one, they told me how great Stevie Ray was. I heard it from Albert King, Buddy Guy, Albert Collins, and Johnny Copeland. Eventually, this blind man saw the light. Then I smacked myself for not having been in the front row of every one of his shows within a hundred miles of me.

I went in deep, and was fortunate enough to see Stevie and his brother Jimmie play together at the 1990 New Orleans Jazz & Heritage Festival.

They were terrific together, and I looked forward to their upcoming album, *Family Style*. I was in the middle of begging magazines to let me interview the Vaughans when I heard the horrible news of Stevie's death at Alpine Valley. A few months later I started working at *Guitar World*, which gave me an opportunity to further immerse myself in Stevie's music, even though it often filled me with sadness; his absence was profound, a ghostly presence hovering over many of my interviews and interactions with guitarists who missed him dearly.

When Jimmie launched his solo career a few years later with *Strange Pleasure*, I found solace in the joyful, swinging music. It was proof that music can overcome grief. Lengthy interviews with Jimmie around his album release and the tribute concert he organized for his brother helped me begin to understand him, and to form a vision of who Stevie really was. I was honored when he asked me to contribute writing to two great releases: 1996's *A Tribute to Stevie Ray Vaughan* and 2000's *SRV* box set. It was clear from our first interview how difficult yet important it was for Jimmie to talk about Stevie. His insights are at the heart of this book, for which we are deeply appreciative.

Stevie continued to have an outsized pull on me when I moved to Beijing in 2005. During my time there, I hired a young musician named Woodie Wu to repair one of my guitars. As we spoke, I saw familiar letters poking out from under his shirt and asked if I could see his tattoo; he pulled up his sleeve to reveal the letters SRV sitting beneath Stevie's face, which covered his left triceps. He had bought a cassette of *Texas Flood* as a teenage metalhead, drawn to the gunslinger on the cover. He had never heard of the blues and didn't know where Texas was, but the music flipped his world upside down.

I couldn't believe I had found a Chinese blues guitarist with a tattoo of Stevie. He couldn't believe the guy who wrote liner notes for his favorite musician had walked into his shop in a Beijing suburb. We became soul mates, formed a band that toured China and changed each other's lives in too many ways to count. I credit Stevie.

Pondering a follow-up to my book *One Way Out: The Inside History of the Allman Brothers Band*, I knew it had to be about someone whose music had impacted me in a similar manner and whose story I found equally compelling. It had to be Stevie, and I knew that to do this right, I had to partner with my friend and *Guitar World* colleague Andy Aledort, who interviewed Stevie four times and had spent decades immersed in the music. I believe that working together, we have truly presented the inside story of Stevie Ray Vaughan. May Stevie's music continue to inspire people from one end of the earth to the other.

ANDY ALEDORT

There are some musicians that you never forget the very first time you heard them play. Robert Johnson and B.B. King, Jimi Hendrix and Charlie Parker, the Beatles and Ornette Coleman are all that way for me. The memory of hearing each one of these visionary artists for the very first time is so vivid— I will never forget exactly where I was and the circumstances surrounding that initial introduction and the impact that it had on me. Experiences like these leave an indelible mark. Stevie Ray Vaughan is one of the musicians on this list.

In the spring of 1983, I was at my mother's house and there was a radio playing softly in the background. A new David Bowie song had come on, "Let's Dance." I wasn't really paying attention to it at all—until the guitar solo. I stopped in my tracks and thought, *"What is this?!* Albert King is playing on a David Bowie record?" The completely unexpected juxtaposition of pure blues intensity over what was essentially a disco/ new wave track was startling, and sounded totally new. As disparate as these two musical styles seemed to be, the combination was brilliant and powerful.

I soon found out that it was a new guitar player named Stevie Ray Vaughan. And as Alan and I discovered in the writing of this book, that unforgettable impact of the very first time hearing Stevie play is one shared by just about everyone we spoke to, from his fellow musicians to the people that would become his closest friends, as well as his musical compatriots in Double Trouble—Tommy Shannon, Chris Layton, and Reese Wynans. All three have vivid memories of that very first moment they heard him play and the impact it had on them.

Shortly after hearing "Let's Dance," I picked up Stevie's debut album,

Texas Flood, and I immediately felt a kinship to his playing and his music. Stevie was about a year older than me and I could hear so many of the same influences in his playing that I had in my own. Along with the musical DNA of the big blues heroes Albert, B. B., Freddie King and T-Bone Walker, the album's final track, "Lenny," revealed the distinct influence of Jimi Hendrix. But there was something else about Stevie's playing that really set him apart: there was a precision in everything that he did that was flawless. And that precision was delivered with an intensity of emotion and a guitar tone that was just beautiful. Another important aspect was that *Texas Flood* sounded like what it was: a three-piece band playing live in the studio with no overdubs. It was about as direct and pure as a record could ever be. The power, the drive, and the focus of Stevie and of the band was undeniable.

Less than a year later, in early 1984, I saw Stevie Ray Vaughan and Double Trouble for the first time, at My Father's Place, a Long Island club that held just over three hundred people and was packed to the gills. Stevie had just finished recording his second album, *Couldn't Stand the Weather*, though it would be a few more months before the record's release. At this point, *Texas Flood* was the only album on the market. Stevie's performance that night was truly phenomenal. Three things struck me immediately: He played the guitar with the natural ease of breathing; his tone—and it was *LOUD*—was the greatest live Stratocaster tone I had ever heard; and his vibrato was absolutely perfect. With his head held down for most of the time, at one point he peeked up for a moment from under his black bolero hat, exposing a grin. It is a moment I will never forget.

Two years later, I met and interviewed Stevie for the first time. I'd brought a guitar and a small practice amp so he could demonstrate some of his songs and guitar parts. After greeting each other, we spontaneously started to jam on a blues shuffle in E for about ten minutes. When I put my guitar down, he asked what I was doing and I replied, "Oh, I have to interview you now." "Aw," he said, "I thought we were just gonna have fun." This gives you an idea of the kind of warm, generous, sweet, and friendly person Stevie was—ever enthusiastic and happy to play and share his love of music and the guitar.

Over the next four years, I interviewed Stevie three more times, as well as his brother Jimmie Vaughan. One of the most fun occasions was when I interviewed them both right before their "brothers" album, *Family Style*, came out. At the time of the interview, the album was still being called by its working title, *Very Vaughan*. It was fantastic to talk to the brothers together, as they picked on each other, laughed at each other's jokes, and shared in the trip down memory lane as only brothers can. Their closeness was crystal clear. Stevie was just as warm and friendly as ever, with a big smile on his face. As he had done previously, he sat back and played my guitar the entire time. At the end of the interview, he stood up, handed my guitar back, and said, "I still love your guitar." It was the last time we ever spoke.

In the years after Stevie's death, I interviewed Chris Layton and Tommy Shannon for their successive projects: Arc Angels, Storyville, and the Double Trouble album. By the end of the decade, they had heard my playing and invited me to record and play some shows with them, a great honor and absolute pleasure. It was through this relationship that I got the opportunity to perform with Jimi Hendrix's bandmates Mitch Mitchell, Buddy Miles, and Billy Cox, as well as Buddy Guy, Hubert Sumlin, Paul Rodgers, Edgar Winter, and many other musical legends.

Regarding Chris and Tommy, this book could never have been as focused, honest, or accurate in terms of their relationship and understanding of Stevie without the many hours of discussion with each of them over the last three decades. The relationships cultivated and that I continue to share with them are ones I will always cherish.

Stevie Ray Vaughan has been the most important and influential musician in the lives of many of the musicians that I have met and communicated with over the last thirty-five years. This is true for people older than myself as well as for people two generations younger. His impact has been felt across every age bracket in every corner of the globe. He remains a true guitar legend and a guitar hero. He set the bar so high, and set an example for performing on the highest level and with the deepest level of emotion. He was a true artist.

For all of these years since his passing, I felt that no one had written the kind of book Stevie deserved, one that would honor his memory appropriately and also tell the story of a life filled with triumph and with no lack of adversity and personal difficulties to overcome. It was a honor to get to speak with and get to know so many of his closest friends and family members, all of whom generously shared their thoughts, impressions, and feelings about Stevie at great length.

Most of all, I have to give great thanks to Jimmie Vaughan. Speaking about his brother is something that has not been easy. After many conversations, Jimmie felt confident that Alan and I would do our very best to tell Stevie's story the right way. The story of Stevie Ray Vaughan could not be told without the guidance of his brother, and we are so thankful for his confidence in us.

I believe this book tells Stevie's story truthfully and completely, and the reader will gain insight into his life as well as a far greater understanding of him as a person and as a musician. Working on this book was a true labor of love, and I dedicate all of the work to the lasting strength of Stevie's music and his spirit. He will continue to inspire for many generations to come.

CAST OF CHARACTERS

STEVIE RAY VAUGHAN *Perhaps the last true blues guitar legend. Born October 3, 1954, Dallas, Texas. Died August 27, 1990, East Troy, Wisconsin.*

JIMMIE VAUGHAN *Stevie's older brother and primary guitar influence. Founding member of the Fabulous Thunderbirds, solo artist since 1991.*

CHRIS LAYTON *Double Trouble drummer.*

TOMMY SHANNON *Double Trouble bassist.*

REESE WYNANS *Double Trouble keyboardist.*

LARRY ABERMAN *Drummer on* Family Style.

ANDY ALEDORT *Coauthor, interviewed Stevie Ray Vaughan four times.*

GREGG ALLMAN *Allman Brothers Band founding singer, keyboard player; died 2017.*

CARLOS ALOMAR *David Bowie guitarist and bandleader.*

CLIFFORD ANTONE *Founder of Antone's, Austin's home of the blues; died 2006.*

SUSAN ANTONE *Clifford Antone's sister, partner in Antone's club.*

CIDNEY COOK AYOTTE *Vaughan cousin.*

LOU ANN BARTON *Triple Threat and Double Trouble singer, 1977–1979.*

MARC BENNO *Texas guitarist, bandleader of the Nightcrawlers.*

RAY BENSON *Asleep at the Wheel founder, guitarist, friend of Stevie's and Jimmie's.*

BILL BENTLEY *Music editor,* The Austin Sun, *1974–1978.*

AL BERRY *Bassist on* Family Style.

LINDI BETHEL *Stevie's girlfriend, 1974–1979.*

DICKEY BETTS *Allman Brothers Band guitarist.*

DAVID BOWIE *Rock star. Hired Stevie to play on his 1983 album* Let's Dance, *which introduced the guitarist to the world (and helped Bowie to his greatest success); died 2016.*

DOYLE BRAMHALL *Songwriting partner and longtime friend and bandmate of both Stevie's and Jimmie's; died 2011.*

DOYLE BRAMHALL II *Guitarist, lifetime friend of Stevie's, son of Doyle Bramhall.*

CUTTER BRANDENBURG *Lifelong friend of Stevie's, crew member 1980–1983; died 2015.*

JACKSON BROWNE *Singer/songwriter who gave Stevie and Double Trouble free time in his Los Angeles studio, where they recorded* Texas Flood.

DENNY BRUCE *Fabulous Thunderbirds manager, 1977–1982.*

FRANCES CARR *Stevie's patron. She funded the band during their crucial early years and formed Classic Management with Chesley Millikin.*

BILL CARTER *Guitarist, singer, songwriter, cowriter of "Crossfire."*

LINDA CASCIO *Vaughan cousin.*

ERIC CLAPTON, *British blues guitar legend; friend and admirer of Stevie's.*

W. C. CLARK *Austin guitarist who played bass in and co-fronted the Triple Threat Revue with Stevie and singer Lou Ann Barton.*

BOB CLEARMOUNTAIN *Recording engineer,* Let's Dance.

RODDY COLONNA *Drummer in Blackbird, lifelong friend of Stevie's.*

J. MARSHALL CRAIG *Writer, confidant of Chesley Millikin.*

RODNEY CRAIG *Cobras drummer.*

ROBERT CRAY *Musician and friend of Stevie's.*

TIMOTHY DUCKWORTH *Stevie's friend; toured with Double Trouble in 1986.*

RONNIE EARL *Roomful of Blues and solo guitarist, friend of Stevie's and Jimmie's.*

JAMES ELWELL *Friend of Stevie's.*

KEITH FERGUSON *The Fabulous Thunderbirds bassist, an important mentor to Stevie during their time together in the Nightcrawlers; died 1997.*

DENNY FREEMAN *Guitarist, fellow Dallas native, bandmate of both Stevie's and Jimmie's.*

JIM GAINES In Step *producer.*

GREGG GELLER *Epic Records executive.*

BILLY F. GIBBONS *ZZ Top guitarist.*

MINDY GILES *Alligator Records marketing director.*

BOB GLAUB *Bassist with Jackson Browne's band.*

DAVID GRISSOM *Texas guitarist, Stevie's friend.*

BUDDY GUY *Chicago blues guitar legend; friend and hero to Stevie.*

WARREN HAYNES *Allman Brothers Band, Gov't Mule guitarist.*

RAY HENNIG *Owner of Heart of Texas music; sold Stevie his "Number One" Strat.*

ALEX HODGES *Stevie's booking agent, 1983–1986; manager, 1986–1990.*

BERT HOLMAN *Allman Brothers Band manager.*

RAY WYLIE HUBBARD *Acclaimed Texas singer and songwriter, best known for "Up Against the Wall, Redneck Mother."*

BRUCE IGLAUER *Founder, president, Alligator Records.*

DR. JOHN *New Orleans blues pianist and guitarist, Stevie's friend.*

EDI JOHNSON *Classic Management bookkeeper.*

ERIC JOHNSON *Virtuoso Austin guitar player.*

STEVE JORDAN *Drummer with Eric Clapton, Keith Richards, the Blues Brothers, and others.*

MIKE KINDRED *Oak Cliff native, Triple Threat Revue pianist, composer of "Cold Shot."*

ALBERT KING *Blues guitar great. One of Stevie's top influences and heroes; died 1992.*

B. B. KING *King of the blues; godfather to all electric blues guitarists; died 2015.*

RUSS KUNKEL *Drummer with Jackson Browne's band and many others.*

JANNA LAPIDUS *Stevie's girlfriend, 1986–1990.*

HARVEY LEEDS *Epic Records head of album promotion.*

HUEY LEWIS *Musician, leader of Huey Lewis and the News.*

TERRY LICKONA *Producer,* Austin City Limits.

BARBARA LOGAN *Wife of Doyle Bramhall, "Life by the Drop" cowriter.*

ANDREW LONG *Photographer.*

MARK LOUGHNEY *Fan.*

RICHARD LUCKETT *Stevie's merchandise manager, 1989–1990.*

RENÉ MARTINEZ *Stevie's guitar tech, 1985–1990.*

TOM MAZZOLINI *Founder and director of the San Francisco Blues Festival.*

JOHN McENROE *Tennis legend, guitarist.*

MIKE MERRITT *Bassist for Johnny Copeland.*

PAUL "PAPPY" MIDDLETON *Dallas guitarist, soundman, and mixer.*

STEVE MILLER *Guitarist and songwriter.*

CHESLEY MILLIKIN *Stevie's manager, 1980–86; died 2001.*

RICHARD MULLEN *Engineer and producer,* Texas Flood, Couldn't Stand the Weather, Soul to Soul.

JACKIE NEWHOUSE *Triple Threat and Double Trouble bassist, 1978–1980.*

DEREK O'BRIEN *Austin guitarist, member of Antone's house band.*

DONNIE OPPERMAN *Stevie's guitar tech, 1982.*

JOE PERRY *Aerosmith guitarist.*

SCOTT PHARES *Bassist in Liberation, Stevie's high school band.*

JOE PRIESNITZ *Stevie's booking agent, 1979–1983.*

MARK PROCT *The Fabulous Thunderbirds / Jimmie Vaughan road manager and manager, 1981–1998.*

JACK RANDALL *Booking agent.*

BONNIE RAITT *Blues great, friend of Stevie's.*

DIANA RAY *Major player in the Austin blues world; wife of Paul Ray.*

PAUL RAY *Leader of the Cobras; died 2016.*

MIKE REAMES *Singer in Liberation, Stevie's high school band.*

SKIP RICKERT *Tour manager, 1986–1990.*

NILE RODGERS *Producer, David Bowie's* Let's Dance *and the Vaughan Brothers'* Family Style.

CARMINE ROJAS *Bassist on* Let's Dance.

JAMES ROWEN *Canadian A&R representative.*

PAUL SHAFFER *Keyboardist,* Late Night with David Letterman *bandleader.*

AL STAEHALEY *Bassist in Spirit and an Austin lawyer who represented Stevie early in his career.*

JOHN STAEHALEY *Austin guitarist in Krackerjack and Spirit.*

MIKE STEELE *Stevie's friend.*

JIMMY STRATTON *Photographer.*

ANGELA STREHLI *Austin blues singer; taught Stevie "Texas Flood."*

JOE SUBLETT *Saxophonist, member of the Cobras.*

GUS THORNTON *Bass player for Albert King.*

JIM TRIMMIER *Saxophonist, member of Liberation and the Cobras.*

CONNIE VAUGHAN *Oak Cliff native; Stevie's high school friend; Jimmie Vaughan's girlfriend and wife, 1972–2000.*

JIMMIE LEE "BIG JIM" VAUGHAN *Father of Jimmie and Stevie Ray Vaughan; died August 27, 1986.*

LENORA "LENNY" BAILEY VAUGHAN *Married to Stevie, 1979–1988; died 2018.*

MARTHA VAUGHAN *Mother of Jimmie and Stevie Ray Vaughan; died June 13, 2009.*

RICK VITO *Guitarist with Jackson Browne's band and many others.*

DON WAS *Producer, bassist.*

MARK WEBER *Photographer.*

KIRK WEST *Photographer, Allman Brothers Band's "Tour Mystic."*

BRAD WHITFORD *Aerosmith guitarist.*

ANN WILEY *Martha Vaughan's sister, Jimmie and Stevie's aunt.*

GARY WILEY *Vaughan cousin.*

1

IN THE BEGINNING

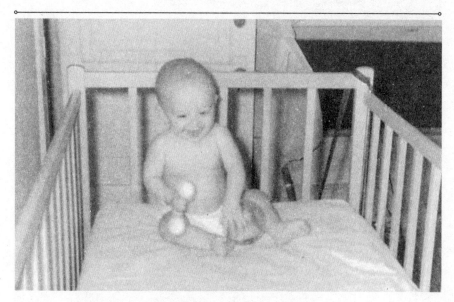

Baby blues: Stevie at seven months, playing in his crib.
(Courtesy Joe Allen Cook Family Collection)

Stephen Ray Vaughan was born October 3, 1954, in Dallas, Texas, three and a half years after his brother, Jimmie Lawrence. Their mother and father, Martha Cook Vaughan and Jimmie "Big Jim" Vaughan, had been married since January 1950 and were striving to establish themselves as part of the growing postwar middle class. Their tenuous grip on working-class stability was a big step up from Big Jim's childhood. He grew up a sharecropper's son, picking cotton in Rockwall County, thirty miles east of Dallas, the youngest of eight children. His father died when Jim was seven, on the eve of the Great Depression.

Big Jim and Martha
Vaughan. *(Courtesy Joe
Allen Cook Family Collection)*

Stevie and Jimmie on the
front porch of their Oak
Cliff home, with Martha
watching over them.
*(Courtesy Joe Allen Cook
Family Collection)*

Big Jim dropped out of high school at sixteen and enlisted in the U.S. Navy with the help of his mother, who lied about his age. "It sounded better to run off to the navy than to pick cotton," Jimmie Vaughan says of his father's decision. Big Jim served during World War II on the USS *Saratoga* aircraft carrier in the South Pacific.

After returning to civilian life, Big Jim got a job at a 7-Eleven in Oak Cliff, Dallas. He worked as an attendant, running out to the cars of drivers who pulled in and honked their horns, to take and deliver orders. He soon had a regular customer in Martha Jean Cook, who lived with her family in Cockrell Hill, just west of Oak Cliff, and worked as a secretary at a lumberyard. Though they met in that parking lot, their romance blossomed on dance floors.

"Once they started dating, they went to dozens of the dance halls around Dallas," says Ann Wiley, Martha's sister. "They both loved to dance." Big Jim and Martha were married on January 13, 1950, and Jimmie was born fourteen months later, on March 20, 1951.

With a new family to support, Big Jim left 7-Eleven and became a union asbestos installer, mixing the "mud" to insulate pipes and ducts in commercial buildings. He had no way of knowing that breathing in asbestos fibers can cause asbestosis, lung cancer, and mesothelioma, a correlation noted in medical texts as early as 1906 but not widely known until the late 1970s. Vaughan's job required constant travel and kept the family moving throughout the South and Southwest. As Steve and Jim, as they were known, grew older, they had to deal with being constantly uprooted from elementary school.

"We trailed around as my dad's job required him to travel all over the South," says Jimmie. "It was real tough always uprooting, going to schools for two weeks at a time. In a way, it was perfect training for the life we eventually lived as musicians on the road all the time. We eventually settled back in Oak Cliff."

In 1961, when Stevie was seven and Jimmie was ten, the Vaughans bought a two-bedroom ranch home at 2557 Glenfield Avenue, which would remain the family abode for more than three decades. Jim and Steve shared the back bedroom. Big Jim had a volatile temper, especially when he was drinking, and could turn violent, leaving his family ever wary. Their Oak

Cliff neighborhood was growing, filled with the young families of World War II and Korean War veterans. Oak Cliff became internationally known on November 22, 1963, when President John F. Kennedy was assassinated in Dallas. The assassin, Lee Harvey Oswald, was arrested at the Texas Theatre in downtown Oak Cliff, after shooting and killing police officer J. D. Tippit.

"It's incredible that we lived in the town where all of that happened," Jimmie says. "I had been to the Texas Theatre with my parents many times. Oak Cliff was a real rough place. Pretty much everyone we grew up with is either dead or in jail."

First cousin Gary Wiley recalls that on Halloween 1962, the boys were mugged and robbed of their masks and candy. Wiley was one of nine first cousins from Martha's side who got together frequently with Steve and Jim.

Big Jim, an intimidating presence with wide shoulders and bulging forearms, was proud of his navy service, telling his boys about seeing kamikaze planes and proudly displaying the "outfit" book of his photos and mementos from the war on the TV stand. "That's where the most important book in the house went," says Jimmie. "He'd show me pictures of where he'd been during the war."

Yet despite his love of music, Big Jim never really shared his own musical background, that as a kid he had a natural ear and could pick out tunes on the piano. He did, however, tell them of a harsh lesson learned when he was ten years old. He had picked cotton for an entire season to save the few dollars required to buy the beautiful string bass he saw advertised in a magazine. After he mailed in the money, he waited anxiously for his instrument to arrive. "He said that six months later, a #10 washtub came, with a broomstick and a string," says Jimmie. "He was pretty disappointed."

Still, Stevie and Jimmie didn't have to look far for musical inspiration; there were musicians on both sides of the family. Martha's two guitar-playing brothers, Joe and Jerrell Cook, were the boys' most direct role models and early influences. When Stevie and Jimmie got their first starter guitars at seven and ten years old, the uncles spent time with the boys regularly, teaching them their first chords and licks.

Along with the influence of their musical uncles, members of the country and western swing legends the Texas Playboys, who were major innovators and stars, visited the Vaughan family home often for card games and dominoes. These gatherings often included off-the-cuff performances that young Steve and Jim watched and soon participated in themselves.

Stevie Ray Vaughan vividly recalled those parties in 1986. "When I was real young, my parents played domino games, like 42, Low Boy, and Nello, and the Texas Playboys hung out at our house all the time. They'd do some playing, and we'd hear their stuff. Mainly, we'd hear them talking about it. I was a little beefheart. Every once in a while, my dad would yell, 'Hey, Jim, Steve, come out here and show them what you can do!' We were little midgets, with guitars hangin' on us that were this big!"

As Jimmie's and Stevie's interest in and proficiency on the guitar grew, their parents continued to encourage them. Big Jim and Martha understood what it was to be profoundly moved by sound, and they were enthusiastic and encouraging of Jimmie's and Stevie's growing interest in music and guitars. They did not object when their sons' passion for music grew into obsession.

STEVIE RAY VAUGHAN: I got my first guitar when I was seven. It was one of those Roy Rogers guitars; it had pictures of cowboys and cows on it, some rope. I had a blanket with the same shit on it, too.

JIMMIE VAUGHAN: I think Stevie and I latched onto the guitar as a way out of Oak Cliff pretty early. My mother's brothers Joe and Jerrell Cook played guitar and were into Merle Travis, who was the epitome of a cool guitar player, riding a Harley with a guitar strapped on his back. My dad always told me stories about his cousins Sammy and Red Klutts, who played drums and bass in western swing, country, and rock-and-roll bands, and another cousin who played trombone with [big band leader] Tommy Dorsey in Los Angeles. My dad's favorite was Jack Teagarden, a Texas jazz trombonist whose style was rooted in blues and New Orleans music.

CIDNEY COOK AYOTTE, *Vaughan first cousin:* There was always music playing in their house, and both Jimmie and Stevie picked up the guitar really, really young.

JIMMIE VAUGHAN: There were thousands of bands everywhere, and music was a huge part of our lives. There was the *Big D Jamboree*, a weekly *Louisiana Hayride: Town Hall Party*–type show from the Dallas Sportatorium with all the great country stars and great guitar players, and we went to these incredible music contests at the Yello Belly Drag Strip [in nearby Grand Prairie], where country, Mexican, swing, and blues bands played. There were huge crowds, and we'd walk from stage to stage.

SRV: We were exposed to every kind of music, and if you listened, you could hear feeling in every style of music we were listening to. Jazz, rock and roll . . . it all goes back to the feeling of the blues.

JIMMIE VAUGHAN: My parents were dancers, and my dad was a honky-tonk man who used to hang out with Bob Wills. Our daddy also worked with a guy who played with Chuck Berry and would come over with his guitar—a big hollow body, with his name in the neck in mother-of-pearl—and show us John Lee Hooker and Jimmy Reed songs. It was a big deal!

RAY BENSON, *Asleep at the Wheel founder, guitarist, and friend of Stevie's and Jimmie's:* Bob Wills was like Elvis in Dallas. Having those guys over at the house would have been something else.

JIMMIE VAUGHAN: When I was twelve, I broke my collarbone playing football, and I was laid up at home for a couple of months. A friend of my dad's gave me this old broken-up guitar, and that's when I really learned how to play. The first thing I learned was Bill Doggett's "Honky Tonk," but I learned it backwards because I didn't know any better.

SRV: I was eight or nine, and I was learning "Honky Tonk," too.

JIMMIE VAUGHAN: I went straight for the blues, because that's what sounded best to me, and I can't tell you why. A lot of my relatives were country musicians, and I never even tried to play country. They were looking at me like, "What in the world are you doing?" I just said, "I like *this*." And I never thought about it again.

SRV: Jimmie turned me on to a lot of different stuff, and I just watched him play. I remember him bringing home Hendrix, Buddy Guy, Muddy Waters, and B. B. King. It was like, "Here comes Jimmie with the Record World, right under his arm!"

JIMMIE VAUGHAN: About a year after I started, Daddy bought me a 3/4 Gibson with no cutaway, about as thick as a 335 with one pickup [a 1957 Gibson 125-T hollow body, serial number U142221], and a little brown Gibson amp. Fifty bucks and I was on my way! School went to hell after that; I just played guitar all of the time and listened to Chuck Berry, Bo Diddley, and Jerry Lee Lewis on the radio.

SRV: I wasn't listening to the radio that much. I was just stuck off in my own little world. When I did listen to the radio, it was a little crystal set, and I listened to Ernie's Record Mart. With a crystal radio, you could pick up like . . . forever. I'd lay there at night and listen to all these blues specials, and they'd advertise thirty-eight record sets! They played stuff that I don't even think was available anywhere except through these Record Mart deals. They had things like Little Milton, B. B. King, Albert King, Jimmy Reed, and on and on. There wasn't very many of us white guys on it.

JIMMIE VAUGHAN: The very first record I ever bought was *Wine, Wine, Wine* by the Nightcaps, young white guys from Dallas playing blues and rock and roll. Stevie and I both learned to play "Thunderbird" from that record. I listened to Jimmy Reed, too. I just always liked that low, deep boogie thing, and I'd get the records of anybody doing that shit. I saw Lonnie Mack on *Dick Clark*, and he played so fast, I couldn't even believe what I was hearing.

SRV: The first record I ever bought was Lonnie Mack's "Wham!" I played it over and over and over and over so many times, my dad got mad and broke it! Every time he broke it, I just went and got another one. I'm glad the first record I bought wasn't the Monkees. I got a lot of inspiration from Lonnie Mack. When we started off, I knew how Jimmy Reed sounded, but I couldn't play it right. And Jimmie would set me straight. When I didn't think it could be any louder, I borrowed somebody's Shure Vocal Master PA, put mics in front of the stereo speakers, and then turned the PA up! It was loud in my room.

GARY WILEY, *Vaughan cousin:* One time, Steve was listening intently to the radio and playing along on Jim's guitar, which he had inherited [the Gibson 125-T]. My brother and I were bugging him to jump on our bikes, but he had to nail that part first. After a while, he went,

First cousins, March 1960: Jimmie in back, Stevie on front left. *(Courtesy Gary Wiley)*

"I've just about got it," and started playing along perfectly. There were multiple guitars, and he was picking each one out, and at the same time putting them into one guitar part, just by listening. He was about eleven. My brother and I were more interested in Stevie's car magazines than his music. He loved cars and had all kinds of *Hot Rod* magazines, which we'd look at while he played guitar.

JIMMIE VAUGHAN: I spent all of my lunch money on records and *Hot Rod* magazines. I loved [revolutionary car designers] Ed "Big Daddy" Roth and George Barris. There wasn't really a difference between that and music; it was just cool stuff. I've never been the same after hearing *The Best of Muddy Waters* and *The Best of Little Walter*. It was just soul and feeling, wild as shit. Hearing the guys screaming in the background of Muddy's "Mannish Boy" was scary! It goes right in your toes and all the way up to the back of your neck. Booker T. and the MG's "Green Onions" hit me the same way. It just made you feel wild to listen to that before you went to school.

SRV: The blues always sounded more like "the real thing" than anything else. It's not like I automatically said, "This is cooler than this," or "This has more emotion." When I heard it, it *slayed* me! There was just not a question. Hearing it all these different ways, from the English blues boom to authorized recordings to shitty bootleg stuff of everybody you can dream of, it was like, if you can hear it, do it. The more I heard, the better I liked what I heard.

Between listening to the feeling in the music and watching my brother, and how much feeling he had with it, I picked up big-time inspiration. What I was getting out of it wasn't so much technical; just the thought of them playing made me want to jump up and play.

JIMMIE VAUGHAN: If you want to be a blues guitar player, there's no better place to grow up than Texas. We can start with T-Bone Walker and Lightnin' Hopkins, and you don't even need to go further, but there's fifty more examples.

SRV: I had a bunch of T-Bone's records, like "T-Bone Shuffle," "Stormy Monday," "Cold, Cold Feeling." A lot of 'em I don't remember the names of; I just know the way they go. T-Bone was the first guy to play behind his head, and on his back, on the floor. Those were all T-Bone tricks. And Guitar Slim.

GARY WILEY: We used to crawdad fish in a little creek near our house in Cockrell Hill. My brother Mark, Steve, and I were down there when a couple of guys in a car came by and started bullying us. Jim, who was about thirteen, came over and stood up to those guys, who were a lot bigger than him. He actually got in a fistfight with one of them, and they left. That's the kind of guy he is. He stepped in against odds and protected us. Jimmie was like the big brother to all of us.

By 1964, when he was thirteen, Jimmie was playing in his first proper band, the Swinging Pendulums, and the gigs would often become Vaughan family affairs.

At home in Oak Cliff. *(Courtesy Jimmie Vaughan)*

SRV: When Jimmie first started playing out, Daddy was trying to manage him, so we *all* went to see him play!

JIMMIE VAUGHAN: He'd put us in the back of his pickup truck and take us to the gig. The band was called the Swinging Pendulums, if you can believe it. In the summer, we had a seven-nights-a-week gig, and I couldn't get in the club alone. The parents had to rotate, and more often than not they would all show up. "We have to take the kids down the club tonight." They enjoyed it, too. They get to see their kids play and hang out in a beer joint on a weeknight with a good excuse.

The Cockrell Hill Jubilee on June 26, 1965, is believed to be Stevie's first public performance; he was ten years old. His first band, the Chantones, performed using the gear of the Swinging Pendulums, who also played and were featured in *The Dallas Morning News* two weeks later. Writer Francis Raffetto wrote that the troupe of fourteen- and fifteen-year-olds "are probably the only combo in town playing in a beer-dispensing tavern but too young to work without their parents. . . . The combo, paid $75 a week each by the Beachcomber, wears red-and-white candy-striped T-shirts."

Stevie in the Chantones. *(Courtesy Joe Allen Cook Family Collection)*

SRV: Jimmie showed me a lot of stuff, but there was also a time when he warned, "If you ask me to show you anything again, I'll kick your ass." Well, I did, and he did. A lot of the time, I just watched him play. The greatest thing was that Jimmie taught me how to *listen* so I could teach myself.

JIMMIE VAUGHAN: I showed him the way initially, but he found his voice himself. I was learning, too. You know, big brothers always bullshit their little brothers a little bit. That's part of their job! They don't know *why* they do it, but they do. When you're a kid, the only person who asks you questions is your little brother, so they've got to be good answers.

The whole notion that we could be musicians was way out. It was an impossible thing, but when you're a kid, you don't know and you don't care because everything's impossible.

SRV: Jimmie had several bands, such as Sammy Loria and the Penetrations. You know the song "Penetration"? It was pretty cool. Obviously, they were into girls.

JIMMIE VAUGHAN: I went from the Swinging Pendulums to Sammy Loria and the Penetrations. I played rhythm guitar opposite Johnny Peebles, who was very much a mentor not only in guitar playing but in life, because he did what he wanted, had a car, played in clubs six nights a week, stayed out all night, and he was a real musician. We did "Bony Moronie," rock and roll, and we wore fancy jackets and did "steps." I was already into it when the Beatles came out in 1964. Then I heard the Yardbirds and said, "Yeah, I love *that!*"

LINDA CASCIO, *Vaughan cousin:* They were always playing us the newest records when we visited. One time, Stevie put on the Doors' "Light My Fire," and we all sat around and listened.

JIMMIE VAUGHAN: When I was about fourteen, I started going to the Empire Ballroom to see guys like Freddie King, B. B. King, T-Bone Walker, and Bobby "Blue" Bland. I'd sneak out, take a cab over, and watch the headliner and the house band, Mo Thomas and the Arrows. The guy at the front door would go around, let me in the back door, and kind of keep an eye on me.

SRV: After "Wham!" I also played along with [The Yardbirds'] "Jeff's Boogie" and "Over Under Sideways Down." Lots of Hendrix, of course. Clapton stuff with [John] Mayall. Get your Rickenbacker bass and go crazy playing "Lady Madonna," just like everybody.

JIMMIE VAUGHAN: A friend of mine had an uncle who lived in England. He knew we were into blues, so he sent the Bluesbreakers record to his little nephew. The guy got it in the mail, called me up, and said, "Hey, man, I got this record you'd probably like." He played it over the phone, and I was like, "Damn! What is that?" It was just wild, heavy, emotional. It was B. B. King, but it wasn't! Clapton sounded really *mad,* but so cool.

SRV: Clapton knew what he was gonna say!

JIMMIE VAUGHAN: He played like B. B. King and Buddy Guy, and it made it seem okay for me to like this because somebody else who's not black was doing it. When Clapton played, he sounded like he knew what the last note of the solo was going to be before he even started. Hearing all that great music as a kid was like developing an appetite and you kept looking for more.

I used to go through the dumpster behind *The Ron Chapman Show,* a teenybopper after-school show on Dallas TV, because they would throw out all the 45s that the record companies sent in. I found a promotional copy of "Purple Haze," which hadn't made its way to Texas yet. I had seen a little bitty article about Hendrix in a magazine, and his name stuck with me because he was holding a guitar. I brought it home, and it sounded like Muddy Waters's stepchild, like Muddy had come back from a tour of Mars. When I heard that stuff, I thought, "That's what I want to be when I grow up."

CASCIO: Stevie was a huge Jimi Hendrix fan. He had this giant three-ring binder with hundreds of pictures of Jimi that he'd show me when we visited his house.

In the summer of 1966, Jimmie joined the Chessmen, a popular band with a record deal, which was formed two years earlier by North Texas State students. Jimmie was replacing founding guitarist and singer Robert Patton, who had drowned in a sailing accident. Jimmie took over his guitar role, while drummer Doyle Bramhall assumed the lead vocals. This was the first time Bramhall worked with a Vaughan; he would remain a crucial member of their inner circle for the rest of his life.

The Chessmen mostly played covers—Beatles tunes as well as the blues rock of Jimi Hendrix, the Yardbirds, and Cream. They were very popular on the club and college circuit, often playing fraternity parties. Jimmie was fifteen.

JIMMIE VAUGHAN: Everyone else in the band was twenty-one, and I was this little kid with attitude and a Telecaster. I knew all the licks.

SCOTT PHARES, *bassist in Liberation, Stevie's high school band:* Jimmie Vaughan was the king of the mountain, the god of Oak Cliff guitar players. Everyone knew his name.

MIKE KINDRED, *Oak Cliff native, Triple Threat Revue pianist, composer of "Cold Shot":* The Chessmen were local rock stars. There were other bands with followings, but none with the same gravity or depth; the Chessmen were head and shoulders above everyone else. We were all in awe of both Jimmie, the hottest guitarist, and Doyle, the great drummer who could sing as well as any black guy.

CONNIE VAUGHAN, *Oak Cliff native, married to Jimmie Vaughan, 1980–2000:* Jimmie was an Oak Cliff star walking through junior high school hallways with a twin on each arm.

DOYLE BRAMHALL, *songwriting partner and longtime friend and bandmate of both Stevie's and Jimmie's; died 2011:* Jimmie was fifteen and I was seventeen when he joined the Chessmen, so I could drive and he couldn't, and I would pick him up, usually just pulling up in front and honking. But one time in 1966, he wasn't ready, so he waved me in. I was sitting in the living room waiting, and Jimmie walked from the back bedroom to the kitchen, and I heard this guitar playing going on from the other direction. I walked down the hall and a bedroom door was a little ajar, and I saw this little skinny kid sitting on the bed playing Jeff Beck's "Jeff's Boogie." As soon as he saw me, he stopped playing, and I said, "Don't stop." He gave me this shy little smile and said, "Hi, I'm Stevie," and I said, "Hi, I'm Doyle. Keep playing. You're very good." Thirty seconds later, Jimmie ran up and said, "Let's go."

I didn't even know Jimmie had a brother, and I was like, "There's another one?" Because Jimmie was so good and it was clear that Stevie had it from the get-go, too.

JIMMIE VAUGHAN: It was crazy. I was making $300 a week—more than my father. I was spoiled by the music, so I didn't do all the stuff that normal kids do. I forgot to be a kid. I made straight As through about fifth grade, then I lost interest and started thinking about cars and guitars. I flunked the ninth grade at L. V. Stockard Junior High. I wasn't doing my work or showing up. The last day of school, Doyle had got a new

GTO, and he said, "I'm gonna come get you," and I said, "Cool . . . let me know when." I knew I had flunked out, so I just ran out the door and jumped in his car, and we drove off to a gig. The next year, the manager of the Chessmen talked to the principal at Browne Junior High, and I went there.

KINDRED: Jimmie and I were in ninth grade at T. W. Browne, and I saw him get thrown out for having long hair. They came right up and grabbed him out of the lunch line. His hair was not even Beatles length, but that was too much for the time and place.

JIMMIE VAUGHAN: We made up the hair story. I got thrown out of Browne quickly for not showing up, and the excuse we used was that they wanted me to cut my hair and I wouldn't. After Browne, I went to Oak Cliff Christian, which was a private school for misfits, and completed my ninth-grade requirements. I had a one-track mind and just wanted to play guitar.

Jimmie moved into an apartment in North Dallas with other members of the Chessmen. He did not come around home too often for a couple of years. With Jimmie gone, Stevie had no shield or distractions between him and his father.

JIMMIE VAUGHAN: My father started drinking in the navy, and though he never said so, he was an alcoholic. The guys he worked with were alcoholics, too, in my estimation. They'd come over and drink. I'd come home from school, and they'd all be sitting around the table with a quart of whiskey in the middle and get real quiet when I walked in. They probably quit talking about whatever they were talking about as soon as they heard the door. That was just normal stuff in those days. My mother would say they were just "drinking men."

SRV: There were a lot of *characters* hanging around. Those guys would come over and get drunk.

JIMMIE VAUGHAN: After I left, they really locked down on Stevie: "You're not gonna do like he did." That just made him try harder!

SRV: By the time I was twelve, Jimmie was gone. Here he was, the hottest guitar player I knew of, considered the hottest guitar player in Texas at age fifteen. I mean, what do you do but get excited when all this is going on?

JIMMIE VAUGHAN: My dad was scared that I'd go down the wrong path. He did the best he could and was trying to warn me and protect me. I grew my hair out, but the long hair was the smallest part of it. People like me were trying to find our way, so we were rejecting stuff, and I had to decide for myself the life I wanted to live.

ANN WILEY, *Martha Vaughan's sister:* Martha was not at all happy that Jimmie had dropped out of school. She did not want to see the same thing happen with Stevie.

SRV: When Jimmie left, they thought they were going to lose me, too. After he moved out, we didn't hear from Jimmie for a long time.

Shortly after Jimmie left home, the Vaughans suddenly moved again, relocating to Graham, Texas, a town of fewer than ten thousand residents about 120 miles from Oak Cliff. Stevie was ripped away from everyone and everything he knew and cared about, including his musician friends. He was beaten up at his new school and suspended regularly. He felt miserable and alienated. After six months, just after he declared to his parents he would no longer attend school in Graham, they moved back to Oak Cliff.

Settling back in, Stevie had his first and last job that did not involve six strings, working as a dishwasher at a restaurant. It did not go well. "One of my jobs was to take out the trash, and I slipped on something and fell about ten feet on top of a huge barrel where we put all the hot grease," Vaughan told writer Michael Corcoran in 1989 in the *Phoenix New Times.* "Luckily, the lid was on or I could've been scalded real bad. Well, the owner came out and saw that I had cracked the lid with my fall, so she started yelling at me. I could've been killed, and all she cared about was her damn lid."

Stevie said that he quit right then and stomped home "as angry as I've ever been . . . put on an Albert King record as loud as it would go and . . . decided that I was going to be like Albert King."

By late 1967, Stevie had a new band, the Brooklyn Underground (preceded by the very short-lived Epileptic Marshmallow), which would last through much of 1968. They played dances at venues, including Candy's Flare, a converted National Guard armory.

The Chessmen opened for the Jimi Hendrix Experience in February 1968 at the State Fair Music Hall in Dallas. "It's embarrassing to even think about, but we opened up with 'Sunshine of Your Love' or some other Cream song—because we couldn't play any Hendrix!" says Jimmie. "I was wearing a jacket with feathers on it because I was trying to be like Hendrix as much as I could."

After the show, Jimi's roadie asked Jimmie if he would swap his Vox wah pedal for Hendrix's broken pedal plus some cash, a trade the young guitarist happily agreed to. Then he and his bandmates were swept into the dressing room for a quick meeting. "They all thought it was funny. 'These guys sound like the Cream.' I was pretty good at copying people."

The Chessmen also opened for Janis Joplin, who took a shine to the young guitarist and invited him to look her up if he ever made it to San Francisco. "I guess she thought I was cute," says Jimmie.

JOHN STAEHALEY, *Austin guitarist in Krackerjack and Spirit:* I met Jimmie when we were both fifteen. It was incredible watching him nail "Jeff's Boogie" and "Crossroads." He was playing a Les Paul through a Marshall, so he had not only the touch but the tone! I lived in Austin, and the Chessmen, along with other great Dallas bands, including Don Henley's, would come down to play University of Texas frat parties and a couple of clubs.

BRAMHALL: I was real spoiled because the first eight or nine years that I played music, I played with either Jimmie or Stevie. At fifteen, Jimmie was already just *real*. He wanted it to be just right.

MARC BENNO, *Dallas guitarist who recorded with the Doors, Leon Russell, and others:* The first time I heard Jimmie, I thought he was the best guitar player I had ever heard. He could play fast. Really fast. He had a style that's in between his own current style and Stevie Ray's. Early on, Jimmie played a lot more like Stevie than anyone realizes. He could play fast as lightning, but he wasn't impressed with that.

CUTTER BRANDENBURG, *SRV friend, crew member, 1980–1983:* Jimmie was the one who created this wild kid. He may not have realized how much his love of music was flowing through his little brother, but Stevie would never love another guitarist more than Jimmie.

SRV: If you want to know what made me go crazy with it, it was watching Jimmie, and, not trying to outdo him, but, shit, what do you do but pick up the ball and run? It's not trying to pass him, and it's not trying to keep up with him. It's more like, "Wow! Look what big brother stumbled onto!"

A lot of people seem to think that we're trying to beat each other at something, but it's not that at all. I saw him get real *exciting*—not just excited, but *exciting*—with something, and that excited me. I didn't know what else to do.

CONNIE VAUGHAN: Stevie was a loner who was bullied because he wasn't a jock in a very jock-dominated school. I was a year ahead of him and started looking out for him in middle school. When we were at Kimball, he would come over and rehearse all the time in the playroom my parents had built above our garage. All he wanted to do was play music.

RODDY COLONNA, *Oak Cliff native, drummer in Blackbird:* I was two years ahead of Steve at Kimball High, which was pretty redneck, and I'd see him in the hallways: a weird-looking little guy wearing hip-hugger bell-bottom jeans, a paisley shirt, teardrop sunglasses that were too big for his head, and a little sash around his waist. I was eighteen and Stevie was fourteen or fifteen. I think he wanted to meet me because I was in a band, and he came up and said, in a low, deep voice with a halting delivery: "Uh . . . hey, Roddy . . . I'm Steve Vaughan. My brother is Jimmie Vaughan."

We started eating lunch together, then jammed, and I was impressed with his chops. Eric Clapton was his idol, and he was playing solos on songs like "Crossroads" note for note. One time, he brought a sunburst Strat that I knew was Jimmie's—it had the stick-on "JLV" letters on it—to the school practice room. And I knew Jimmie would have hit the ceiling if he knew Stevie had that guitar in school!

Stevie played with the Southern Distributor in the spring of '69, covering the Doors, Beatles, Yardbirds, Byrds, Kinks, Jimi Hendrix, Cream, Rolling Stones, and other popular rock hits. Playing in a band provided Stevie the opportunity to escape his home environment as much as possible.

COLONNA: Stevie had a difficult home life; his dad was pretty rough on him. From when I first met him, he always talked about how mean his dad was.

BRANDENBURG: Mr. Vaughan was rough on Jimmie about all the music, and now his other son was following along, which made Mr. Vaughan very tense. He sometimes held that against Jimmie, and Stevie got it from both his brother and his dad.

JIM TRIMMIER, *saxophonist, member of Liberation and the Cobras:* I was scared of Big Jim. He came out and looked me over, wondering, "Is this guy gonna fuck my son up, or is he gonna be okay?" My hair was getting long, which was not cool in '69 Dallas. Mean dads were pretty common, including mine.

COLONNA: I only sat down with Big Jim once, and he started bringing out mint-condition B. B. King 78s that had belonged to one of Stevie's uncles, and I was blown away. It wasn't always grim over there. But there were a few times Stevie called me up and said, "Hey, Roddy, my dad hit my mom. Can you come pick me up?" He'd be crying. There were nights when he didn't want to go back home.

SRV: I learned how to be afraid all the time, because it wasn't very constant at home. I don't know if everybody else in the family perceived it the same way. Probably not. But I learned real quickly not to know what to expect, so therefore I'd just stay out of the way, keep my feelings out of the way. If I did have feelings, it must have been my fault, 'cause that's what I heard when the fights were going on.

2

LEARNING TO FLY

Intoxicated by success, the Chessmen fell apart by the end of 1968. Jimmie had had enough of playing the hits of the day, and as soon as Bramhall regained his strength after contracting hepatitis, the two formed Texas, focusing on blues and R&B. The band's name fluctuated; Texas became Texas Storm and eventually just Storm. Bramhall was sometimes both drummer and singer and sometimes just the front man.

Stevie was continuing to make a name for himself, a fifteen-year-old guitarist astounding people who often checked him out simply because he was Jimmie's brother. He used this fact as a badge of authenticity, a secret entrance code into clubs and onto bandstands.

BRANDENBURG: A friend told me I had to hear this kid who was playing at Candy's Flare. I walked in, and he was whipping through Freddie King's "Hideaway" like warm butter on hot pancakes. In that moment, my life truly changed. I was twenty, and this skinny fifteen-year-old kid with a guitar that almost covered him just knocked me over. After the show, I told Stevie that I had traveled all over to see Jimi [Hendrix] eighteen times. We just fell into each other, and I started driving him to gigs and sometimes even to school.

COLONNA: When I met Stevie, he loved Clapton. He'd put on an album and play air guitar, putting his fingers exactly on the right frets of the imaginary guitar. Later on, he'd study different people just as intently.

Stevie asked to borrow Albert King's *Live Wire: Blues Power,* then re-fused to give it back! He learned that record inside and out.

BRANDENBURG: I worked at an old folks' home, and Stevie would some-times go with me to pick up my paycheck. He wanted to meet a few great patients I had told him about, and he'd bring his guitar and play for some of the old-timers, who would yell for him to come to them. There was this old black man, Jefferson Seedman, who had a guitar he always carried but couldn't really play because his hands were so crippled. Stevie would play for him, and he would rear back, slap his leg, and say, "Now dat boy has got it!" Once, he started to cry, and Stevie hugged him and said, "Come on now, you know I'm coming back. I ain't ever gonna not come see you." Mr. Seedman said, "Oh, I know. I just like the way you play so much; it sure makes me feel good." Stevie said, "Well, that's what music is supposed to do, make ya feel good."

COLONNA: I had a Dodge van, and Stevie would call me up and ask me to pick him up. We'd go cruising through Dallas, and he was already known around town as a great guitarist—at fifteen! We'd make the rounds of clubs, and they knew him everywhere. He'd sit in at the Fog, the Aragon, and the Cellar, which was a rock-and-roll strip club that was open till daylight and had girls walking around in bras and panties.

BENNO: I was playing at a place called the End of Cole Avenue, and a kid who looked like he was eleven came up and said he wanted to sit in. I was like, "Not really," and he said, "I'm Jimmie Vaughan's little brother," and I said, "Oh, man. Okay." Because Jimmie was already a legend who everyone agreed was the best guitar player in Texas.

I asked Stevie if he wanted to borrow a guitar, and he said he had one and went out to a car and came back carrying a '51 Broadcaster, which was Jimmie's guitar, no case. He plugged into a borrowed amp and just made it happen. He had real pure tone and was fast and smooth; he really played pretty. He hadn't put it all together yet, and his motor skills weren't all there, but his vibrato and tone were right on, and he would hit certain licks that made everyone scream like a bolt of lightning had hit. What he was playing combined with how he looked—maybe eighty-five pounds in his shorts and T-shirt—just made people go crazy.

Already feeling burned out at seventeen, Jimmie took Janis Joplin up on her offer, showing up at her door in Haight-Ashbury; she escorted him to the Fillmore to see Chuck Berry and Tony Joe White. "It was the first time I'd ever been there, and I got to go with her," he says. "It was a trip. I was just a little kid."

Joplin had assured Jimmie in Texas that if he came west, she could get him a record contract, and he returned with the whole band in tow.

"I kept going out to LA and walking up and down Sunset wishing that I had a gig there. There was always the big record deal around the corner that was gonna make you a big star," he says. "Texas Storm ended up getting a gig opening for Junior Walker at the Whisky A Go Go, and we got booed off the stage and fired, and nothing ever came of it."

He soon moved back to Dallas where his wife, Donna, was pregnant with their daughter Tina. Disillusioned with the music business, he started working as a garbage collector for the city of Irving.

"I thought that you practiced real hard and got a record deal because you were good, and that a deal was the reward for being a good musician. It was a real rude awakening when I found out that it had more to do with the way you look and who's your manager.

"I had to get a job, so I became a trash man. I did that for a few months but didn't like it too much. Then I got a job at a lumberyard, saved enough money, and said, 'We're moving to Austin and playing blues.' I wasn't interested in any other music."

The full-time move to Austin would take a bit more time, but the switch to blues was immediate and pronounced, and Jimmie and Storm started spending more time driving to the capital city, about two hundred miles south.

BENNO: A lot of people were honestly disappointed when Jimmie began playing just blues and no rock. With his creativity and songwriting, he could have gone to the moon. Him dropping rock was like Bob Dylan going electric to those of us who knew and loved his playing. People were shocked and upset. He could have developed that direction and been a very creative hit guitarist, but he just wasn't interested. Playing fast didn't impress him the way it impressed the rest of us. He was only interested in Jimmy Reed and other black blues artists.

JIMMIE VAUGHAN: Part of it was seeing Muddy Waters the very first time, at the Family Circle in Dallas. I decided right then that what I really liked was the music, and the rest of it was bullshit. Really, it was totally selfish, and I'm sure I neglected my family, totally focused on music as only a kid can do.

BENNO: People like Steve Miller and Don Henley were coming out of a blues background and making a mark. We had all played clubs together, and they all knew Jimmie and how great he was, but he wasn't interested in any of that pop business. He wasn't going for it at all.

JIMMIE VAUGHAN: I used to try to play fast, but I got bored with all these guitar players going "hidla-hidla-hidla, didlee-didlee-didlee." So I started thinking of the instrument differently and listening to how saxophonists phrase solos. When someone like [saxophonist] Gene Ammons plays, it's like having a conversation with somebody who's real comfortable with themselves. Guys like B. B. King or Junior Walker, when they play, they talk. So that's all I want to do, with my own voice. It's about communication.

In late '69, Texas found themselves in need of a bass player, and Jimmie asked his little brother to fill in. The fifteen-year-old Steve played bass in the band and was soon being called *Stevie,* the first time that became his name.

"We got a gig at the Vulcan Gas Company in Austin [October 31–November 1, 1969], with Phil Campbell on drums and Paul Ray and Doyle Bramhall singing, but we didn't have a bassist, so Stevie played bass, sort of," recalls Jimmie. "We tuned a Barney Kessel hollow-body guitar down to D, so it sounded more like a bass. All we ever did around the house was us trading back and forth between playing the lead parts and the rhythm parts and bass lines."

Still, Stevie's tenure in the band was brief. "I was 'little brother,' especially then," Stevie told *Guitar World*'s Bill Milkowski in 1984. "He was moving ahead a little faster than me, and I guess I was dragging it down a bit, so that didn't work out too well. But I think with any brothers there's a period of time when the little brother always gets in the way. That's just brother-to-brother shit."

Stevie next auditioned to be the bassist in the nine-piece horn band Liberation, but guitarist Scott Phares suggested they switch instruments as soon as he heard Vaughan play.

"One of the horn players said he knew a kid who would be a good fit on bass if his mother would let him do the gigs," Phares recalls. "This skinny fifteen-year-old shows up and plays a few songs, and we all agreed he was very good. Then we took a break, and Stevie asked if he could play my guitar. I was a decent guitar player, but he cleaned my clock, blowing us away on my white Telecaster. We all immediately decided that we'd switch instruments, and he handed me his '60s sunburst Fender Jazz bass."

Liberation played a lot of Chicago and Blood, Sweat & Tears material, as well as some Led Zeppelin and Jeff Beck and a handful of blues, mostly to appease Stevie. "We knew about Jimmie, but he was way up there in a different stratosphere," says singer Mike Reames. "He'd already done things like hang out with Janis Joplin!"

In addition to the horn section, led by saxophonist Jim Trimmier, the band had several lead singers, including Reames and Christian Plicque, a handsome, charismatic African American.

MIKE REAMES, *Liberation singer:* Stevie was very shy and seemed nervous, with that little shit-eating grin, like a jackass eating briars. He was fifteen, and I was a freshman in college, and he could be frustrating to deal with, like we'd be trying to get work done and he was messing around. There were other issues with having a kid in the band.

PHARES: Stevie loved to get high. He liked to do speed and play guitar. He liked methamphetamine pills like Desoxyn—"Yellow Ds"—and Dexedrine—"White Crosses" or "Crossroads." He would do speed, drink Colt 45 or Schlitz Bull malt liquor, and play guitar all day long.

In 1970, we played an SMU fraternity party at a Marriott, and at the end, Stevie drank all the half-empty drinks left on the tables. We all thought we were bulletproof.

JIMMIE VAUGHAN: Stevie was aware I had gotten into drugs. I was in Austin for a fraternity gig, and I went over to some guy's house to smoke weed and listen to blues records. He said, "You know what these guys are doing, right? They're shooting speed." So I started shooting speed, only on the weekends. You'd smoke marijuana on top of it and could play nonstop for a couple of days. You would get so high, and so *tuned in* that if someone dropped a pin across the room, you knew what the pitch was—in your mind anyhow.

TRIMMIER: Stevie transfixed me; the first time I heard him, he was the best guitar player I had ever heard. He was fleet of fingers and just in joyful control of the instrument. He did not practice—he played guitar, which was Jimmie's old Broadcaster with "Jimbo" carved in the back.

Stevie had stripped this 1951 Broadcaster, serial number 0964, of its clear finish and fitted it with two volume controls instead of one volume and one tone.

COLONNA: I was over at Stevie's house one day, and he said, "Check this out," and showed me the Broadcaster. He said, "This was in the closet, all in parts, and I put it together."

TRIMMIER: Stevie would play records for hours. He'd pick the needle up, play a lick, then run it back and play it fifty or a hundred times trying to get everything precisely right. He was listening intently and on a high level—and he listened with his fingers. I know that sounds mystical, but his fingers were part of his senses. They were in tune with his ears.

PHARES: Stevie could play anything note for note exactly like the records. He could sound just like Clapton on "Crossroads" and Jeff Beck on "Jeff's Boogie." Learning those songs note for note was a rite of passage for every Dallas guitar player.

SRV: If you played at the Cellar, you had to know "Jeff's Boogie." And nobody knew that it was really the Chuck Berry song "Guitar Boogie."

TOMMY SHANNON, *Double Trouble bassist:* In 1969, Uncle John [Turner, drummer] and I played Woodstock and recorded three albums with

Johnny Winter. When that band broke up, I flew back to Dallas and went to the Fog, the same club where I had first met Johnny. Walking up, I could hear the guitar from outside, and it sounded really special. I knew from those first few notes that I was hearing something great. Stevie's inner dynamic was coming through, with the exact same spirit everyone would know eventually. A bunch of people were talking to me, and I ignored them, looking to see who was making this big sound and was shocked to see a scrawny fifteen-year-old kid. He was awkward and shy and had real big feet. When we spoke, I told him the truth: "You're already better than all these other guys you're looking up to." He gave me a big smile, and we made friends right then and there.

PHARES: Many of our gigs were dances, but people would stop dancing to watch Stevie solo. At the high school, people would sit around the stage to get a close look at him. He had a long, white curly patch cord and he'd take a flying jump off the stage right into the middle of the dancers, walking around and playing his ass off. He was a showboat, but he could pull it off.

TRIMMIER: He just boogied. Everybody was older than him in all his early bands—and he made them all. Even at that age, there were no false notes. He was always true to the music.

PHARES: One night, ZZ Top walked into Arthur's with instruments in hand and said, "Hey, we're a South Texas band fixing to release an album, and we want to take two of your sets tonight to get some exposure." Mike said, "Are you guys any good?" and Billy Gibbons said, "We'll play, and if you don't like us, we'll leave." They got up there, and Stevie just about wet his pants—he couldn't wait to play some blues with Billy. They squared off and traded licks, and it was amazing.

BILLY F. GIBBONS, *ZZ Top guitarist:* Frank and Dusty and I had just teamed up, and Arthur's was a swanky nightclub. A young gunslinger announced, "I'm Jimmie Vaughan's brother, and I'd like to sit in. My name's Steve." And play he did! That was the first encounter of many.

TRIMMIER: I had a car and would drive Stevie around, often with him playing guitar in the passenger seat. He would talk about John Lee Hooker, trying to get those licks just right.

REAMES: I never needed to have a radio in my car. He'd sit in the back playing his acoustic guitar.

BRANDENBURG: Stevie would often ask me to drive him to Arnold and Morgan Guitar Shop, where he would buy three picks or a set of strings while breaking six or seven strings. He'd break one, hand me the guitar to put back, get another one, break a string. He'd also blow up tubes and speakers on amps playing so loud. Larry Morgan knew Stevie was never gonna buy anything. He'd always say, "I'll handle it," only occasionally asking Stevie to play a little quieter. The man was in business, but he and his techs would extend themselves to Stevie. This was something I saw all through Stevie's life; people just wanting to help him.

Vaughan was often sleeping through classes at Justin F. Kimball High School after late-night, speed-fueled gigs. He struggled in most classes, including music theory; an inability to read music kept him out of the school's stage band. The only class where he showed real promise was art, and he was proud to have some cartoons published in the school newspaper. His art skills were good enough to earn him a scholarship to Imagination's Growing Place, an experimental art class at Southern Methodist University.

In September 1970, Stevie cut two songs for a compilation album of Dallas teen bands with the group Cast of Thousands, fronted by Stephen Tobolowsky, who would go to become a successful character actor, notably playing Ned Ryerson in *Groundhog Day*. They were his first studio recordings. By January 1971, Vaughan had dropped out of school just months away from graduating, quit Liberation, and after short stints in several groups, including Lincoln and Pecos, formed his own band. Blackbird focused on psychedelic blues/rock and was fronted by Christian Plicque. Roddy Colonna was on drums, along with keyboardist Noel Deis, second drummer John Hoff, the well-established David Frame on bass, and Kim Davis on second guitar, often playing harmonized Allman Brothers lines with Stevie.

COLONNA: Stevie, Christian, and I would go listen to records at Cutter's house, who would tell us what songs we should play in the dream band we hadn't formed yet. By fall '71, we were gigging as Blackbird, and a

big influence was the Allman Brothers, which is why we added a second drummer. Stevie started playing slide on songs like "Statesboro
Blues," and he even sought out a Goldtop Les Paul like Duane Allman's.
He found a trashed-out Les Paul for about $200 with frets that were
turning green.

He started using a glass bottle to play slide after we saw the Allman
Brothers at the State Fair Music Hall [September 27, 1971], sitting up
in the balcony right above the stage, watching Duane Allman, Dickey
Betts, Jaimoe, and the rest. It was *unbelievable,* and we were heartbroken when Duane died a month later [October 29, 1971]. That night
we played at the Funky Monkey, and Stevie played the Goldtop in
honor of Duane and played his heart out.

One of Blackbird's regular gigs was at the Cellar, a rock-and-roll strip club
that was an important venue for Dallas bands playing original music and blues.

Blackbird, Austin, 1972. *(Courtesy
Cutter Brandenburg Collection)*

COLONNA: The Cellar was a small room with spotlights everywhere, and the band set up behind a little runway where the girls would dance. A phone onstage would ring; I'd answer it, and someone would say, "Y'all play a long instrumental," so a girl could get up for a striptease. Right before she showed it all, the lights would go off and she'd run offstage. Every once in a while, a professional stripper would come in and wow everybody.

We'd play a set, then two other bands would play, and we'd play again. We'd be off from 11:00 to 1:00, so we'd jump in the van and go jam at the Fog, Mother Blues, or the Funky Monkey.

PAUL "PAPPY" MIDDLETON, *Dallas guitarist, soundman, and mixer:* We used to sneak Stevie in to sit in with my band at Mother Blues, which was, shall we say, a full-service club. You could get anything there, so they were very careful about underage people on the premises. The owner would be up on the third floor playing poker with guys like Freddie King, and when he heard Stevie playing—because he was louder and different than anyone else, even then, he'd run down and chase him out.

COLONNA: We'd sit in with the soul guys at the Aragon Ballroom, or go smoke a joint somewhere and go back to the Cellar for the second set. ZZ Top played after us one night and called Stevie up to jam. Stevie sang "Thunderbird" with Gibbons yelling, "Sing it, Little Stevie, sing it!" That was one of the first songs Stevie would sing: "Get high, everybody get high!"

GIBBONS: "Thunderbird" was one of those pass-around fast shuffles that everybody knew.

COLONNA: His main guitar was a red semi-hollow Epiphone [a 1963 Epiphone Riviera], which he got cheap because it had sat in a store window and the sun had faded out the color of the guitar.

JIMMIE VAUGHAN: I left the "Jimbo" guitar for Stevie, and he took it to school and routed it out and put two P-90 pickups in it, or attempted to, which might explain why it had two volume knobs. He didn't want me to see what he'd done, so he traded it for the Epiphone Riviera. But it wasn't a secret weapon that we figured out how to rule the world with—it was just a $175 guitar. Guitars were like hot rods: everybody took them apart and customized 'em. It was like a '40 Ford.

COLONNA: It was all about tone with Stevie, even then. He started moving to larger string gauges, an idea he got from Jimmie. Stevie would make fun of guys that used thin strings. But the Epiphone was falling apart from the heavy string tension, and I constantly drove him to the store to get that guitar epoxied back together. The strings were also wreaking havoc on his fingertips, and he started using Krazy Glue to fix the holes in the ends of his fingers, which came from bending those heavy strings.

BRAMHALL: Stevie and Jimmie were the first ones I was ever around who were as into tone as anything. They weren't satisfied with just playing the notes. Most players at the time didn't think tone was that important, but Jimmie and Stevie definitely concentrated on having their own sounds from the beginning.

3

AUSTIN CITY LIMITS

Over the course of several months in 1970, Jimmie Vaughan and Doyle Bramhall both moved to Austin, along with several other musicians who would form the core of the city's blues scene. They didn't all know each other well or at all, but they were all lured by the city's more laid-back, less restrictive feel. Stevie would not be far behind.

"It was an environment that attracted musicians and people who liked to have fun," says guitarist Denny Freeman. "A lovely place with trees, funky houses with cheap rent, lots of pretty girls, and a lot of freaks where it felt safe to have long hair."

The state capital was still a sleepy town of 250,000 and, of course, the home of the University of Texas, where most of the Dallas crew had been playing parties for years. The city was full of advantages for young blues-obsessed musicians. Jimmie was no longer a rock star, and that was fine with him; in Austin, he could pursue his blues vision unimpeded.

BRAMHALL: The Cellar was really the only place in Dallas where you could play Muddy Waters on ten. In Austin, there were more places like that, and it was cheaper to live. It was like a little San Francisco; you could come down and express yourself, and people left you alone to do your thing. We started having a little scene.

DOYLE BRAMHALL II, *son of Doyle Bramhall, guitarist, friend of Stevie's:* Jimmie's house was sort of home base for everybody. It was a blues

Denny Freeman and "Little Doyle," Doyle Bramhall II.
(Connie Vaughan/Courtesy Denny Freeman)

commune vibe, a village, one big musical family, and everyone was very tight. Jimmie was like my uncle, and his daughter, Tina, was like my sister.

JIMMIE VAUGHAN: My daughter, Tina, had been born, and I was working construction because I'd stopped doing fraternity gigs and was just playing blues. I got the Monday night gig at the One Knite and played there with the Storm every week for five years. There would always be a line of dozens of motorcycles out front . . . you could get in a lot of trouble there if you weren't careful.

DEREK O'BRIEN, *Austin guitarist:* The One Knite was a super funky place with a coffin-shaped door and no cover. It was the greatest joint in town, and the Storm were the greatest band, playing authentic '50s / early '60s blues. Jimmie was like nobody else, nailing B. B. King's style and vibrato. He had a great ear and could hear something and just *do it,* picking up licks from all the great blues guitar players. He was playing through a black [Fender] Bassman [amp] with a single fifteen-inch speaker, instead of the four ten-inch speakers. Jimmie knew all those secrets for great tone.

JIMMIE VAUGHAN: On the cover of Willie Nelson's "Cowtown Jamboree" album [*Live Country Music Concert*], his steel guitarist is playing though a 1×15 Bassman. In those days, you could send your Bassman back to Fender and they'd recover it and change the speakers from 4×10 to 1×15, if you liked. It was real loud and clear. When that speaker blew up, I plugged my Silvertone 6×10 cabinet, fitted with Jensens, into the head.

W. C. Clark was an Austin guitarist, bassist, and singer who was on the road playing with soul singer Joe Tex. He would play at various East

Side clubs while home. Hearing young white Dallas bluesmen like Jimmie, Denny Freeman, singer Paul Ray, and Doyle Bramhall made him rethink his path.

W. C. CLARK, *Austin guitarist and bassist, member of Stevie's Triple Threat Revue:* Those guys were not playing music to make money, but for the feeling, and I felt the same way. We were all scholars and seekers of the blues. When I heard those guys laying it down and Doyle singing like Bobby Bland, I knew I wanted to be involved, so I quit Joe Tex, moved back to Austin, and became a hippie.

BRANDENBURG: Blackbird went to Austin one weekend to see Storm at the One Knite, where we could hardly get in the door. People would pass your money to the bar and they'd pass back a beer. Storm's music made everyone go nuts. The next night at the New Orleans Club, Storm opened for Krackerjack, which was the hottest band in town.

SHANNON: After we left Johnny [Winter] towards the end of '70, Uncle John and I moved to Austin and put Krackerjack together, and we were drawing huge crowds. Austin was a hippie town—all of the bands had beards, long hair, and played in shorts, blue jeans, and T-shirts. Unc and I learned about cool clothes in New York and dressed in a way no one in Austin had ever seen: velvet bell bottoms, Jimi Hendrix shirts, and high-heeled, square-toed boots, with shag haircuts. Led Zeppelin was our model, and we heard all the time, "Just a bunch of guys dressing like a bunch of girls!"

Inspired by Jimmie and his friends and by the encouragement of several people they met on that weekend visit—most importantly, Krackerjack booking agent Charlie Hatchett—Stevie and Blackbird moved to Austin in March 1972. "We'd been going back and forth between Dallas and Austin almost every weekend, so moving there made sense," recalls Colonna.

Blackbird played clubs while also opening for national touring acts, including Wishbone Ash, Zephyr featuring Tommy Bolin, Wet Willie, and Sugarloaf ("Green-Eyed Lady"). The band was playing blues/rock while the still-developing blues scene in Austin was steeped in traditionalism.

JIMMIE VAUGHAN: Stevie called and said he was coming down. He stayed with me for a bit, but I was married, with a kid and a day job, and trying to get something going myself. Stevie had his own friends and pursuits.

COLONNA: As soon as we got to Austin, we could see that there was a big divide between the blues people and the rock people. At a late-night party, Jimmie went off on Kim Davis, and he didn't seem to respect Blackbird, a rock/boogie band playing Allman Brothers songs.

DENNY FREEMAN, *guitarist, fellow Dallas native, bandmate of both Stevie's and Jimmie's:* By then, Hendrix had died and Cream had broken up, and a lot of us had turned towards hard blues and were getting pretty snobby about it. Blackbird was a rock band, but Stevie's role was inserting blues. Like Jimmie, Stevie had exceptional, obvious talent that couldn't be denied. Every once in a while, someone comes around who has a specialness that people just respond to, and that was the case with them both.

COLONNA: Charlie Hatchett kept us booked at places like the Abraxas in Waco, the Nickel Keg Saloon in San Marcos, and the Rolling Hills Club outside of Austin, which became the Soap Creek Saloon. I copied Uncle John Turner's way of doing business: you get your girlfriend to collect the money at the door and count every head so the club owner can't cheat you, buy a keg for thirty-five bucks, give away free beer, and let the girls in free. Do anything to get 'em in there dancing.

SHANNON: Blackbird was drawing big crowds because of Stevie's guitar playing. They were a really good band, with two drummers, organ, two guitarists, a bass player, and a singer, but everyone was talking about Stevie, who was playing Peter Green and Duane Allman licks. All of the musicians would be back at the bar saying, "Listen to that guy!"

COLONNA: Stevie *always* had a guitar in his hands—he played all of the time. As soon as he woke up in the morning, he'd get the yogurt, put it on the table, and play to an Earl Hooker or Albert King record, whoever his idols were that day. He was completely dedicated to the instrument, and he'd work on his playing constantly. He was real sincere about it—there was nothing phony-baloney about him. Listening to music and playing guitar were the biggest things in his life. He'd always be saying, "Listen to this!" Whatever he was into, he was into it *all the way*. His main amp then was a 4×12 Marshall bottom with a black-face Fender Bassman top that had "Euphoria" stenciled on it, and Stevie was convinced that Clapton had been in a band called Euphoria and that it might have been his amp.

JIMMIE VAUGHAN: Stevie was really good very young, but he really picked it up after moving down to Austin. He went from a really good kid to a real badass who just kept getting better and better.

COLONNA: We all moved into places that were too expensive for us, so when [Krackerjack singer] Bruce Bowland moved out of the band house on Sixteenth Street, my wife and I moved in. Shortly after, Stevie and his girlfriend, Glenda Maples, lost their place and crashed with us. We were all crammed into a tiny shotgun house, and all of these loser drug-dealer people came by all of the time. It was a bad scene. Early one morning, there were these two really seedy guys hanging around my back door, and when they came walking in, I yelled at them, and they said, "Oh, we're here to see Tommy." It was the break of day, and Tommy's speed connections were rolling in.

One was a wild-eyed, crazy rich kid from Houston with a brand-new Corvette. He was a super mean guy. I walked into Tommy's bedroom, and he wouldn't let me leave. He pulled out this Bowie knife and said, "Now, hold your foot still," and threw the knife into the floor, just clipping the edge of my boot.

SHANNON: Krackerjack got a record deal with Atlantic, and then we broke up! Flaring egos. Blackbird was also sort of falling apart, so we merged and called ourselves Blackbird—me, Stevie, Roddy, and Bruce Bowland.

COLONNA: Blackbird didn't have any original material, so a record deal was even more unlikely. Christian was getting junked out, hanging out with the really bad heroin crowd. He got busted, and we had to bail him out of jail. It got to where we just couldn't work with him anymore.

SHANNON: That band only lasted a few months, because we were all so crazy into drugs, then Krackerjack re-formed, with me, Uncle John,

Bruce, and Stevie and Robin Syler on guitars. Robin was very good, but he was intimidated by Stevie.

COLONNA: Tommy was really heavy into speed, and it soon made its way to Stevie and I. Maybe because of the drugs, the band was just wearing down. I was coming down with hepatitis but didn't know it. I was getting weaker and weaker, and they replaced me with Uncle John by the end of '72. I still lived in the house with all of them, and Tommy and Stevie told me one day that Uncle John was going to join, so I went home and cried! I was heartbroken.

Vaughan's stint playing alongside Shannon and Turner in the re-formed Krackerjack furthered his reputation and provided validation of his skills and of the possibilities inherent in expanding rather than mimicking classic blues. Unc's preference for flamboyant production and stage attire would prove to be Stevie's undoing.

"Stevie tried to get into the stage-clothes thing," says Shannon. "He came to a gig dressed in leotards and the weirdest shit I have ever seen! But Uncle John fired Stevie because he was onstage with a bulging wallet in his back pocket, which Unc thought wasn't cool. I was too messed up to intervene.

"Stevie was trying to find his place in the world and didn't realize how deep his talent was, that he was already better than all the older musicians he admired so much. He was very sensitive and very confused. All of his role models, guys like me, were out of our fucking minds on drugs and alcohol, and he was going to live that life. None of us understood where that would lead."

As Stevie's stint in Krackerjack came to an end, he joined Stump, with David Frame on bass, playing with them from the end of February to the beginning of May 1973. During this time, Vaughan was also bonding with Bramhall, as the two shared a desire to expand their repertoire beyond the blues, a feeling decidedly not shared by Jimmie.

"I was playing straight blues with Jimmie, but Stevie and I both wanted to branch out a little more," Bramhall said. "We were listening to Marvin Gaye and Sly Stone and wanted to incorporate some of that stuff into our music, so Stevie and I found each other getting together more often. Then he called and said that he had gotten a phone call from Marc Benno, who had a deal with A&M and a big tour lined up, and needed to put together a Texas blues-rock band."

Benno had partnered with Leon Russell in the band Asylum Choir in the late '60s. By '73, Russell was riding high, having played with Bob Dylan, Eric Clapton, George Harrison, and many others. Benno's many high-profile session gigs included playing guitar on the Doors' *L.A. Woman* album. Being in Benno's band was a big deal, and the group he put together and named the Nightcrawlers featured Doyle on drums, Stevie on guitar, Tommy McClure on bass, and ex-Chessmen and ZZ Top member Billy Etheridge on keyboards.

BENNO: I called Jimmie and offered him the gig, but he said, "I'm not interested. I don't want to do any rock and roll. Why don't you get my brother?" I asked if he thought he'd do it, and he said, "He will if I tell him to. Y'all are gonna go to Hollywood, huh?" And I said, "Yeah, I'm signed to A&M, and we're going to go make a record." And he goes, "I'll tell him to do this. Give him a call."

BRAMHALL: We went out to LA to record, and it was a kick for us just to be out of Texas. Other than little trips to Oklahoma or Louisiana, I don't think any of us had even left the state. We were in LA for two weeks, riding around in limos and living like rock stars. We recorded seven songs, including "Dirty Pool," the first song Stevie and I wrote together, and three of them are actually good. Then we went on a short tour with Humble Pie and the J. Geils Band. We played seven or eight gigs in places like Detroit, Chicago, and New York, and it was our first time out in the big world. Unfortunately, music took a backseat to drinking and drugging—especially for me—so while we played some good music, it was pretty much a mess.

BENNO: It was just a complete blur. We could do it pretty good but were drinking and drugging heavily, and there was a lot of shenanigans going on. Like we went to Barney's Beanery and there was a line around the block, and Billy Etheridge said, "We'll be sitting in there in a minute,"

Doyle Bramhall in the Nightcrawlers, Armadillo World Headquarters, 1973.
(Kathy Murray)

and he walked around the corner, phoned in a bomb threat, the place emptied out, and we walked in. It was crazy times, and stuff like that didn't even seem like a big deal.

BRAMHALL: I guess the label hated the record.

BENNO: They said it didn't sound like me. The music was good, but there wasn't really a category for it. It was kind of like the Allman Brothers, but it was more blues, and they didn't hear anything that they could really promote. They were kind of right; we missed the mark. There was some great stuff on the album by what you could call a great cult band, but it wasn't developed and it never even got mixed properly. They just called the whole thing off. I had invested a lot of time and money, and it just fell completely apart.

The Benno-less Nightcrawlers continued with a new bassist, Keith Ferguson, who quit Jimmie's band to join. The band built a bit of a following, and Stevie would occasionally bust out Stevie Wonder's "Superstition" or a Jimi Hendrix song.

BRAMHALL: We decided to keep the band together. We still wanted to branch out from Jimmie's Muddy Waters and B. B. King–style blues. Mostly we just knew we wanted to keep writing and playing together.

JIMMIE VAUGHAN: Doyle had a great voice, and Keith had played with Lewis Cowdrey and all of these people that had come to Austin from California. Doyle and Keith weren't just older than Stevie; they were older than me, and Stevie learned a lot from playing with such experienced guys.

MIKE STEELE, *friend of Stevie's:* Keith was a huge influence on Stevie in terms of both music and style. Jimmie and Stevie were really close, and there was a deep admiration between them, but Stevie wasn't always playing what Jimmie thought he should be playing, and he would tell him in no uncertain terms. Stevie was always trying to get big brother's approval, while Keith would tell him to play what he wants. He was a different kind of big brother, telling Stevie, "Be yourself, and you will be all right."

JOE SUBLETT, *saxophonist, member of the Cobras:* I heard about the Nightcrawlers playing at this little joint La Cucaracha. Those guys were so cool, and Stevie stuck out. His playing had less Albert King and Jimi Hendrix and a lot more B. B. King, Otis Rush, and Buddy Guy as well as a Kenny Burrell / Grant Green soul/jazz vibe. Doyle was singing from the kit, and he was great. It was exciting.

O'BRIEN: My car broke down late at night, and Stevie offered me a lift. I was going to get someone to try and look at my car, and he said, "What are you talking about? Just hang out and we'll deal with it in the morning." He was living with Doyle, and the next morning, the two of them were playing together in the garage, working on songs.

GIBBONS: That was one stellar combination with a stalwart and solid sound. The combination of Doyle's remarkable singing and Stevie's guitar-stinging was something to behold.

LINDI BETHEL, *Stevie's girlfriend, 1974–1979:* I saw the Nightcrawlers with Stevie and Storm with Jimmie at Soap Creek. My girlfriends had

Stevie Ray Vaughan in the Nightcrawlers, Armadillo World Headquarters, 1973.

(Kathy Murray)

been raving about Stevie, and there was lots of love for him and Jimmie in the graffiti on the walls of the women's bathroom, with hearts all over!

At the end of the night, Stevie came over and put his head down on the table. I said, "Are you okay?" and he said, "Oh, I'm fine—just tired." When I went to leave, I had a flat tire. I saw Jimmie driving away, so I yelled and asked for a ride. I got in his car, and as we started driving, the door opens, and Stevie jumps in next to me. Our legs touched, and I felt a shot of electricity. We didn't say a word to each other.

We pull up at my house, and as I'm getting out, Stevie asks, "Do you want to go to a party at my brother's house?" and I said, "Okay!" But there was no party—it was just me and Stevie. We talked all night and spent the night there. That's when we fell in love and became a couple for the next five years.

The Nightcrawlers signed a contract with ZZ Top manager Bill Ham, who recorded their show at the Warehouse in New Orleans and threw the group out on the road for extended runs. They opened for Kiss and Electric Light Orchestra (ELO) in Detroit and Atlanta before breaking up somewhere in Mississippi. Ham demanded they repay the money he had invested. A dispirited Vaughan felt broken. He was not yet twenty years old.

"No one really knew what was going on with them and Bill Ham, and there were always rumors that he signed all these guitarists like Van Wilks, Stevie, and Eric Johnson just to stop them from being competition to ZZ Top," says Freeman. "All I know is they were a great band who never made any money or recorded. All they did was go out on the road and starve to death eating mayonnaise sandwiches. With Stevie, Keith, and Doyle, that band could have been a real powerhouse."

Adds Colonna, "Stevie wanted out of that contract with Bill Ham. Kim Davis and David Frame had a similar situation with their band Point Blank, which Ham also managed. They were held back and never had any real success."

By September, the Nightcrawlers were broken up, and Stevie was frozen due to contractual obligations to Ham. He sat in with some people but did not form a new band. Bramhall, worried about his health and growing drug habit, moved back to Dallas. Stevie auditioned for a Dallas fusion band, playing some of the music to Derek O'Brien and asking him his opinion. "I didn't know what to say because it seemed like the only reason he'd do it was because he really needed the money," says O'Brien. "He turned them down."

When Benno called Vaughan and told him he was hanging out songwriting in Bolinas, a hippie oasis in Northern California, Vaughan asked him to send a ticket. He had nothing going on—and very likely wanted to put some distance between himself and the debt-seeking Ham. Among the musicians they jammed with was Jerry Garcia, who told them that he would be signing acts to the Grateful Dead's new Round Records and wanted to work with them. But with Benno still signed to A&M, which wouldn't release him from the deal, signing with another label was impossible. Benno and Vaughan eventually cut more sides in Los Angeles. When nothing happened, Stevie returned to Austin, where a new band had recently taken shape: Paul Ray left Storm and formed the Cobras with bassist Alex Napier and guitarist Denny Freeman. Stevie Ray Vaughan would soon join them in what was to become Austin's hottest band, providing immeasurable momentum to his development as a guitarist, singer, and performer.

4

STEPPIN' OUT

The Nightcrawlers reunited for a night to open for Paul Ray and the Cobras on New Year's Eve 1974, at Adobe Flats in Dallas, and Stevie asked Ray if he could join his band, which had a growing club reputation. Before welcoming him into the fold, Ray checked with his bandmates. It was particularly important for Ray to get the approval of guitarist Denny Freeman, whose nickname was the Professor due to his thoughtful manner and thorough knowledge of guitar styles and music history.

"I was the Cobras' sole guitar player, so it was a little tough to have Stevie join, but it was also really exciting to play with him, and I loved the guy," says Freeman, who was already a friend and occasional roommate of Jimmie's. "I've heard people say that I taught Stevie how to play, and that's ridiculous. He was great the first time I heard him. I sometimes helped him find chords or a note outside the blues scale, but there is nothing he could have learned from me about blues playing. He wasn't as strong a rhythm player as he would become and didn't fully grasp unusual chord changes that well yet, but his lead playing was there, and any fan of his later music would immediately recognize him."

STEELE: Stevie learned so much from Denny, and his playing grew tremendously. His self-confidence and charisma blossomed, and he started moving away from the Clapton-influenced rock style into more of an Albert, Freddie, and B. B. King blues style.

Stevie and Denny in Paul Ray and the Cobras.
(Mary Beth Greenwood)

JIMMIE VAUGHAN: When you first get going, you've got an idea in your head about how you want your playing to be and look for like-minded guys you don't have to explain everything to. It took Stevie a little while in Austin to find the right combination as his playing evolved. It all started coming together when he joined the Cobras. In about a year and a half, he went from a kid playing guitar to "Stevie Ray Vaughan."

SUBLETT: Stevie's approach to music was fully formed, but chores like having money to pay rent or buy a car were kind of secondary. It could be irritating, but he was a lovable guy, and you couldn't really get mad at him.

FREEMAN: He was younger than the rest of us, and he could be frustrating to deal with. Say we were getting ready to drive to Lubbock for a gig and we're supposed to meet at the drummer's house at noon. By 12:30, everyone's there except for Stevie. Someone tries to call him and his phone's cut off, so you say, "Somebody ought to drive by and get Stevie."

So you go by his house, knock on the door, he answers and he just got out of bed and says, "Hey, let me take a shower." So you wait, then he comes out to the car and goes, "Hey, can we take my girlfriend to work?" "Okay, Stevie." So we drop her off and start back, when he says, "Anyone need to go to the music store?" "No, Stevie, we've all been there." "Well, could we stop by because I need to get some strings?" "Okay, Stevie." Then we're on the way and he'll go, "Hey, have y'all eaten?" "Yes, Stevie, we've all eaten." "Well, could we run into Dan's Hamburgers so I can grab me a few?" Then we'd get there and it would be, "Could someone lend me five dollars?" Then we'd finally get out of town.

SUBLETT: There was always that thing with Stevie: "Joe, you got any money?"

RODNEY CRAIG, *Cobras drummer:* One time we went to pick him up on our way out of town, and there was a note on his door that said, "At the Laundromat." So we went down there and had to wait for him to finish his laundry. But he was a great bandmate who never copped an attitude.

FREEMAN: It was really difficult to get mad at Stevie and harder to stay mad at him, because he was sweet, funny, and nice. And he kept that sweetness throughout his life. I loved the little guy. We all did.

JIMMIE VAUGHAN: Stevie was very kind, soft-spoken, personable—truly a sweet, gentle person that would give you the shirt off his back and do anything for people he liked.

STEELE: Stevie always had a positive outlook on life. Despite not having money, struggling, and being on the couch circuit, he was always upbeat and looked to the positive side of things. Music was his driving force, and he figured the rest would fall in place. And he was right. He was great to have as a friend; he always had your back.

B. B. KING, *king of the blues:* He reminded me of my sons when they were about seven or eight years old. He just had so many questions and would follow me around, happy and smiling and eager to please.

DR. JOHN, *New Orleans blues pianist and guitarist:* Stevie had this real boyish charm. He kept this very appealing childhood innocence about him even when he wasn't really innocent at all.

CLARK: I wouldn't call him childlike. To me, he always seemed older than his years because he could be so serious and intent about life and music.

BETHEL: Though he was only twenty-one, he was very mature in how deep, sensitive, and aware he was. He was like the first real man I'd ever met. He was a very soulful, humble person and would never talk bad about anyone. But he could be insecure. It seemed like he needed a lot of love.

FREEMAN: Stevie almost didn't talk about anything except guitars and music. He was completely obsessed with it, and so was I. We had similar tastes and were always trying to turn each other on to new stuff. Those were fun, exciting days because we were excited about everything. We would sit around for hours talking about music. That might sound boring, but with someone with a burning passion like Stevie, it's anything but. He was just consumed with playing the damn guitar.

SUBLETT: He was focused on what he was doing as a player. He had a vision of who he wanted to be, and everything he did was towards that end. I always figured that he would get famous and make a lot of money and have someone to take care of all the other stuff for him.

BENNO: Stevie never put the guitar down. He would walk around the house with it around his neck. Like a basketball star dribbling everywhere, whatever little chore he was doing, he had the guitar.

SUBLETT: He was our honorary roommate and lived with us all the time. I'd come home from gigs and see him lying on the couch, dead asleep with a guitar in his hands, like he fell asleep playing.

CIDNEY COOK AYOTTE: Even when he was a little kid, Stevie always had a guitar in his lap.

CRAIG: I never once went to his house when he wasn't playing along to records by Django Reinhardt, Jimi Hendrix, or Albert King. He was incessant.

RAY HENNIG, *owner of Heart of Texas music:* I've owned a guitar store since 1960, and I've seen a lot of great musicians, but I don't believe I've ever come across anyone half as obsessed with the guitar as Stevie was. He

Bottoms up at the After Ours Club Austin, 9/25/77. *(© Ken Hoge)*

used to hang out in my store, just noodling on guitars all the time. I would say that he was one of my best customers except he didn't have any money. He was broke all the time, so he never paid for anything in those days. He used to come by on his way to a gig and ask for a pack of strings. I'd toss him one, and he'd say, "Hey, if I make any money tonight, I'll pay you." And he would. I lent him guitars all the time. He'd take them for a week or two, then bring them back.

FREEMAN: We liked our Strats and Fender amps, but the gear was not the main thing. The focus of our passion was songs and records that we hadn't heard before.

CLARK: He would not pass by a music store; he had to go in there and check out the guitars, and he was not looking for beauty. He was looking for sounds and tones. One time someone just walked up to him and gave him a guitar, and I thought, "Goddamn. People do that?" People would see how good he was and want him to have their instrument or to play something on it and hope that gives it some soul.

HENNIG: One day in '74, he brought back a nice Strat he had been borrowing and was looking through all the instruments when he came to this ol' beater. He picked it up and must have played around with it for a half an hour, just making chords, turning it over, looking at it, weighing it, before he asked if he could plug it in. I said, "Sure, but it sure is ugly." So he plugged in and played for an hour or so, then told me he wanted it and asked if he could swap it for the one he had just returned. I said, "Well, you're ripping yourself off. That has got to be the cheesiest Strat I've ever traded for. It's raggedy assed and beat to death. What do you want it for?" He said, "It just feels good, Ray. It feels real good." I figured he'd bring it back in a day or two, but he never did. That became his Number One.

5

BLUES WITH A FEELING

I n 1974, Jimmie Vaughan and Storm, with Lewis Cowdrey on harmonica and vocals, were playing at Alexander's Place in South Austin when Kim Wilson, a singer and harmonica player from California, sat in. Jimmie thought he was fantastic and soon flew to Minnesota, where Wilson was living, to play together for a couple of weeks. They returned to Austin to form a new band, whose name they had already settled on: the Fabulous Thunderbirds.

In their first months, the T-Birds played with different rhythm sections at the Rome Inn, the One Knite, and any other place that would have them. Jimmie was also still playing with the Storm, and at one of their gigs, he discovered another great singer, the sultry Fort Worth native Lou Ann Barton, and decided that his new band would have two dynamic front people, one male and one female.

"I was visiting Austin with my friend [drummer] Mike Buck, and we went and sat in with Storm at the Rooster Tail, and Jimmie flipped out and said, 'I'm putting you in my new band,'" Barton recalls. "I said, 'I don't live here, honey.' He introduced me to Denny [Freeman], then took me over to a house where Denny, Stevie, and [Cobras bassist] Alex Napier lived and said, 'This is where you're going to stay.' It wasn't a question. I didn't know any of these people, but Jimmie was like a madman on the guitar, the best white player I've ever known. He had the tone and touch and played in a style that made me go crazy and get up and move. There was power and groove and sexiness in everything he played. When I heard him, I thought, 'That's the guy for me.' So I stayed in Austin."

The Fabulous Thunderbirds did not become a steady gigging band with a consistent rhythm section, bassist Pat Whitefield and drummer Fredde "Pharaoh" Walden, until July 1975, when twenty-five-year-old Clifford Antone opened Antone's nightclub on East Sixth Street, at the time a desolate stretch of town. The club grew out of late-night jam sessions in the back room of his sandwich shop and import/export business. A blues fanatic from Port Arthur on the Gulf Coast, Antone was on a mission to both expose the growing crop of great young blues musicians in town and to shine a light on the music's giants, many of whom were struggling to continue careers at all.

"Clifford was just so passionate and serious about the blues, and he so much wanted to have the club so he could just hear the music, and so the guys could have a place to play," says Susan Antone, Clifford's sister, who was involved from the club's start. "He just wanted people to know about and see the great blues men and women."

Many blues musicians found themselves with staggering careers in 1975, including some of the sidemen who crafted the music's classic sounds alongside their iconic bandleaders, including Jimmy Reed's guitarist Eddie Taylor, Howlin' Wolf guitarist Hubert Sumlin, Little Walter's guitarist Luther Tucker, and Muddy Waters's guitarist Jimmy Rogers and pianists Pinetop Perkins and Sunnyland Slim. All became Antone's regulars, usually arriving solo and playing with a house band, often the Fabulous Thunderbirds, who would regularly open shows and then back the star attraction. Antone also went out of his way to reunite blues stars with the sidemen who helped them forge their signature sounds, such as Reed and Taylor or John Lee Hooker and harmonica player Big Walter Horton. Reigning blues stars like B. B. King, Albert King, and Muddy Waters also came to Antone's with their bands.

JIMMIE VAUGHAN: Stevie and I had been playing at different clubs around town three, four nights a week in different lineups. Between Austin, Houston, San Antonio, and Dallas, you could play somewhere every

Jimmie Vaughan and The Fabulous Thunderbirds with Angela Strehli sitting in at Antone's. Kim Wilson and Keith Ferguson in the background.
(Watt M. Casey Jr.)

night of the week. And then Antone's opened, and all kinds of incredible stuff happened. It was the only place that wanted blues music all of the time.

FREEMAN: The hippie country thing was really happening, and everyone jumped on that bandwagon, which made it tough for us blues guys to get good gigs. Antone's was our ground zero from day one.

JIMMIE VAUGHAN: We played Antone's the first week it opened, and we were there three or four times a week.

CRAIG: Clifford was such a blues fanatic. He said, "You're not going to believe this: I've got Jimmy Reed for *five nights*!" There were twenty people there on Wednesday, and Clifford couldn't understand why the place wasn't packed.

TERRY LICKONA, *Austin City Limits producer:* Clifford was on a mission with a different vision and dream. Everyone else thought he was crazy opening up a music club in a converted men's store in a sketchy, pretty dead part of town, but he was able to book these incredible blues acts, and the opportunity to see them for a relatively cheap ticket was remarkable for anyone with any roots music knowledge.

FREEMAN: Clifford brought in people we never dreamed we'd ever see, much less meet, much less play with. It provided us with incredible opportunities to get to know and learn from the masters.

ANGELA STREHLI, *Austin blues singer:* Clifford's whole idea was to educate people to the blues by having the masters there and to have the rest of us open and back them. The blues' biggest supporters were often purists who thought that we shouldn't devote our lives to this, so those were not very happy times. Our heroes themselves were the ones who encouraged us and were delighted that we were devoting our lives to something they created.

JIMMIE VAUGHAN: We were all scared shitless the first time we backed Muddy Waters. After our second song opening the show, Muddy lifted the curtain, looked down from upstairs, and gave me a big smile and nod. He took us in after that, getting us a bunch of gigs in Boston—the first time the band left Texas. He really encouraged us to keep doing what we were doing.

LICKONA: A lot of these legends didn't have bands, and once they realized there were amazing musicians in Austin who could not only play the parts but excel at it, word spread very quickly. Then they looked forward to coming to a place where they would be treated well and play with great musicians.

JIMMIE VAUGHAN: We would open most shows and then back up guys like Jimmy Rogers or Eddie Taylor, who would often come for extended stays, so we would really spend a lot of time together. Blues is a circle, and Antone's put us in the middle of it, playing with our heroes and even our heroes' heroes. We had to know our shit! It was like going to college. It was amazing to be able to meet your heroes and have them approve of you.

Barton left the T-Birds within a year, and the rhythm section shifted to drummer Mike Buck and bassist Keith Ferguson, a quartet that grew together through their regular Antone's gigs.

DENNY BRUCE, *Fabulous Thunderbirds manager, 1977–1982:* I started working with the T-Birds when mutual friend Ray Benson got us together. I flew to Austin, went directly to Antone's, saw them backing Hubert Sumlin, and then playing their own set. The first song was "Scratch My Back," and I could hear what their first album would sound like in my head, so I became their manager.

BILL BENTLEY, *music editor,* The Austin Sun, *1974–1978:* Jimmie and Stevie didn't hang out much. They were both busy establishing their own careers. Jimmie never looked ambitious, but he knew how good he was. He was a professional musician since he was fourteen. He started the T-Birds, and that was it; he was going for it. As Stevie started to rise, the T-Birds were the hottest band in Austin. Kim was a fantastic singer and harmonica player, and Jimmie was a little wilder then, when they had so much time to fill up.

BRUCE: They were very ambitious and wanted to get on the road, to become a national act. I couldn't get them any kind of record deal despite a year of trying hard. The punk invasion was in full swing, and a white blues band wasn't what people wanted, so though they had a lot of interest from big music people, it was hard to nail anything down.

[Producer] Joel Dorn said he was about to get them signed to Island. [Songwriter] Doc Pomus loved them and said something would happen soon. One of Bob Dylan's girlfriends knew Kim. She said Bob was getting his own label with Columbia and wanted them. Bob's person said they'd be in touch after they made the deal. At least six months went by, and I was set to make a deal with Chrysalis for a new label, Takoma; I would co-own, sign, and produce acts. I told the band they could be the first act and start recording the next week, and they jumped at it. They went into the studio and played live.

In 1976, Albert King played Antone's for the first time, on three consecutive nights, April 29 to May 1. Unlike some of the other blues greats, King had never given up his band or stopped touring regularly. He had his own tour bus, which he drove himself, and he arrived in Austin with his customary flair.

Albert King at Antone's, Home of the Blues.
(Watt M. Casey Jr.)

King was an intimidating man who stood six foot five with broad shoulders and usually had a pipe clenched between his teeth, which sparkled with gold. Onstage, his Gibson Flying V looked like a ukulele in his massive hands. His tough tone and aggressive playing style, marked by huge, multiple-string bends, were equally macho. The lefty held his right-handed guitar upside down and tuned in an enigmatic fashion that is still debated, the combination of which gave him a highly distinctive style that's been oft-copied but rarely duplicated. Stevie Ray Vaughan was an exception; Albert King's style was at the very heart of his playing. He was not going to miss an opportunity to see his idol perform and hopefully to interact with him. Clifford Antone, who died in 2006, said that Stevie begged him to ask Albert to let him sit in.

JIMMIE VAUGHAN: We could argue about who's the greatest, but Albert King is in that conversation. He was absolutely amazing. And he came to Antone's with his great band and all his hit records. We're all there. It's a packed weekend night, and Clifford says, "I'm gonna ask Albert to let Stevie sit in." Well, nobody asked Albert King to sit in. That really was the rule, but Clifford tells him, "There's this kid we call Little Stevie, and you gotta hear him." Albert tells him to do you-know-what to himself.

STREHLI: Albert was a gruff person and wouldn't take any nonsense, so for Clifford to even ask him to do this was quite incredible.

JIMMIE VAUGHAN: Clifford didn't give up easily, so he does it again the next night: "That kid's here . . ." Albert can't believe he's being asked again, so he says, "Now I'm curious. This better be good." It was so far out; nobody would ask Albert King to sit in unless you were dumb or something. I don't even know if Jimi Hendrix would do it.

GUS THORNTON, *Albert King bassist:* I played with Albert for years and only remember a few people sitting in. It's not something he usually did.

SUBLETT: I was sitting right next to Stevie when Clifford came over and said, "Albert said you can come up." None of us could believe it, but if Clifford wanted you to do something, you were going to do it—apparently even Albert King!

STREHLI: Of course, Stevie just burned, like he always did. There was Little Stevie up there with Big Albert killing it, and it really tickled Albert— and all of us! He started playing Albert King licks and doing it really good, and Albert looks down and shakes his head.

JIMMIE VAUGHAN: It was badass. We all stood there with our mouths open as Stevie played really good Albert King licks.

SUBLETT: Stevie was shredding, and Albert turned away his fretboard as if to say, "This young punk is ripping me off. I'm not going to let him see what I'm doing." He was paying big respect to Stevie because he couldn't believe the skinny little white kid was pulling it off. Stevie was never intimidated onstage with his guitar, no matter the setting.

O'BRIEN: Stevie shocked Albert, who put on a show; when Stevie was soloing, Albert was taking his guitar and bunching the curtains around it, pretending to be scared. Stevie was winning Albert over. Albert knew Stevie was something different, and he let Stevie know that. It really felt like a milestone for Stevie.

THORNTON: Albert loved Stevie and his playing. A lot of people play Albert's music, but Stevie was about the only one who could get the touch and feel right.

ALBERT KING, *Blues guitar great:* If you play too fast or too loud, you cancel yourself out. Once you lose the feeling, you got nothing but a show going on. It's not deep. No doubt about it, Stevie had what it takes.

JIMMIE VAUGHAN: Albert didn't like anyone, but he liked Stevie! He put his arm around him, and from then on, it was Big Albert and Little Stevie. Everybody went, "Whew, that was scary." I would never have tried that, but you've got to admire the audacity.

6

CRAWLING KINGSNAKES

The Cobras' weekly gig at the Soap Creek Saloon, dubbed "Tuesday Night Cobra Club," became one of the hottest nights in town, in the process helping expand the scope of one of Austin's cosmic cowboy hubs. Fifty-cent shots of tequila helped lure blues lovers out to the country on Tuesday evenings. The Soap Creek was a roadhouse atop a hill down a rutted dirt road bumping off Bees Cave Road, about five miles outside of central Austin. It was owned and run by George and Carlyne Majewski and known as both "Dope Creek" and "the Honky Tonk in the Hills." The old wooden farmhouse had two big rooms, a rambling structure that was one of the first Austin places where rednecks and longhairs happily rubbed elbows. Asleep at the Wheel, Willie Nelson, Townes Van Zandt, and Jerry Jeff Walker were all regular performers, along with Doug Sahm, who lived across the parking lot in a little house hidden by trees.

There was a giant doorman named Billy Bob, a couple of pool tables, an eclectic jukebox, rough-hewn wooden walls covered with posters of past and future shows, and a dance floor that was usually packed. While disco was beginning to rule the nation's clubs, Paul Ray and the Cobras had Austinites jumping up to boogie to old-time upbeat blues and R&B by the likes of Bobby "Blue" Bland and Ray Charles. Their original music was in the same vein. Stevie began to step to the front more often, digging into a slow blues or two every night, and the crowd had to get used to his extended

Paul Ray and the Cobras, 1976. Denny Freeman far left, Stevie far right.
(Watt M. Casey Jr.)

soloing, sometimes using the guitar excursions as an excuse to go out in the parking lot and smoke a cigarette or joint.

FREEMAN: The Soap Creek Saloon was the hot place that only wanted country, and we finally got in there when someone asked for us to open—I think it was John Lee Hooker, because our friend played bass with him. We turned it into a regular Tuesday-night booking, and "the Cobra Club" became the hottest thing in town, probably because a lot of pretty girls loved us—and where they go, the guys follow. We were a fun band stretching out from three-chord blues playing dance music with multiple singers. And, of course, we had Stevie.

CRAIG: I said to Carlyne, "If you give us the gate, you can have the bar." Within three months, we had five hundred to six hundred people on a Tuesday night. At two dollars a head, we starting making real good money.

CHRIS "WHIPPER" LAYTON, *Double Trouble drummer:* Joe Sublett was my friend, and I heard so much about the Cobras and finally went to check them out at the Soap Creek. Walking up, I could hear a guitar solo playing as loud and clear as if the band was outside the building, and I thought, "That's kind of wild."

I walked in and saw Stevie, who had stepped to the front and was soloing on Number One, and I was mesmerized. When I was younger, I snuck into a place and saw Freddie King play from the back of the room. This reminded me of that. Stevie's playing was great, and he had this very demanding charisma; you couldn't not look at him. I loved the band, but I was really taken by Stevie's playing. He and Denny and Joe would play harmonized lines and two-guitar, one-horn stabs, like a horn section, that sounded great. I later learned Denny did those arrangements.

TRIMMIER: Stevie's style had become really bluesy and soulful. He was playing through a tweed Peavey Vintage with no feedback or heavy sustain. It was more like a turned-up Howard Roberts jazz thing. He was starting to find his sound. Stevie made that band pretty damn special.

CRAIG: I helped book three nights at a club in my hometown of Lubbock. I called the guy to book some more, and he said, "I'd love to have you guys back, but that guitar player is just too loud." His clientele had given him shit about that. We tried to get Stevie to turn down, and he'd fiddle with his knobs, but nothing happened! He had to get the tone, man.

In May 1977, the Cobras were named Band of the Year by *The Austin Sun,* boosting their stock. *The Sun* wrote, "They play hard but smooth, don't talk or waste time between songs, and don't need any stage histrionics. . . . Then there's guitarist Stevie Vaughan, cited by many observers as the man who'll one day take his place among the great Texas blues guitarists."

Says Freeman, "It was a big deal and a good feeling. *The Austin Sun* was very meaningful around town. When we got that award, our manager said, 'Our price just doubled.'"

Around the same time, the Cobras did some recording, cutting "St. James Infirmary," sung by Ray, and "Thunderbird," the Nightcaps' song that had been a local favorite, sung by Vaughan, who was just starting to get comfortable fronting the band as a singer as well as a guitarist.

SUBLETT: Stevie always sang one song a set, usually a slow blues like "Tin Pan Alley." He was learning how to sing and felt a little insecure about it, but his soloing was fully developed, and he would take full advantage of the moment: one blues would be ten or fifteen minutes. The truth is, a lot of people would step outside because they weren't ready for a long, slow blues, but Stevie played great and kept getting more comfortable out front. At some point, everyone got on board. It was,

Stepping to the fore with the Cobras at the Soap Creek Saloon. *(Kathy Murray)*

"There's Stevie Ray Vaughan," and then he could play slow blues songs all night long.

LAYTON: When Stevie first started singing, he was real sheepish and had to be encouraged. He'd do "Crosscut Saw," by Albert King, inching his way to the mic, and you could barely hear him; [*whispers*] "I'm a crosscut saw . . ." He almost never opened his eyes while singing; he would sort of brace himself, and if he kept his eyes closed, he wouldn't see anyone looking at him.

As Vaughan slowly became more comfortable as a front man, he asked Angela Strehli to teach him "Texas Flood," a simmering slow blues by Arkansas bluesman Larry Davis that was a nightly showstopper for her.

STREHLI: He said that he always liked "Texas Flood," which I had been doing for years, and asked if I could teach him the words, which I did.

FREEMAN: I had a 45 of Larry Davis's "Texas Flood" that Keith Ferguson had given me, and Stevie asked to borrow it because he was learning the guitar part. He returned it with a big chip! It was still playable, and I still have it.

DIANA RAY, *major player in the Austin blues world; wife of Paul Ray:* At least he returned Denny's record! Paul always complained about Stevie borrowing records and never giving them back. You couldn't stay mad at the guy, though.

STREHLI: He needed encouragement to sing; he was still a little scared. But he took the song and made it so associated with him that I quit doing it, because eventually everyone thought I was imitating him.

ERIC JOHNSON, *virtuoso Austin guitarist:* Stevie had some real magic with that song from the very beginning. He was very sensitive and concerned about the gravity of the composition, and putting himself into it, so the focus became the song. The dexterity and elevated playing only become timeless in the context of a strong vehicle and, like all artists, he understood that. I admired his singing as much as his playing, It was just part and parcel of the whole thing.

COLONNA: Bill Campbell, a very influential white blues guitarist in Austin, told Stevie, "Man, you gotta start singing. Find a singer you really like and copy him." And Stevie decided to copy Doyle, who had copied Ray Charles and Bobby "Blue" Bland. Doyle had a tremendous voice, and he was Stevie's model.

BRAMHALL II: Stevie told me many times that he wanted to sound like a combination of Bobby Bland and my dad.

SUBLETT: He really wanted to be a good singer, and he worked hard at it. Stevie wasn't gonna just learn the words and make do. He approached it with the same seriousness and intent that he did his guitar playing. I walked into our apartment one night, and Stevie was sitting on the floor singing along with a Ray Charles record. He sang it one time, then stopped and said, "Is it this way or this way?" and then sang it a

Stevie's last gig with the Cobras, Soap Creek Saloon, 10/77.
(© Ken Hoge)

slightly different way; his ears were so acute, and he was homing in on the minute subtleties.

I said, "Dude, they both sound great!" He was focusing on this one little phrase, listening to the microtones, the really tiny units between the notes which most of us can't hear. He was thinking about it on a much deeper level because his hearing and analysis of things were really deep.

LAYTON: The second time I saw the Cobras, Rodney Craig overslept and was late, so Joe said, "Chris, come up here and play with us!" He vouched for me, but none of the band knew me, so they kept saying, "Let's just wait." But the Soap Creek was packed, so they finally called me up and we launched into a song. I looked around for a cue, and Stevie was looking back at me, giving me a nod of approval and a couple of winks. It's cool that my first encounter with Stevie was us playing together.

CRAIG: I had a family and would work construction all day, come home, take a nap, get up to play a gig, come home at 3:00 a.m., go to bed, and start over the next day. I ended up oversleeping occasionally, and that one turned out to be historical. Chris was in the right place at the right time.

LAYTON: I've got to thank Rodney, because if he hadn't overslept, I might never have gotten the chance to play with Stevie.

7

COME ON (PART 1)

The Cobras had a growing reputation and were drawing large local crowds when Ray developed vocal nodes in July 1977 and had to stop singing for several months. The rest of the band decided to fill in at the mic and keep pushing on. Stevie's exposure and experience as a front man continued to grow, and the next month he abruptly left the Cobras just after Ray returned. While his bandmates accepted the departure as inevitable, it was a blow to a group riding high on their Band of the Year award.

"I wasn't surprised when he left, but I was upset," says Sublett. "His energy was one of the things that made playing in the band so much fun. Standing between Stevie and Denny was incredibly inspiring and exciting. He asked me to join him, but I didn't have the foresight to follow him out of a popular band making decent dough."

Adds Freeman, "It wasn't surprising when Stevie decided to go front his own band. He was picking up fans along the way, and it was just time for him to go become Stevie Ray Vaughan. It was obvious that he had some sort of destiny, and we were all rooting for him. He was taking a big chance, but Stevie wasn't afraid."

On September 23, 1977, Jeff Nightbyrd wrote in *The Austin Sun*, "The reason for the split appears to be that Paul Ray's moving in a more mainstream direction while Stevie wants to play blues; also Stevie Vaughan lately has been recognized as a star in his own right, and he wants a band."

Vaughan formed the Triple Threat Revue, so named because it featured three front-people: Stevie Ray, blues belter Lou Ann Barton, and the sweet-singing bassist W. C. Clark. The drummer was Fredde "Pharaoh" Walden, and the keyboardist was Mike Kindred, an old Oak Cliff friend and former member of Krackerjack and Storm who had already written the great moody tune "Cold Shot," which quickly became a Triple Threat staple.

Triple Threat Revue, 12-4-77, L-R: Mike Kindred, W. C. Clark, Lou Ann Barton, Fredde "Pharaoh" Walden, Stevie. *(© Ken Hoge)*

KINDRED: I was playing in the Antone's house band and pumping gas on South Lamar when Stevie pulls up, walks over, looks at me, shakes his head, and the talks began. He told me about Lou Ann and his plans for this band, and I said, "We need Fredde Pharaoh on drums." Then I got into his car, and we went to McMorris Ford, where W. C. Clark was one of the top mechanics, and starting laying our propaganda on him.

CLARK: Stevie was always on the black side of Austin because he was really interested in learning the black culture. He kept coming by my job and telling me that he had decided to put a band together and needed me to play bass. I wasn't looking for a gig, because I was getting a steady paycheck and relaxing for a change, but he kept pestering me.

LAYTON: Lou Ann led the way initiating Triple Threat Revue. She grabbed Stevie and said, "You gotta get out of the Cobras, and we should form a new band."

MAY 28, 1977, LOU ANN BARTON DIARY ENTRY

Stevie and I talked again about doing something last night . . . Saw Paul Ray and the Cobras, and they asked me to sing. . . . It was so great to see Denny. Stevie played so great I fell out. We spoke later and he asked me for my phone number. He said he's enjoying what he's doing now but he thinks we can work together in the future.

LOU ANN BARTON, *Triple Threat and Double Trouble singer, 1977–1979:* I knew that Stevie's time in the Cobras was running out. We put together a dream band. They were all killers.

KINDRED: We all sang lead and would chorus behind Lou Ann with four male voices, and it was just killer. We were a happening band!

JIMMIE VAUGHAN: They were a fabulous band. Fredde Pharaoh had done a lot of playing in my bands, with a killer shuffle, and he could really swing. He played simple, aspiring to play like the guys on the early Albert Collins records, and he did. And W. C. Clark is a great singer, bassist, and guitar player.

CLARK: I had seen Stevie around a lot, and I knew how unique he was: how clean a tone he had, how nasty and low-down he could be, and how he could play licks exactly like Chuck Berry, Albert King, and B. B. King. I knew he was for real, that he was a seeker, a warrior. And that's why I not only agreed to join his band but to play bass, which I had given up to focus on guitar. I really had no interest in playing bass again, but Stevie had such a fire and I was so impressed by how

Just another "midnite to 5 am" gig: a Triple
Threat Revue flyer. *(Courtesy Mike Steele)*

much he had already improved that I wanted to see where he could
take it.

On October 7, after just a few shows, Margaret Moser wrote in *The
Austin Sun,* "Triple Threat Revue's first week of performances promises
to give Austin's blues bands serious competition . . . Fort Worth chanteuse
Lou Ann Barton . . . skimmed the cream of the crop of Austin's rhythm
and blues musicians. Besides Miss Lou Ann's cat scratch vocals, she handpicked Freddie [*sic*] Walden and Mike Kindred, who thundered their way
through Storm, on drums and keyboards, respectively; W. C. Clark, bass
and former lead guitarist for Southern Feeling; and the whiplash guitar of
Stevie Vaughan, who just retired from a two-year tenure with Paul Ray and
the Cobras. This ain't no empty threat."

CRAIG: Lou Ann was terrific, a great singer in her prime and a huge presence.

LAYTON: Lou Ann was very dominant, very imperative, very demonstrative, and she knew exactly what she wanted. Lou Ann had the reins of Triple Threat. Stevie slowly asserted himself.

CLARK: Stevie got down every inch of the way. There was no slack in him. His endurance and perseverance were unreal. Guys like B. B. and Albert and Freddie King and Albert Collins had that mean, soulful endurance, always trying to get every possible tone out of a single note, just digging deep into the guitar to satisfy something deep within their own souls. Stevie had that, and it changed me. Like a lot of black people at the time, I wasn't getting down that hard on the guitar, instead focusing on my singing and the groove, but he opened my eyes.

BRAMHALL: When you're up there that high musically, you're always looking around the corner for something new to add. I think that with any great artist or athlete, you can see them move through different levels of growth and continue to improve. It never surprised me that Stevie would surprise me. You kind of expected it. It was like, "What are you gonna do next?" Then he would do it, and it would be like, "Let's build on that."

BENTLEY: Stevie completely burned it down when he started Triple Threat. He was possessed. Jimmie was the king of cool, and you could feel Bill Campbell in your bones, but you could feel Stevie from the back of the club before he played a note. Some nights, there were only five or six of us at the Rome Inn for Triple Threat, but we were all completely breathless.

CLARK: We didn't need a leader in Triple Threat. Everything just worked, but after a while we all looked up at Stevie because his name was the one that was selling the band, and we all knew who was drawing the people.

KINDRED: He was the strongest member. The first time they billed his name was in Dallas. W. C. pointed it out to me, and I said, "We might as well get used to it." Stevie was a phenomenon. When you see a blazing meteor, you don't argue with it. Give him his due, and we can all only prosper. He was a six-shot killer, and you take the stage alert and aware when you take the stage with Stevie Ray Vaughan. I loved that about him. He wasn't trying to make anyone look bad, but he immediately established a level which said, "Do not approach if you're bullshitting."

RONNIE EARL, *Roomful of Blues and solo guitarist, friend of Stevie's and Jimmie's:* I met Jimmie when he toured the Northeast and then stayed with him for a month in 1978, and he told me to go see his brother. I had never heard blues with so much passion, intensity, and force, and it really affected my playing. Hearing both Stevie and Jimmie was a heavy awakening. Their styles were different, and Stevie was very loud, but he was not playing rock. The biggest difference between them was Jimmie was in an ensemble and Stevie was more the centerpiece of the band. Yeah, he had W. C. and Lou Ann, but it was Stevie Ray's band, and that was unmistakable.

CLARK: He still wasn't really singing more than a song or two a set. Somewhere in there, Stevie started doing "Pride and Joy."

BETHEL: We were living together in Hyde Park, and one night, I woke up and he wasn't next to me; he was kneeling down by the window, sitting in the moonlight, writing. He had his beret on—his "security" hat—and nothing else. I said, "What are you doing?" and he said, "I'm writing this song." The next morning, he showed it to me, and it was called, "Sweet Little Thang." He later changed the name to "Pride and Joy."

ERIC JOHNSON: My girlfriend Mary Beth [Greenwood] shared a cottage with Lindi, and Stevie and I saw each other there. One night, we passed one guitar back and forth and talked about music. He was a very sweet, affable guy, down to earth, and just *easy*. He was not complicated, edgy, or murky, but entirely genuine and generous about music.

BETHEL: Mary Beth and I would tell Stevie that he had to come with us to see Eric play, but he didn't want any part of it. One night, Eric was playing at the Armadillo, and Mary Beth said, "I go to all your gigs, Stevie, so you are coming with me to Eric's gig." As soon as Eric started playing, Stevie flipped out; he stood on the chair, screaming, "Yeah!" He loved it, and they became very good friends after that.

Stevie, 3/77, new tattoo peaking through. *(© Ken Hoge)*

KINDRED: We were both wondering about our spirituality, and some of my fondest memories of him are the long rides back from playing Stubbs in Lubbock. W. C. was always driving, bless his heart, and Lou Ann was passed out, usually across our laps, and Stevie and I were talking about trying to treat everyone the same and trying to be spiritually up-

right. There was a soft side to him that was very different from what
you saw onstage.

SHANNON: Stevie was very interested in certain spiritual quests. That was
one of the things that drew us together, but we expressed it in the weirdest ways. We were into the *I Ching,* the power of crystals, color therapy,
and certain prophecies that we'd read about. We were into the *Urantia,*
a big ol' thick book supposedly written by an alien. He always had a
spiritual ideal, but, like me, he had a hard time living up to that ideal.

BETHEL: He basically lived with me and Mary Beth. We used to get into our
PJs, and Stevie would read to us from *The Urantia Book.*

LAYTON: Healing oneself—spiritually, physically, and mentally—was
something Stevie was very interested in. He was into investigating healing modalities uncommon to Western culture and believed that people
could be healed via color light therapy. He came up with this idea for
a chair, like a dentist's or massage chair, with a pattern of lights or
LEDs that would correspond with the energy points/meridians in the
body. You could then orchestrate the kind of light that went through
the chair and develop a therapeutic protocol specific to the ailments or
needs of a given person. It would be directed to every part of the body,
using ultraviolet light, or blue or red lights. This concept is not that
far out; the roots of color light therapy go back to ancient cultures of
Egypt, Greece, China, and India.

The T-Birds were well established as Austin's top blues band by
April 1978, when Stevie and Jimmie were featured together on the cover
of *The Austin Sun.* Jimmie told writer Bill Bentley that it was the first time
he had ever been interviewed.

"Though not actually the leader of Triple Threat . . . Stevie is the one
who keeps the fire burning," Bentley wrote. "And, as Jimmy [*sic*] is sometimes known to point out in explaining the brothers' difference, 'Stevie
sings.'"

BENTLEY: When we finished the interview, I asked Stevie for his address to
send him a copy when it came out. He replied, "I don't really have a
place to live." He was still sofa surfing. His home was his guitar.

STEELE: One day, I asked Stevie, "Where are you living?" and he said, "Well, um . . . nowhere, really." I invited him to live with me, which he did, staying on the sofa sleeper for about six months.

JAMES ELWELL, *friend of Stevie's:* I spent a lot of time moving his stuff because I had a pickup truck and he lived out of boxes. He was definitely a struggling artist. I worked at a bicycle shop close to where he was living—the "Custom" sticker on his Number One guitar came from there—and he walked in and asked to borrow five dollars for food. I said, "Stevie, I have a moped in the back of the shop; why don't you take it so you don't have to walk everywhere?" He had a blast riding the thing around Austin with his beret on and people saying, "Goddamn, get a car, son!"

Hubert Sumlin, Howlin' Wolf's right-hand man, sitting in with Triple Threat Revue at the Soap Creek, 6/78. *(© Ken Hoge)*

By mid-May 1978, both Clark and Kindred had left Triple Threat and were replaced by a pair of Barton's Fort Worth buddies, bassist Jackie Newhouse and saxophonist Johnny Reno. No longer a triple threat, the band changed its name to Double Trouble, after the Otis Rush song.

KINDRED: With five *el jefes* in one band, I'm amazed it lasted as long as it did. Like his brother, Stevie's music became more focused, and he became less interested in variety. Storm was a very restrictive band; Jimmie didn't want to play any rock and roll, and we all knew it. Stevie was far more accepting on the front end, then we went through a natural shaking-out period where we discovered that we weren't on the same page; people's musical drives were different. My imagination was becoming pretty active, and I wanted to play more than blues shuffles. Look where Stevie ended up: with a trio playing Texas to Chicago blues. Triple Threat started out with a wider scope than that.

CLARK: One reason I pulled back is I wasn't ready for the life on the road I saw him headed towards. He had a destiny, and I felt for a long time like I let him down, because he struggled for a few years to find a bassist to do what I did: set him up, anticipate him, cut out the drummer, push him to a new thing.

BARTON: They all quit because of differences with Stevie. I stuck with him. We were a team, and I also felt sorry for him. I felt that I had to help this guy out. He didn't have two dimes to rub together or any decent clothes. I said, "Don't worry, we'll regroup," called my buddies in Fort Worth, and got Jackie and Johnny Reno in the band.

KINDRED: My one regret is we didn't get a great recording—which we captured one night at the Armadillo opening for Toots and the Maytals. We played an incredible show that they recorded. Being young and dumb, we let some guy have the tape, and we never saw him or it again.

BARTON: We changed the band name. Stevie and I were the Double Trouble. When I quit, it worked out perfect for the rhythm section to just pick that up and become a trio.

JACKIE NEWHOUSE, *Double Trouble bassist, 1978–1980:* Right from the start, we were usually playing five nights a week. Every Friday and Saturday was either Antone's, the Rome Inn, or Soap Creek, and we had a lot of great gigs at After Ours, which was open till 5:00 in the morning. We had a regular Wednesday at the Soap Creek and Sunday at the Rome Inn, but otherwise I never knew where we'd be, and Stevie's communication wasn't great. I often had to look in the newspaper to see where we were playing that night! The drummer situation was in flux. Fredde had a family and a roofing business in Dallas, so he couldn't always make the gigs, though he was the perfect drummer for the band: a hip, cool guy with the best flat-tire shuffle you ever heard. He would usually come down for Friday and Saturday, but we were always scrambling to get somebody for the weekday gigs.

BARBARA LOGAN, *Doyle Bramhall's wife, "Life by the Drop" cowriter:* We went to see Stevie and Lou Ann one night and she came over and said, "We'd love to have you in the band, Doyle." He thought it might happen but he also had just stopped drinking and was hesitant and was working with Rocky Hill [brother of ZZ Top bassist Dusty Hill] and happy with what he was doing.

On June 19, Double Trouble played Houston's Juneteenth Blues Festival, one of the biggest free blues fests in the world and the first time they played before a massive outdoor crowd. Other artists on the bill included Buddy Guy, Junior Wells, Big Mama Thornton, and Albert Collins. It was, recalls Newhouse, "a big deal" for the band, but their lineup was still unstable.

In July, Pharaoh finally left Triple Threat, replaced by Jack Moore, a University of Rhode Island student who was spending the summer in Austin and had been introduced to the scene by mutual friends in Roomful of Blues. When Moore left town, Vaughan was looking for a drummer again.

Sublett recommended his friend, roommate, and Corpus Christi homeboy Chris Layton, who Stevie knew a bit from the time he sat in with the Cobras.

"I moved from Corpus to Austin with a band called La Paz that played funk and jazz fusion," recalls Layton. "Joe Sublett left the band to join the Cobras and recommended me to Greezy Wheels, a cosmic cowboy band with a big following and a major label deal. It was a good, steady-money gig."

SUBLETT: Stevie told me he needed a drummer, and I asked if he would give Chris Layton a shot. He asked if he was a blues drummer, and I said, "No, but he's a good musician, and he can learn." I told Chris, and he started woodshedding. Stevie came over, and Chris was in the back room with headphones on playing Albert Collins's "Frosty." Stevie thought he sounded good and was impressed that Chris had strung together all these wires to make headphones run through our apartment.

LAYTON: The next day, he came over and we realized we had a lot of the same musical influences and interests like Stevie Wonder, James Brown, and Earth, Wind & Fire. We were both flipped out over the Donny Hathaway *Live* album. I told Stevie that I wanted to play with him. He was this amazingly talented guy, and I thought that we could do great things together. I had never seen anyone like him.

SUBLETT: He basically told Chris, "If you play what I want you to play, I'll give you a shot," and Chris didn't have any ego issues, so that was fine. Stevie told me that he preferred a guy that he could teach how he wanted him to play, because he was a really good drummer himself. He could sit down and show you how to play a few different shuffles, and he said, "I've had drummers who are set in their ways and get offended if I make suggestions." With Chris, he had a guy with an open heart and open ears who could grow with him. He said, "If Chris can play in sync with my right hand, what more can I ask? We'll build anything beyond that."

LAYTON: Stevie found it *attractive* that I wasn't a dyed-in-the-wool blues player. He had this yearning to not be just another blues guitar player, but he was expected to be faithful to the blues because of his brother. He was fascinated with me *because* I had never played blues, not in spite of that.

He didn't offer me the gig right away, and I went out to see them at Soap Creek. Fredde was back, but he had a bad speed problem and wasn't reliable. Fredde would ask if I wanted to sit in, then leave and sometimes be gone for two weeks! Lou Ann came up and said, "Are you gonna join our goddamn band or not?" Stevie added, "You wanna play with me?" and I said, "I do."

JOE PRIESNITZ, *Austin booking agent and manager, booked Vaughan, 1979–1983:* I booked Greezy Wheels, who were making good money. One day, I saw Chris and Joe Sublett walk by my office a few times before coming in. Chris, staring at his feet, said, "I'm thinking about leaving Greezy Wheels." I said, "You can't do that! We've got so much going on!" He said, "Yeah, well, I'm thinking of teaming up with Stevie Vaughan." My jaw dropped, and I said, "Really? Can you make any money doing that?" And he said, "We're gonna give it a go!"

LAYTON: I was getting a $350 weekly check, which was really good money. When I told Cleve Hattersley of Greezy Wheels that I was quitting and why, he put his hands on my shoulders and said, "Kid, you're making a big mistake." Everyone thought I was nuts to quit a good, steady gig to go out on the road with this drug-crazed, unfocused guitarist. But Keith Ferguson said to me, "I'm glad you are with him. He really needs you."

BARTON: I liked Chris as soon as we met, and I wanted him in the band. I told him, "When you get up there, just pop the snare. Hit it hard every time!" And he got up there and did it. He and I were very close.

SUBLETT: No one ever told a drummer, "Hey you didn't play enough licks tonight." It's all about the groove, and Stevie worked with Chris to build that. On off nights, he would call Chris and me to meet at some little dive like the AusTex Lounge, very often with just Chris and Stevie playing. There was a lot of learning going on.

LAYTON: I'd like to say those gigs were because we were learning to play together, but it was because Stevie was so disorganized that he'd forget to give the other guys enough notice, so no one else could make it! We'd play for free to about five people! The AusTex was a real dump with no windows.

Shortly after I joined the band, Stevie invited me to jam at Hole Sound, a small studio in a church basement. I walked in and was surprised to see W. C. Clark there with Stevie. I sat down at the drums, and W. C. said, "Play a shuffle. I'm gonna talk over your shoulder, but just keep playing." He started talking in my right ear: "Play really, really lightly." He knew I was from Corpus Christi and began talking about the ocean: "Think about being down at the beach watching the waves come in and break on the sand."

CLARK: I said, "You know the way the waves just roll in on the shore? That's what you should be thinking of when you're playing this groove." Chris said it helped him to not push the beat.

LAYTON: He kept describing metaphorical imagery as I played along, and something changed in the way I thought about and played a shuffle. Stevie grinned and picked up his guitar, and we jammed for a while. I truthfully hadn't heard a lot of the great blues drummers.

CLARK: Chris had been playing in a country band, and he hadn't played very many blues shuffles, and we were just getting that together. I helped him understand how to play what he wanted to play and make it right in the category of what we were doing because of the mathematics of it.

LAYTON: Talk about a great music lesson and the conversation had nothing to do with music. That experience gave me a different perspective on playing. A lot of learning to play an instrument involves approaching the instrument from a technical perspective; on the drums, there is an idea that if you practice rudiments enough, you will be a great drummer. But that's not really true. Same thing on the guitar: you need to know your scales, chords, inversions, but ultimately, you have to apply it all to making music. Playing music is not just the technical side of studying an instrument. This key had been put in and unlocked the door to a new perspective.

Around this time, Stevie's increased drug consumption and erratic behavior had drawn his bandmates' concern and criticism. He responded with a letter, stating, *"If band members are so dissatisfied with my leadership of the band they should make matters more to they're [sic] advantage and go on they're [sic] own. I will be more than able to carry on with my career—recording, working gigs and on a much higher level. I do understand some of the complaints concerning my health—actions, etc. But also understand all circumstances involved and evolving because of them."*

LAYTON: The letter came from his belief in his talent and that if we just played our asses off, the business would fall into line. But there was so much insanity that rational people had to make a distinct choice between "I can't hang around here" or "I'm gonna join the party." This played out in every part of his life: his personal relationships, the way business was conducted, the drugs and the alcohol. I was fucked up, too; I had to be.

Stevie was deep into speed, staying up three or four days straight and not bathing. He was crashing with me and Joe, but he was like an alley cat; he'd show up to eat, then vanish for a week. One night, I woke up at 4:00 a.m. and heard someone walking around. I go downstairs and there's Stevie in his underwear, sitting in a lotus position, staring at an office organizer plastic set of drawers. I asked what he was doing, and he looked up at me with these wide, wildcat eyes and said, "Trying to get organized."

8

TROUBLE IS KNOCKIN'

Layton's first gig with Double Trouble was September 10, 1978, at the Rome Inn, and the band played seventeen more shows the rest of a busy month. Layton was a stabilizing presence, musically, socially, and business-wise. He was almost twenty-three, a year younger than Stevie, upbeat, outgoing, and less grizzled than many in their orbit, taking on some of the duties of both a manager and booking agent. Layton, whose father owned a successful Chevrolet dealership, had a bit of business sense and had put in some time at Del Mar Community College.

Double Trouble, which now included Layton, Jackie Newhouse, and Johnny Reno backing Stevie and Lou Ann, had established themselves as regulars at a handful of Austin clubs while traveling north to Dallas, Fort Worth, and Waco, south to San Antonio and San Marcos, and east to Houston and Nacogdoches.

"The band wasn't exactly packing them in when I joined," Layton says. "It was actually in disarray. Johnny lived three hours away in Fort Worth and did not want to come down for low-paying gigs, and Stevie sometimes gave us a few hours' notice, which led Lou Ann to refuse, and sometimes Jack wasn't available. People recognized Stevie as a great player, but it's not like the world was following him to whatever gig he did. People wondered if the band would even show up."

One of the things Layton addressed was the lack of a band vehicle.

"When I got in the band, we didn't have transportation, and I said, 'Look, it's crazy to have everyone finding their ways to gigs however they can,'" he recalls. "I took the little credit I had, went to a bank, took out a loan, and a got a Dodge van so we could drive to gigs together. I cosigned for the band, and we all committed to making a monthly payment. When we eventually crashed it, it was hard for me to explain to the other guys why we had to finish the payments!"

In the summer months before Layton joined, Stevie had started dating Lenora "Lenny" Bailey, who would become his longtime love interest and wife and the muse for several great compositions, starting with "Love Struck Baby." They met at the home of Lenny's then-boyfriend Diamond Joe Siddons, a guitarist whose abundant supply of drugs attracted musicians like Stevie into coming over to play with him, according to Mike Steele. It backfired when Stevie left with his girl.

"Lenny was a real trip, and I never did see what Stevie saw in her," says Craig. "Every time I saw them together, I thought it was crazy and that he was getting far deeper into cocaine. I'd known Stevie for years, and suddenly he was always asking where the blow was coming from."

Early in 1979, Vaughan did some recording, backing W. C. Clark on both sides of a single in January, adding guitar to "Rough Edges" and "My Song." In March, he and Double Trouble cut a full album-length demo, eleven tracks recorded in the basement of country station KOKE on a four-channel mixer and produced by Joe Gracey. A popular DJ who was no longer on the air due to voice problems, Gracey was a Stevie believer looking to help.

"Everything was done live with four microphones and all of us in one tiny room," recalls Layton. The recordings included blues classics sung by Barton, including "Shake Your Hips" and "You Can Have My Husband," as well as the first recorded versions of three Stevie originals that would remain at the heart of his repertoire: "Love Struck Baby," "Pride and Joy," and "Rude Mood," the blistering instrumental based on Lightnin' Hopkins's "Hopkins Sky Hop."

A few months later, Reno left the band, which pushed on as a four-piece. Later that year, with financial backing from Austin businessman John Dyer, Gracey took the band into producer Jack Clement's Nashville

One of the first Double Trouble promo photos, with Lou Ann Barton, Chris Layton, and Jackie Newhouse. *(Courtesy Joe Priesnitz)*

studio, where they cut ten tracks that Stevie hated and refused to allow to be circulated, even as a demo to get gigs.

BARTON: None of us liked the recordings. We went there to get a Sun Records–style old sound—raw, playing in one room—but it sounded tinny, with no depth, and all the songs were way too fast. It's easy to guess why that was the case. We didn't get what we were after.

NEWHOUSE: There were a lot of bad habits going on, and we all had them. But as long as you could get Stevie to the gig, it would be great!

LAYTON: We had all kinds of problems, but Stevie not playing his ass off was not one of them. That was the bedrock anchor of how the band could continue under out-of-control and unmanageable circumstances. If Stevie was in the building, everything was good. But the question often was, "Where *is* Stevie?" There were countless times I had to hunt him down on a gig night. At 7:00 or 8:00, I'd ask if anybody had talked to Stevie, and the answer often was, "Fuck no!" He didn't have a place to live, and I'd have to track him down an hour beforehand.

STEELE: Poor Chris was like the border collie that had to herd Stevie, and later Tommy, nipping at their heels, running around barking and chasing them to get their shit together.

LAYTON: One night, we had a big show at Antone's, and I found Stevie completely unconscious on Mike Steele's couch. He'd been up for two days on a speed high and crashed. I knew that once I got him in the building, he would tear it up. I never knew anyone else you could jar out of a total speed crash, get him upright, strap a guitar on, and he'd play his ass off. He finally came to, stood up, and looked at a pile of clothes on the floor. He was naked and picked up a scarf and started walking around. I said, "Stevie, what the fuck are you doing? We've got a gig at Antone's in forty-five minutes!" He's got the scarf in one hand and grabs the ironing board and tries to plug the iron in, and I'm yelling, "Fuck that! Let's go!" It was kind of hilarious in a tragic way how his life was totally unmanageable and chaotic.

NEWHOUSE: Despite it all, Stevie was a really sweet, funny guy and pretty easygoing as a bandleader; he never told me what to play.

Layton was well aware of Stevie's big brother, Jimmie, but had not had much interaction with him until Stevie suddenly said, "We're going to my brother's place for a party." Walking into the crowded bash, Layton recalls being excited and intimidated to meet the guitarist he had heard so much about. After Stevie introduced Layton as his new drummer, Jimmie instructed him to stay put, left, and returned with a copy of the Junior Wells live album, *It's My Life, Baby!*

"He stuck it in my chest and said, 'You need to listen to this!'" says Layton. "He thought listening to that record would help me out, and it did. It's one of the greatest live blues records ever made."

By 1979, the Fabulous Thunderbirds had begun establishing themselves nationally, which also impacted Stevie and Double Trouble, as all of their names began to be known by blues fans outside of Texas. In April, Joe Priesnitz of Rock Arts began booking Stevie and Double Trouble, and six months later, in October 1979, The T-Birds' eponymous debut album, often referred to as *Girls Go Wild*, was released by Takoma Records. Both bands finally had some forward momentum.

"Getting an agent was welcome relief," says Layton. "Booking our own gigs, handling our own gear, playing the gigs, and then getting down the road was exhausting. And having somebody say we were worth caring about on a business level was a good feeling."

Double Trouble played the San Francisco Blues Festival in August, their first big show outside of Texas.

TOM MAZZOLINI, *founder and director of the San Francisco Blues Festival:* Word had spread about the Austin scene, and I booked the red-hot Fabulous Thunderbirds in 1978. They were a sensation whose impact could be felt on many bands here, with musicians cutting their hair and dressing cooler. We wanted to bring more acts from Austin, which led to booking Stevie Ray Vaughan and Double Trouble featuring Lou Ann Barton the next year.

LAYTON: I helped book all these gigs around the San Francisco Blues Festival, and none of them paid more than two hundred bucks. We only had enough money to buy gas for the van and loaves of bread and bologna. We couldn't afford to eat a square meal, but it was a lot of fun.

MAZZOLINI: No one had heard of Stevie Ray Vaughan out here. He was a complete mystery, and what took place was a stunning performance. The

The band played San Francisco and Berkeley around the San Francisco Blues Festival, August, 1979. *(Bill Narum)*

crowd was overwhelmed and asking, "Who are these people, and where are they from?" I sensed that there was a kind of destiny happening, that something was about to change the direction of the blues. Barton gave a gut-filled Texas roadhouse set alongside Double Trouble's driving sound, and on a day of many great performances, theirs was the most memorable. Vaughan was the real surprise: so young, yet so sophisticated and inventive. How fortunate we all were to have experienced someone who would change the direction of the blues!

MARK WEBER, *photographer:* I was drinking beer with Stevie and Lou Ann in front of an old blue Cadillac when the promoter drove up in a van with [Muddy Waters's guitarist] Jimmy Rogers and [Muddy Waters's and John Lee Hooker's guitarist] Luther Tucker. Jimmy was just getting back on the scene, and I'd heard him play the day before, and I said to Stevie, "That's Jimmy Rogers." For those of us that know, that's all I had to say, and Stevie only said, "Oh, man, oh, geez, that's Jimmy Rogers!"

LAYTON: We played the festival and did a live radio broadcast on KFAG in Palo Alto, where we opened up for Robert Cray, who was starting to have a big name on the circuit out there.

ROBERT CRAY, *musician, friend of Stevie's:* It was actually early in our own California touring as well, and we didn't have a turnout. One of the shows had nine people in the audience. Stevie was, of course, a great guitar player, and we all had fun hanging together.

LAYTON: We became good friends and started to make a name for ourselves, because anyone who saw Stevie wondered who the hell he was.

CRAY: We didn't know anyone who wasn't from the West Coast, and they were different in the way they looked and dressed and acted. We had a day off in Santa Cruz and were invited to a barbecue at a friend's house and invited them all. I knocked on Stevie Ray's door, and he answered wearing an Afro wig and a black kimono with a sash around it, looking like Jimi Hendrix. He went to the party like that and stayed in character the whole time. He was a total character, as was Lou Ann Barton and her cat-eyed glasses, and we loved them. They were easy to have a lot of fun with.

NEWHOUSE: Stevie bought his first kimono in San Francisco. He really bought it for Lenny, but ended up borrowing it and some of her other clothes; they were the same size.

BARTON: Stevie borrowed my kimono and scarves a few times and returned them drenched in sweat, and I said, "You can have it. I don't want it back!" That California trip was a sweet time for our band.

Stevie and Lou Ann on the Santa Cruz boardwalk, August, 1979.
(Courtesy Lou Ann Barton)

During this whole era, we all had nicknames and alter egos. We were just a bunch of kids getting road crazy and having fun, going back to Triple Threat. I became *Maw* then *Mudda*, and Mike Kindred was *Paw*. Stevie had three personalities: *Patrick, Brady,* and *Ed Roy,* Brady's retarded cousin. Chris was *Harold,* and Jackie was *Buford.* This is just infantile, sixth-grade humor, but it was good fun. Other friends all wanted in and got names, too.

LAYTON: We'd slip into our alter egos to keep ourselves from going crazy. Brady or "Bwady" was kind of a good-hearted goofy redneck: "Brady play geetar reel good!" We wrote Brady songs like "Hangnails and Boogers."

PRIESNITZ: Chris would check in from the road and tell us how things were going. He called and said, "Hey, it's great out here, but we are out of money." I thought we'd had it planned out where they'd be able to make it there and back, though it would be tight. We wired some money, even though we didn't have much ourselves. They managed to play a couple more shows on the way home to make it work out.

In September, the band cut another demo with Gracey, nine songs in all, once again starting with "Rude Mood." Remarkably, this version of the instrumental is virtually note-for-note identical to the version recorded for *Texas Flood* more than three years later.

Stevie's alter ego Bwady. *(Courtesy Tommy Shannon)*

"'Rude Mood' is like a thoroughly composed classical blues piece," says Layton. "All of the hits, accents, and breakdowns were always in the exact same place every time we played it."

Adds Newhouse, "This is around when Stevie began to write more, and those tunes became staples of his set for years to come: 'Love Struck Baby,' 'Rude Mood,' 'I'm Crying,' 'Empty Arms,' and 'Pride and Joy.'"

Despite winning converts one by one, Vaughan was still struggling to develop an audience beyond Austin and outside a smallish circle of blues fanatics, some of whom rejected Stevie's love of Jimi Hendrix and tendency to inject any number of influences into the music. The conflict even extended to the band itself, a constant source of tension between Vaughan and Barton, who was still treated as the de facto star by taking the stage after the band had warmed up the crowd.

NEWHOUSE: We were encouraging Stevie to take more of a leadership role. He really came along as a singer, and Lou Ann was more of a featured vocalist; we would do twenty to thirty minutes without her, then we'd bring her up and she'd do four or five songs.

LAYTON: Stevie and Lou Ann had a fiery relationship.

BARTON: I truly loved him and cared about him. When he finally got a house, I took sheets, drapes, plates, and cutlery over to set up house for him.

LAYTON: She wanted to play straight blues and had no patience for anything else. Jimi Hendrix was one of the biggest, most important musicians to both me and Stevie. We started doing "Little Wing," and it rubbed Lou Ann the wrong way: "We don't need to do any goddamn Jimi Hendrix!" They were totally at odds about that.

NEWHOUSE: Lou Ann was more of a blues and R&B purist, but she certainly liked Hendrix's music.

BARTON: I love Jimi Hendrix! Who wouldn't? I just didn't understand Stevie wanting to do covers of his music in our blues band.

The quartet incarnation of Double Trouble came under serious stress during a monthlong East Coast tour in the fall of 1979, coming to a head

Stevie and Lou Ann onstage. *(Mary Beth Greenwood)*

November 13 and 14 at New York's Lone Star Café. Many music industry insiders were there to check out the swashbuckling Texans with a growing reputation. Among those in attendance were New Orleans piano master Dr. John and his friend Doc Pomus, composer of "Save the Last Dance for Me," "Little Sister," and other early rock classics.

DR. JOHN: Doc kept telling me about this Texas guitar player I had to see, so we went to the Lone Star Café. Stevie was a hell of a guitar player, but he wasn't showing he was special yet.

LAYTON: There was some good word out about Lou Ann and the band, and we knew this was a potentially important gig with record company people in attendance. We opened with a few tunes without Lou Ann, during which time she drank herself into obliteration. When Stevie called her up, she tripped on the last step, grabbing onto the mic stand to catch her fall and pull herself up. Stevie said, "C'mon, Lou Ann, get it together!" She turned, thinking she was off mic, and said, "Fuck you, motherfucker! You worry about your own shit, and I'll worry about mine!" We could see the record company people running for the door. The show was a disaster, and Stevie was livid. It was the straw that broke the camel's back between them.

NEWHOUSE: Lou Ann was drunk and breaking glasses. It wasn't the first time something like that had happened—but it was the last time.

BARTON: We were both so drunk, and I threw a shot of whiskey at him and walked offstage. I was just sick of being shit on. Sick of him treating me badly, hogging the stage, and looking at me as an afterthought. My feelings weren't hurt. They had been before, but I was pissed. At the beginning, it was all Lou Ann, and he started doing more and more singing. It got to where we'd play from 12:00 till 2:00, and at 1:30, I was still sitting in the back with people asking, "When are you going up?" I think he wanted the spotlight for himself and saw me as competition, and I finally had it with him.

LAYTON: The same thing happened the next night, and Stevie told Lou Ann that she needed to stop drinking so much. She said, "You do as much of that bullshit as I do." He said, "Yeah, but I keep my shit together." That was mostly true. Then it was "Fuck yous" back and forth, and he says, "Get out of the fucking van! I'm firing you!" And she goes, "You can't fire me. I quit, motherfucker!" Back and forth: "I quit!" "You're fired!"

NEWHOUSE: It was the breaking point. Stevie fired Lou Ann in the middle of the night in the van.

LAYTON: Then she looked at me and asked, "What about you, Harold? I was the one that asked you to join this goddamn band! Where are you at?" I said, "I'm playing with Stevie, which is why I joined the band."

BARTON: We both drank way too much, and it's really hard to have a relationship with bottles of Crown Royal between you all the time. Drinking leads to nothing good, and we had big fights, and I was ready to get the fuck out of there. I don't know which of us was meaner to the other. We all loved each other, but it wasn't working with me and Stevie anymore.

LAYTON: A week later was Thanksgiving, and the band was in such bad shape as we limped into a shitty diner on a cold, rainy night. The food was no good, it seemed like the band was falling apart, and we're on the other side of the country, away from our families. We felt pretty desperate and very low.

The band stayed together for the rest of the tour. Barton's last show was at Lupo's Heartbreak Hotel in Providence, Rhode Island, on November 24, after which she joined Roomful of Blues, with whom they had played several shows on the tour.

"I never regretted it for a moment," Barton says. "I was sick of being mistreated. There's a reason all the other guys quit Triple Threat, and I held on trying to help Stevie as long as I could. Roomful of Blues had been after me for six months, and it was time to make the change."

Reno had left the band a few months prior, so Double Trouble was now a blues/rock power trio. With their focus sharpened, there was an immediate change in the group's setlist.

LAYTON: When Lou Ann left, we moved away from an R&B approach to blues and dropped a lot of songs.

JIMMIE VAUGHAN: Stevie had made the decision that he wanted to play with just bass and drums, where there was room for a twenty-minute guitar solo, which could be a good thing.

NEWHOUSE: It was clear that a trio was the best thing for Stevie, who rose to the occasion. Lou Ann no longer felt like a really good fit. She needed a more traditional R&B/blues band and sounded better than ever in Roomful of Blues.

ERIC JOHNSON: Stevie had an open mind and wanted to create his own signature, to open up to the potential that music has, unencumbered by genre lines or ceilings. That allowed him to become as big as he did emotionally and musically. People like that create a new alphabet but it requires sacrifice, slowing your career velocity by removing you from the categories of blues, jazz, or rock that people rely on.

PRIESNITZ: When the band returned to Austin, they came into the office, and Stevie explained what happened. His general feeling was relief, but I was concerned about the ninety days of shows we had booked. Lou Ann was the front person. Stevie was a phenomenal soloist, but I wondered if they should bring in another person. I posed the question: "We got all these dates, so who's gonna sing?" And I got this ice-cold stare from Stevie, who said, "Well, I am, motherfucker!"

LAYTON: There was some talk about getting another woman singer, but I think Stevie always wanted to be the sole front man. He had to get over the hump of feeling timid about his singing. Not everyone is Aretha Franklin, and you don't have to be to put your message across.

BARTON: I taught him everything I knew—to sing hard and loud and project, and I think I helped him. He was a hell of a lot better singer in Triple Threat than he had been in the Cobras. I thought he became quite good and got his point across with a lot of guts and soul.

PRIESNITZ: Our agency was right above Steamboat, which my partner Hank Vick booked, and they came in and started rehearsing that day. We could hear them working up the set with him as the singer and improving.

STEELE: One night at Steamboat, I walked up the stairs behind the stage, and Stevie was right in front of me. He was playing a slide song, and this guy comes to stand next to me, and it's George Thorogood. He was in town playing at the Opera House and was really riding high. Stevie finishes the song and turns around and sees George and yells, "Hey, c'mon up and play!" and George said, "No, no, I don't want to play." And I said, "I don't blame you."

On December 5, 1979, Double Trouble opened for Muddy Waters at the Palace in Houston. Stevie and Lenny were busted for cocaine possession when an off-duty police officer saw them snorting in front of a picture window after their set. They were released on $1,000 bail after a night in jail.

NEWHOUSE: Chris and I were watching Muddy after we played, and a friend found us and said that Stevie and Lenny had been taken to jail. Ironically, Muddy was playing "Champagne and Reefer" at that moment. We only missed one gig but had to bail him out ourselves with all of the money I had in my bank account.

BARTON: Drugs and alcohol are no good in a relationship, and that one . . . oh my God!

Lenny and Stevie, June, 1980. *(Daniel Schaefer)*

On December 23, just a couple of weeks after the bust, Stevie and Lenny got married in the band room at the Rome Inn during a Double Trouble set break.

SUBLETT: All of a sudden, Stevie and Lenny said, "We're getting married upstairs." It was just a room where we hung out before we played. Keith Ferguson poked me with his elbow, and we looked at each other like, "What is this?" We were highly amused because the last thing anyone thought was that Stevie was going to be married, and where he chose to do so kind of says it all.

COLONNA: I had moved to Seattle and was passing through Austin when I stopped at the Rome Inn to see Stevie play. I got there early when he was setting up, and he said, "Hey! I'm getting married tonight!" He had twisted Juicy Fruit gum wrappers into wedding rings. I said, "What's your anniversary present gonna be, a newspaper?" and I could see that hurt his feelings.

NEWHOUSE: Some guy with a collar did the ceremony. Then we went back down and did the next set. We all brought gifts and tried to make it as much of a real wedding as we could. It was real sweet and pretty crazy, but that's the way he rolled!

COLONNA: People threw little rice packets, and after Stevie and Lenny left, her father said, "They better pick up that rice, because that's about all they will have to eat."

STEELE: I was in the club, and he came down for the second set, saw me, and said, "Hey, we just got married!" I thought, "Oh, fuck."

NEWHOUSE: Their relationship was tumultuous, dysfunctional, passionate, violent. [Rome Inn manager] Clayton "C-Boy" Parks, who was kind of a godfather to the blues scene, did not predict good things for that union; he thought they were too much alike, crazy in the same way. Neither was what you would call emotionally available, and they ended up bringing out the worst in each other. She certainly was no good for his bad habits, and the drug use escalated the extreme behavior.

STEELE: Their relationship was always volatile, and it got worse as the coke use escalated.

NEWHOUSE: We were driving back from a gig in Houston with Chris and I in a car following Stevie, Lenny, and the crew in the van. We came up to them pulled over on the side of the road, and James [Arnold], our driver, was leaning against the back door as we pulled up. We asked what was going on, assuming they had car trouble, and he rolled his eyes and pointed to the back of the van. Lenny and Stevie were inside, crying and hugging, with everything in the van completely trashed. They had a knock-down, drag-out fistfight in the back of the van. Physical fights were not uncommon.

SUBLETT: Stevie and Lenny were in that zone, partners in crime. A lot of the time, they seemed to get along fine, and I liked her. It just seemed nuts to get married in the middle of so much craziness—that such a marriage was bound to crash and burn.

NEWHOUSE: Their marriage came completely out of left field, and neither seemed like the marrying kind. I wouldn't have been surprised if they had broken up, so I was surprised they got married. Deep down, I think Stevie wanted to have a normal relationship. But he and Lenny would pick on me and my wife, Jody, saying things like, "Oh, you guys are so normal, happy, and boring!" Maybe that came out of being a little jealous of a less rocky relationship.

LAYTON: Stevie was a sweet person, but he was difficult to have a relationship with. He was kind, decent, and morally put together, but he didn't always function that way. Lenny would say, "The drugs have gotten way out of control, and I'm really concerned," and the next minute they'd be doing drugs together. Their relationship was just haywire.

STEELE: The problem was you never knew which Lenny you were going to get. She had as many personalities as Heinz has varieties. I didn't trust her, and I didn't think she was right for him, and I couldn't understand why he wanted to be with someone like that. I thought that Lenny would be his downfall, because she was so into drugs, and his abuse increased once they got together.

LAYTON: Stevie needed a lot of basic help, and Lenny wanted to give it to him. She tried to help him get his shit together, but trying to *make* someone do things can become part of the dysfunction of the relationship.

You can't help people that don't want to be helped. It turned into codependent enablement.

STEELE: Once while Stevie was out on the road, she was so high and hysterical that she brought their Caprice convertible into a mechanic and told the guy he needed to get the snakes out from underneath the seats. She'd been up for days and was hallucinating.

Eight days after his marriage, Stevie and Double Trouble rang in the new year and a new decade at Antone's. The blues club, which continued to be so vital to the Austin blues world, was not a regular gig for the band, though Stevie was often there sitting in on off nights or after his own gigs.

LAYTON: We had a circuit of places we played regularly, and it didn't include Antone's, which had legitimate blues legends playing there, and the Thunderbirds as the house band. Our homes were the Steamboat and the Rome Inn, which got its name because it was originally an Italian restaurant. It was vacant and left for nothing, with broken-out windows and splintered doors, and C-Boy Parks brought in a cash register and some whiskey bottles and just set up shop. The door was always open for us there; we played every Sunday, and eventually the Thunderbirds started doing "Blue Mondays" there. C-Boy would always say, "I take care of all my people," and would bring in barbecue and feed us.

NEWHOUSE: Stevie was never as traditional as Jimmie, and he wanted to differentiate himself and get out from his brother's shadow. Some of that included changing the way he looked.

LAYTON: When I first saw Stevie, he was wearing an early '60s retro style: applejack hat, sharkskin pants, and vintage satin or bowling shirts. He was getting all of his clothes at thrift stores.

NEWHOUSE: Stevie went from wearing a suit and vest in the Cobras, which was more or less the standard way traditional blues bands in Austin were dressing, to cutting the sleeves off his T-shirts and wearing kimonos and a full-length leopard-skin coat. One night in New Orleans's French Quarter, the ladies of the night offered Stevie all kinds of things for that coat. Other times, I thought we were gonna get our asses kicked, stumbling out of the van at rural rest stops in the middle of the night with Stevie wearing that coat. But he was oblivious to all of that. It was like he never came off the stage. It became glammed-out, punked-up blues, which was also part of separating himself from his brother.

SUBLETT: I heard there was a rivalry, but I never saw that. Jimmie was loyal to the core if you asked him about Stevie: "Oh, he's great." And Stevie would always say about Jimmie, "He's the best. He's the reason I play." If you tried to disrespect one to the other, they'd jump on you in a second. They didn't jam together or hang out all that much. They had to find out who they were, and their styles were very different, but man, did they love each other and love playing together.

NEWHOUSE: If we were in town, we'd always go see the T-Birds Monday at the Rome Inn. I can't say I remember seeing Jimmie at our gigs too much. Occasionally, Stevie would sit in with the T-Birds. He idolized his big brother. I saw Jimmie do things that I don't think he would be proud of, and I imagine alcohol was involved. We went to a Thunderbirds gig in Dallas when Stevie was scrambling and the T-Birds were one of the top regional bands in the state; Jimmie could go to Dallas and *own* that town. Afterwards, Jimmie was riding Stevie in the parking lot, saying that he and his band weren't worth shit. It got physical, and Stevie pinned Jimmie down and was on top of him. I think that was a turning point in their relationship, like when you stand up to your dad for the first time. I never saw anything like that happen again.

Cutter Brandenburg, who had spent years in California, touring the world as a crew member for Ian Hunter, Jo Jo Gunne, Andy Gibb, and others, became Double Trouble's first real crew member in 1980, after returning to Austin and seeing Stevie for the first time in several years at his wedding.

"Stevie and Whipper asked me if I could come work with them," Brandenburg recalled. "Stevie hugged me and said, 'I need ya.'"

As a very old friend with years of experience working with successful rock and pop bands, Brandenburg had Stevie's trust and definitive ideas about how to boost Double Trouble's odds of success. Over the next year, Cutter's influence would help create "Stevie Ray Vaughan."

Recalls Layton, "Cutter said, 'You guys need help. You have to get your shit together because you have no idea what you are doing.' He had been out in the world with very successful acts, so we listened to him and his list of how we should present ourselves and what we should do."

"I had learned a lot about touring and artists and said, 'Stevie, you are a white boy playin' the blues, and we're gonna start from scratch,'" Brandenburg said. "We had to take a direction and do things that get him in the position to be the artist he wanted to be."

As Stevie was establishing his own musical and stylistic persona, his future partner Tommy Shannon was struggling through his own drama, wrestling the demons he would have to vanquish before he could become Stevie's right-hand man.

SHANNON: I got worse and worse after Krackerjack broke up in 1973. Stevie and I went our separate ways, and I began my descent into a drug-filled hell. The lower bardo of existence! I got really strung out and was put on ten years' probation, which was revoked three times because I had dirty urine specimens. I was in and out of jail and institutions for five years, falling totally out of touch with music. I had no friends; they all turned their backs on me, thinking I was too far gone to help.

I finally spent a year in the last possible place—a farm in Buda where all of the other guys were old derelicts from under the bridge. I was lost. It's a terrible thing when someone else has control of your life, like the judge who told me that I couldn't play music anymore because he didn't want me in bars. When I finally got out, all I had was a broke-down car, some clothes, a few pictures and memorabilia—and my '63 Fender Jazz bass, which I'd kept under my bed at the farm. One night, I opened up the case and just started crying. I loved it so much, but I was so far away from it that I couldn't even pick it up. I just put it back under the bed.

I got out in '78 and stayed in a halfway house in Austin for four months and started working as a mason with my cousin laying rock and brick. During this time, I drove my '64 Volkswagen Bug to the Rome Inn and heard Stevie playing his ass off. Afterwards, we talked for a long time outside. I had gotten a better probation officer, who let me play, and I started playing with Rocky Hill. I moved to Houston to play with Rocky and Uncle John, then quit to join Alan Haynes in the Texas Boogie Band. All this got me back into music and away from the bottom.

9

BLUES POWER

In October 1979, Stevie met a person who would change his fate. Edi Johnson was a bookkeeper at the Manor Downs horse track outside of town and, after getting to know Stevie for most of a year, she asked her boss, Frances Carr, if she might back the guitarist, whose talent and need for help were equally obvious. Carr was from a prominent South Texas family and a friend of the Grateful Dead's. Sam Cutler, ex-Dead and Rolling Stones road manager, helped her open Manor Downs in 1975. Chesley Millikin, an Irishman who had been general manager of Epic Records in Europe and was also close to the Dead, was another friend and the track's general manager. Carr and Millikin formed Classic Management specifically to manage Vaughan, starting in May 1980. Stevie finally had some backing to help propel him beyond the club circuit.

After eight years of honing his craft and finding his own artistic voice, the twelve-month period from January 1980 to January 1981 would prove to be pivotal in Stevie Ray Vaughan's career. After years of toughing it out in beer joints, couch surfing, and riding in broken-down vans for weeks at a time, with no place to call home and no money in his pocket, the essential elements to Stevie's success began to fall into place one by one. His old friend Cutter Brandenburg was back by his side, along with bassist Tommy Shannon, who would become his closest friend. With the financial backing of Frances Carr and the music industry connections of Chesley Millikin, Stevie finally had the tools he needed to break through.

"It was like watching a Polaroid develop," says Layton. "What was once a cloudy picture was coming sharply into focus."

EDI JOHNSON, *Classic Management bookkeeper:* I took karate classes at the Rome Inn Monday afternoons, and people there kept telling me I had to see Stevie, because I loved the blues. I realized immediately that he was on a different level than anyone I'd ever seen; he took you to a place where you only hear music and nothing else in your life matters. At one point, he and Lenny asked me to read a contract from Denny Bruce and Takoma Records. I told them not to sign it and said they needed someone with more knowledge than me. Stevie then asked me to be his manager, which was ridiculous!

    I thought he was worthy of going places, and it wasn't going to happen being paid by the door at the Rome Inn. I saw Stevie over a period of months, getting to know him a little bit before I was comfortable suggesting to my employer that she get involved. I figured Frances, who was known to have resources and connections in the music business, could help.

LAYTON: Frances was good friends with the Grateful Dead, and Chesley knew the Rolling Stones.

EDI JOHNSON: I told her that this guy was really good and had a chance to go somewhere and that maybe her friend Chesley could fly in and see him. They went down to the Rome Inn and were impressed and started talking about setting up Classic Management. Frances said, "I need to have someone watching the books, so you're going to have to do more work, and I'm going to have to pay you more." I offered to do it for free—that would be my contribution to this project. It had become clear to me that one reason Stevie did not have management was his involvement with drugs and reputation for being unreliable. Anyone backing him had to be willing to not make any money for a few years.

LAYTON: All of that happened without my knowledge. All of a sudden, we had a manager. It was kind of bizarre.

EDI JOHNSON: Chesley realized that the guys needed to play a lot more, and Frances was concerned that they needed money to pay rent and have places to stay. The band and crew were put on a weekly salary, and the money to cover it was transferred from Classic Management to a Stevie Ray Vaughan and Double Trouble band account. All the money that the band earned was deposited into that account. They were only making $500–$1,000 a gig, and I don't think the band started to pay any of the loans or 10 percent commission back for about three years.

NEWHOUSE: Stevie saw Frances as a guardian angel who could finance the band's day-to-day operations, but I made more money when we were self-managed, paid our expenses and the Rock Arts booking fee, and split what was left. All of a sudden, we're on salary and making less. It was a regular paycheck, but we didn't see any extra money from the windfall of a really good gig. We got $200–$250 a week, which wasn't bad, but there were clubs in Lubbock where we'd make $800 at the door, and now that money went to Classic Management and we were getting peanuts.

LAYTON: Nothing was really any different than it had been before, though at least we felt like we weren't doing it all ourselves.

EDI JOHNSON: Stevie and I both had to sign every check, and that could prove challenging for me. Stevie and Lenny moved out to Volente [about forty miles from downtown] because she wanted to get him away from all the people who were giving him drugs. Every Friday, I had to bring the paychecks out there and get them signed so the band could get paid. I would bring any bills as well, and it could take all night to get him to sign everything. Stevie wasn't responsible, and like most really artistic people, he didn't have a grasp on money. He was totally consumed by his music.

STREHLI: Stevie was so compelling that we all figured that sooner later he was going to grab a lot of people. But there were so few businesspeople in the Austin music world. As good as he was, he could have kept grinding his gears for years. Just having a manager was a big deal.

NEWHOUSE: Chesley would tell us, "You guys have got to watch out for Stevie; keep him away from the drug dealers, and make sure he's not doing coke." Then twenty minutes later, we'd see him shoving coke up Stevie's nose.

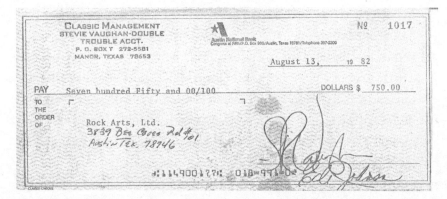

After Stevie signed with Classic Management, he and bookkeeper Edi Johnson had to sign every check from the band account. *(Courtesy Joe Priesnitz)*

LAYTON: Chesley was a very high-rolling guy with a lot of great ideas but with very little attention to what it meant to the bottom line.

JIMMIE VAUGHAN: I mean, who likes managers, anyway?

NEWHOUSE: We used to make fun of Chesley behind his back. We didn't have a lot of respect for him because he was an older guy with some affectations: he wore an ascot, and we just thought he was ridiculous and out of touch. But he was Frances's boy, so we had to accept him.

EDI JOHNSON: He was Irish and he had an accent, so the way he dressed didn't seem that strange to me. He was European.

LAYTON: Chesley had some stock phrases that were ridiculous, all said in this grandiose Irish accent. "Top dollar! Nothing but the best!" "You've never had it so good, you little cocksucker!" And my favorite: "You'll be eating shad roe on the gefilte fish highway!" The idea was, "Stick with me and we'll all be eating caviar, or fuck it up and we'll be eating gefilte fish."

BENTLEY: Chesley . . . well, he wore an ascot around Austin and treated the local scene and certainly a mere writer like me as being beneath him.

EDI JOHNSON: Chesley could charm a snake. He was funny, and he was a crowd-pleaser who made people laugh. He was protective of Stevie.

BRANDENBURG: He was uniquely hard to read; Chesley just kinda rolled with it. He had a master plan, and he did a lot of great things like hiring publicist Charles Comer, who was well respected in the industry and had a lot of connections.

EDI JOHNSON: Charles Comer was extremely helpful.

PRIESNITZ: One of Chesley's big problems with Stevie, who he called Junior, was the lack of original material. He'd say, "All Junior wants to do is play the blues." The band would work around Texas, and we established a tour through the Southeast and Northeast, anchored by the Lone Star Café in New York City. It was a grind.

NEWHOUSE: After a gig at No Fish Today in Baltimore [February 15 or 16, 1980], Stevie was speed rapping at the bar with someone for two hours. It was twenty degrees out, and we were huddled in the van. Finally, I walked in and said, "C'mon, let's go to the rooms," and Stevie turned around and told me to fuck off. Soon we were yelling in each other's faces—not for the first or last time. I said, "We're tired of waiting on you; get your ass in the truck!" And he said, "Suck my ass! It's my truck, and it'll leave when I tell it to!" It was forgotten the next day, but Chesley embellished the story into me knocking Stevie out, which led to weirdos calling my house and threatening to kill me years later.

LAYTON: Speed was everywhere—it was cheap, and it brought total chaos to everyday life. One day, I got a call to jam with Stevie at Hole Sound. I pull my car around back, and there's the van sitting there running and burning up, with the radiator overflowing and on the verge of stalling out. Stevie was passed out in the driver's seat with the door hanging open; he'd been up for days and finally crashed. I reached in and turned the motor off. The drug-induced mayhem and chaos was endless.

BRUCE: Stevie was always snorting what he called *cocaine* and I call *crank*—"coke" that made his nose bleed with every line. He'd get going on long raps that made very little sense, such as, "In addition to being a recording artist, I need money for a medical research laboratory and to hire skilled people, because I'd like to cure poverty and starvation." It was a speed freak's rap. I thought he should calm down and get sober, but "Just Say No" was not going to work. He just wanted to rock on his own terms.

April 1, 1980, Steamboat 1874 show broadcast live on
KLBJ radio and released as *In The Beginning* in 1992.
(Courtesy Sony Music Entertainment)

On April 1, 1980, the Double Trouble show at Steamboat 1874 was broadcast live on KLBJ radio. This oft-bootlegged show was released in 1992 as *In The Beginning*. It's a solid document of what the band sounded like at the time: raw, powerful, and unrelenting.

LAYTON: A gig like that was special. KLBJ did live broadcasts once or twice a month, and they'd tape it as it was being broadcast. The "Tin Pan Alley" from that show became the most requested song KLBJ ever had. We beat "Stairway to Heaven"!

WARREN HAYNES, *guitarist, Gov't Mule, the Allman Brothers Band:* The Fabulous Thunderbirds had started to infiltrate our scene a little bit, and I already loved Jimmie when a friend saw Stevie at the Double Door in Charlotte, North Carolina [July 9, 1980], a little bitty blues club. He said, "Jimmie Vaughan's little brother is pretty fucking amazing. Oh, and it was the loudest thing I ever heard."

GARY WILEY: I was going to Texas Tech in Lubbock when Steve and his band came to Fat Dawgs, which held about two hundred people [September 18–20, 1980]. I visited him at his cheap motel, and he asked if I was coming to the show. I said I couldn't afford it, and he said he'd take care of it and to bring three friends. We walked into the packed club, past a line of people who couldn't get in, just waiting outside so they could listen. We discovered he'd given us the best table in the house, three feet from the stage. He got into a very long version of "Voodoo Child," squirted lighter fluid on his guitar, and lit it on fire with his cigarette while still playing it! It was incredible, and the place went berserk. At their break, Steve came over and sat down with us. We were all mesmerized; all the people in the crowd were raving about how great he was.

NEWHOUSE: We opened for Willie Dixon at the Bottom Line in New York [October 17–18, 1980], and it felt like we had reached another level, playing a place we had heard about for our whole lives. Billy Gibbons was there, along with other important musicians and celebrities. And,

Early promo flyer for the trio. *(Courtesy Joe Priesnitz)*

of course, sharing a bill with Willie Dixon was especially significant to Stevie.

On October 27, Stevie and Double Trouble played at Rockefeller's in Houston, one of their regular gigs. Old friend Tommy Shannon was living in town, still working as a bricklayer and day laborer when he came to see them.

SHANNON: Seeing Stevie again was a revelation. I thought, "That's where I belong." He played "Texas Flood," and I got goose bumps; after just a few notes, it was like I woke up and thought, "I'm going for this gig with everything I've got." His guitar playing had crossed the gap from straight blues, incorporating some rock and Hendrix. At the break, I went up to Stevie and said, "I belong in this band." I was almost frantic about it. I sat in, and it sounded so good!

BRANDENBURG: Tommy had been through the worst part of his life, and his hands were cut, calloused, and crusty from laying bricks. You could see the pain and anguish in his eyes: one of the best bassists of all time forcibly kept away from music by legal rulings. I think it was slowly killing Tommy because he *is* music. It was so sad to see him dying for someone to give him that opportunity. There was an immediate connection between Tommy and Whipper that did not exist with Jackie. It was on, and Stevie had the foundation he needed—a rhythm section that he knew would follow him wherever he went.

LAYTON: I thought, "Well, all right!" Big Jack was losing enthusiasm. He and Stevie weren't that close. It was just a gig for him. Jack didn't like the band to play loud, and Stevie was getting louder and louder. Cutter told Stevie, "Man, we could get Slut in this band! Fuckin' Tommy Shannon! You need to hire him." Stevie was hitting methedrine, snorting cocaine, and drinking like crazy, but he had reservations because of Tommy's past drug abuses. I was thinking, "What are you talking about? You've got a rig in your sock right now!" Cutter said, "No, man, he's cool." And I said, "Let's get him! Call him up now!"

BRANDENBURG: Whipper and I talked about it on the drive back from Houston. When we talked to Stevie, he agreed that this thing had to include Tommy Shannon. We went to tell Chesley, and he didn't want to do it. He felt the investment had been made in Jackie, but we said, "Chesley, if this does not happen, we are going nowhere." The next time we went to Houston [a month later], he came to hear Tommy sit in with us, watching from the back with me as the energy level jumped ten times. He said, "You're right, Cutter, it's what we have to do." He asked what I knew about Tommy, and I said that Stevie and I had known him for a very long time, and he said, "I've seen enough and have never heard Stevie and Chris so alive. It's now on you. Get these boys back to Austin, and we will start all over." I could hardly contain myself.

10

GET EXPERIENCED

Jackie Newhouse's last gig with Double Trouble was January 3, 1981, at Skip Willy's in San Antonio. The next day, Layton drove to Houston in his Datsun 510 station wagon to pick up Shannon and help him move to Austin. The Stevie Ray Vaughan and Double Trouble lineup was set for the next four years.

"We all felt bad because Jackie was a great person and a real good bass player, but he wasn't Tommy Shannon," said Brandenburg. "I think he recognized that, too, when it came down to it."

Indeed, decades later, Newhouse says there were never any animosity between him and Stevie, noting that they had stopped socializing outside gigs. And, he adds, "all of the drugs and alcohol were getting harder to deal with."

Shannon's presence shifted the dynamics and sound of Double Trouble in ways that were immediately apparent. "When I saw Stevie with Tommy and Chris, it was obvious that the guy was about to blow up," says Eric Johnson. "You can't say too much about the magic, chemistry, and alchemy between a group of musicians, because those guys had it."

The local *Buddy* magazine reviewed the February 20–21 shows at the Steamboat, writing, "Stevie may be the best guitarist playing anywhere in the country. With the addition of bassist Tommy Shannon, Double Trouble has become a virtual blues machine, while Stevie is leaning more and more towards blues Hendrix style."

Layton says that Tommy's arrival eliminated all thoughts that they were a traditional blues band, bound by any genre restrictions. Millikin, who had originally hesitated to sign off on the change, quickly understood what was happening. He came to Shannon's first rehearsal and happily proclaimed, "Night and day, the difference is! Night and day!"

"Things started to roll with Tommy," Brandenburg said. "We now had a rhythm section that was intense, tight, full, and rich, and Stevie's confidence level as a front man grew with every single show. Stevie could really soar, and Whipper and Tommy were his wings."

With Cutter's encouragement, Vaughan also further developed his sartorial style, dressing in a more flamboyant, personal way that matched the music's increasing originality and aggression. Both onstage and off, his clothes became more outlandish and Hendrix-inspired, heavy on the kimonos and scarves, and topped off with the gunslinger's bolero hat that would soon define him. "He needed an image to get beyond making a little living on the Austin blues scene," Brandenburg explained.

LAYTON: Cutter thought that Stevie was downplaying himself too much. He'd say, "Stevie, you are one of the fucking greatest guitar players

One of the first Stevie Ray Vaughan and Double Trouble business cards. *(Courtesy Denny Freeman)*

ever! You need to start dressing that way and acting that way!" He had the hat made for Stevie at Texas Hatters and said, "Here, man, put this fuckin' thing on!"

BRANDENBURG: Stevie was wearing applejacks or berets while I had been wearing a large black cowboy hat for years. One night at some funky honky-tonk, he had misplaced his cap, so he used mine—with a scarf on to make it fit his little head—and we all liked the gunfighter image. Stevie also liked how the broad brim helped shield his eyes from the lights.

LAYTON: Cutter also said, "You should use your middle name; *Stevie Ray Vaughan* has a ring to it. A few years from now, people will be saying "'Stevie Ray' this," and "'Stevie Ray' that!" Stevie just went with it. It wasn't part of his personality to think, "How can I promote myself and present myself as a flashy guitar badass?"

BRANDENBURG: I was the only person who called him *Stevie Ray,* and I just thought it sounded good—as did "Stevie Ray Vaughan and Double Trouble."

PRIESNITZ: They were playing a series of Steamboat shows, and he changed his name and the name of the band. Chesley thought it was ridiculous to have Double Trouble as part of the billing.

LAYTON: People did pick up on the name thing right away. "Stevie Ray!" And "Rave on!" for *Ray Vaughan.* People dug the hat, too, and distinguishing himself through what he wore kind of opened the door to everything else.

BRANDENBURG: Now Stevie had an image that we all felt good about. Besides the talent, we had a good name, a look, and they were working hard on songs and communicating with an audience. I also wanted them to get out of the "bar gig" attitude. All the tours I had been on had shown me that this was show business and it was showtime. I felt we could really stand out if we presented ourselves differently than other bands in Austin with a more polished look and approach.

SHANNON: Some of the confidence he began to feel about his playing started with the clothes. He believed he could really break out and develop his own vision.

One of the first promo posters for "Stevie Ray Vaughan and Double Trouble."
(Courtesy Joe Priesnitz)

JIMMIE VAUGHAN: We always made jokes about the way that Stevie liked to dress crazy. He just liked to dress up. He would wear anything but the kitchen sink. He wore all the scarves because of Hendrix, of course.

SHANNON: Hendrix's example inspired him clothes-wise, too. He got some shit from the blues purists for that, but who cares? Being a purist is like being a religious fundamentalist. If you can't see beyond the little circle you draw around yourself, how are you gonna move out of it?

JIMMIE VAUGHAN: I don't know who these "purists" were that didn't like Stevie; probably some guy who was jealous in the corner that nobody paid any attention to. You had guitar players standing around having a big dick contest. Most of those guys shouldn't be there. People get playing mixed up with ego, and it's not always the same thing.

SUBLETT: I don't recall Stevie ever being disrespected. Every time he stepped into Antone's, Clifford had him onstage with whomever was there. Clifford always loved him and had open arms to anyone with talent and the right intent.

DAVID GRISSOM, *Austin guitarist:* Stevie was at Antone's *a lot,* sitting in with everybody: Albert Collins, Jimmy Rogers, Eddie Taylor. One of the greatest things I've ever witnessed was him and Otis Rush going toe to toe, full on. They were *staring* at each other, just going *at it.* The roof was blown off that night. It doesn't get any more intense than that.

ANDREW LONG, *photographer:* Stevie was around a lot. What a gift to be able to witness him over several years go from student to master as he played with his teachers. But to say "student" is a joke and disrespectful. Was Yo-Yo Ma ever really a student? Genius is genius, and it was all there from the beginning. That was obvious to anyone. He didn't need to learn what to play, just what not to. All the greats he sat in with— Hubert Sumlin, Otis Rush, Albert Collins—Stevie became one of them.

BENTLEY: Stevie's abilities were beyond scrutiny, but there was always a stuffy, too-cool-for-school clique who made a point of saying, "I like real blues, and Jimmie is the real thing." Jimmie, on the other hand, would be the first to tell you how great Stevie was.

JIMMIE VAUGHAN: Stevie loved playing so much, and that came through in everything he did. That was infectious, and no one who knew anything criticized Stevie for trying different things.

Austin's Auditorium Shores, 7-15-81. *(Watt M. Casey Jr.)*

LICKONA: Stevie was such a sweet kid with no attitude, and there never was any skepticism about whether he had talent. Even when he was basically a kid, he was the talk of the town as much as anyone I can remember. He was sensational, and there was such a charisma about him and a magic about the way that he played and his whole onstage persona. He was completely consumed by his music. Everyone knew he was the real deal as soon as they heard him, including people like B. B. King and Buddy Guy.

BONNIE RAITT, *singer / slide guitarist:* Long before I met Stevie or saw him perform, I had heard all about him from guys like Albert Collins and Buddy Guy, who kept running into him and being blown away.

BUDDY GUY, *Chicago blues legend:* I'm from Louisiana, which is close to Texas, and I had no idea white people there would come out to hear you play blues, so I was astounded as soon as I walked into Antone's the first time. Last I knew, those guys were listening to Hank Williams and Bob Wills, who I liked, too. Then they slipped Stevie up there behind me. I'm like, "Wait a minute, man. Who the hell is this?" He was hitting them notes and made me feel like I should go in the audience and watch so I could learn something 'cause he had that Albert King tone and attack. I was just thinking, "I gotta know who this guy is." I really couldn't believe what I was hearing.

SHANNON: A neat thing happened when younger people started to come to see Stevie, because they didn't think of what we were playing as blues. They responded to it as a new sound. It had more of the rock energy to it. He wanted to put his foot over the line but for a long time was afraid of people asking, "Who does he think he is, playing Jimi Hendrix songs?" I kept bugging him to work up "Voodoo Child."

LAYTON: He'd get kind of quiet and shy away from it, like it would just go away as an issue.

SHANNON: We also played "Red House" and "Spanish Castle Magic," and one day, he played me the whole "May This Be Love" solo, note perfect. The cool thing was watching the transformation happen. When he began to trust his instincts and finally became comfortable in that role, he really took off, and I saw the biggest change in his playing. And it wasn't just about playing Hendrix stuff, because it translated to the way we played everything. That's when he became the Stevie that everybody knows.

BENSON: I remember standing side stage the first time I heard him play "Voodoo Chile" and thinking, "Holy shit! Stevie's channeling Jimi now."

ELWELL: Double Trouble had a box van with dual fuel tanks, and one day, the switch underneath wasn't working. Stevie asked me to take a look at it, so I jumped underneath and started wrenching around. He comes out with a long orange extension cord and his Fender amp, which he sits down on and starts playing "Little Wing," "Manic Depression," and a few other Hendrix songs. He'd just started adding this stuff to his sets and asked if I thought people would like it or feel he was "infringing too much." I was rocking out under the truck and said, "Hell no! You are killing it!"

DR. JOHN: Stevie started blowing me away one night when we was hanging at his pad. He put on some trippy, difficult Hendrix album and started playing along with it, which impressed me. Then he started playing off it, getting down, improvising, and I thought, "Man, this kid is jamming with Jimi Hendrix." That's when I saw something real unique in what he was going for and realized that this guy was something altogether different, someone who was taking the instrument somewhere new, really striving for something big.

STEELE: Stevie liked to jam to Jimi Hendrix records. He'd sit on the couch with his guitar, headphones on, eyes closed, zoning out while playing along to *Band of Gypsys*. I also saw him lift the needle on "Voodoo Child (Slight Return)" a thousand times, wearing out *Electric Ladyland*.

One Halloween, Stevie took his infatuation with Jimi Hendrix to the hilt, transforming himself into his hero for a night. It was a heartfelt tribute from a guy who long carried a Polaroid photo of Jimi and a Hendrix autograph in his wallet. Stevie wore a ruffled shirt, a sparkly vest Shannon lent him, and an Afro wig that was a gift from Hendrix impersonator Randy Hansen.

"He looked so much like Jimi Hendrix, it was eerie," says Shannon.

"I think it was a lot of fun for Stevie to get out there with a good excuse to 'be' Jimi Hendrix for the night. He admired and deeply respected guys like B. B. and Albert King, but he was awestruck by Jimi Hendrix, who Stevie considered in a category of his own."

With the incorporation of more Jimi Hendrix songs into his set, Stevie decided to tune his guitar down a half step all of the time, just as Hendrix had done. Detuning the instrument facilitated the move to even heavier string gauges, all the way to .013s, several steps thicker than the norm. Detuning serves to decrease the tension and make the heavy strings easier to bend while yielding a better tone and a meatier sound. Playing them required enormous hand and arm strength and a level of sacrifice in terms of ripping up his fingertips that few would be willing to embrace.

SRV: I started getting into using different fret wire because I noticed that I had an easier time playing when I had a little bit more fret. With normal guitar frets, I was wearing them out so fast, and I found out that I could put bigger frets on the guitar, raise the action, and use bigger strings. For me, all that made it feel easier to play. This works better for me because I can play hard with both hands.

The gauges vary because it's based on the shape my fingers are in. I go from an .011 to an .013 on the high E, which is the only one I lighten up on. As a rule, the others are .015, .019, .028, .038, .054 to .056 or even .058. The good thing about such heavy strings is that you can hit 'em hard and they don't move—when you *pop* 'em, they stay there.

BRAMHALL II: He paid a price for being as committed as he was to the kind of string bending he was known for. He had a "callus kit" to make new calluses on the spot: a wallet with compartments for nail files, manicure scissors, super glue, and baking soda. He often had massive holes, like a quarter-inch deep, in his fingertips. Before shows, he would fill the holes with baking soda and put super glue over it and stick it to the other palm of his hand let it dry and rip a new piece of skin off to form the new callus. Then he'd file it down smooth so it wouldn't catch on the strings. He was very ingenious and inventive.

SHANNON: He would literally glue his fingers back together after burning them up. His method was very scientific. He would make this concoction of glue, put it on the end of the finger he wanted to fix, and the finger he was taking the skin off of, push the two fingertips together, and then slowly pull away the finger that he was grafting the skin from.

LAYTON: He would also add some skin oil to help the skin peel away, like peeling back a sticker real slow, so that it won't rip while you're pulling it off.

SHANNON: You'd be sitting there talking to him, and he'd suddenly rub his finger on your face to get some skin oil. This would last most of the gig, but by the end, he'd worn through it.

DONNIE OPPERMAN, *guitar tech:* Stevie was a brutally physical player. I sometimes changed his strings two or three times the same night! When I first met him, he would push extra high E and B strings through the bridge and he'd tape them to the face of his guitar. If he broke one of those strings, he'd just grab one of the new strings, pull it straight, and wind it himself onto the peg. He had this technique where he could bend the very end of the string down and then snap it off in one move before sticking it in the tuning peg. Super strength in his hands. I can't do that, and I've tried hundreds of times.

BONNIE RAITT: Just when you thought there wasn't any other way to make this stuff your own, he came along and blew that theory to bits. *Soul* is an overused word, but the fire and passion with which he invested everything he touched was just astounding, as was the way in which he synthesized his influences and turned them into something so fiercely personal.

DR. JOHN: He took something where there wasn't much space to be unique and made it his own.

ERIC JOHNSON: You forge your own voice by combining all of the heroes who have an emotional impact on you, and finding an original way to put it all together into an original voice, with your own concept, attitude, and influence. You can hear Stevie's influences—Albert King's microtonal bending, the power of Freddie King and Otis Rush, Jimi Hendrix, T-Bone Walker—but his own personality, attitude, and intention overshadows that. He also loved jazz guitar players like Wes Montgomery, George Benson, and Kenny Burrell, and organ trio stuff by Jimmy Smith and Groove Holmes.

SHANNON: Stevie loved organ jazz and horn players like Miles Davis, John Coltrane, and Ornette Coleman as well as rockabilly and old rock and roll like Little Richard and Chuck Berry.

LAYTON: He loved to play horn lines on the guitar, instead of just copping cool guitar licks.

SRV: Kenny Burrell was big for me. We play [Burrell's] "Chitlins Con Carne." I also listened to Wes Montgomery a lot. Django [Reinhardt]. Grant Green's *Live at the Lighthouse;* he's got some *tone,* man. [Willie Nelson's guitarist] Jackie King. [Austin jazz guitarist] Fred Walters. The Wes stuff is his recordings with trios and quartets. My favorite Wes record, *In the Wee Small Hours,* had an orchestra on it. God! Sometimes it sounds like Muzak, but what he played on it . . .

Every once in a while, something just comes out. I can't read music; I can't read a note. But every once in a while, I feel the "Wes" thing coming. I can't do it just sitting here. I've got to be groovin' out!

BRAMHALL: I had great admiration for him as a musician and a person because he always lived life to the fullest. Every time you were around him, he was a constant reminder that today is all we have guaranteed. Even in the early days, whether he was buying a pair of boots or trying out amps, he was just completely into it. He was never satisfied with staying in one spot. He wanted to stretch, and that is what made him one of a kind. Several times, when it seemed like he couldn't get any better, he took it to another level. He was always pushing the doors open and never wanted to stay the same.

SHANNON: Stevie was a very funny, spontaneous person. He could be acting like Brady, just completely goofing off, then pick up the guitar and immediately go into that other mode. He couldn't play the guitar without doing it right. One time we were imitating heavy metal bands at sound check, and Stevie was trying to play all nervous and hyper, doing all of these weird vibratos. But it didn't really work; he was too good to sound bad.

BRANDENBURG: A very cool thing happened one night at Skip Willy's. We had a $300 guarantee, but there were only about twenty people there in a new club for us, and I wanted to make sure they would want us back. Stevie agreed and told me to make a deal, so I told the guy we would not hold him to the guarantee. He said, "What do y'all want to do?" I said, "Give us fifty dollars and this dang milk bottle." He says, "You nuts? That milk bottle is from 1890, and Pancho Villa shot a pellet through it!" He showed me the hole. I said, "Okay, just fifty dollars, then." He said, "Okay, and here's some draft beer."

We played a great show for those twenty people, with the owner out there having a great time. Stevie said, "It was a great live practice, and we will eat this one," so I told the guy that we didn't even need the fifty bucks. It would be good for us in the long run. We shook hands and said goodbye, and when I opened the door to the truck, there in the driver seat was the milk bottle with three hundred-dollar bills in it. I looked back, and the guy was smiling and said, "Great show! Thank you, guys." I walked back to him, dumbfounded, and said, "Man, you don't have to do this." He said, "I want you to have the milk bottle, and Stevie and the guys deserve the money. What a great show." It was again one of those things where people wanted to help us, and losing money was not a point of contention. So I ended up with this 1890 milk bottle with a hole in it from Pancho Villa.

MINDY GILES, *Alligator Records marketing director:* Denny Bruce told me about Jimmie's kid brother, a sizzling guitar player who loved Jimi Hendrix and Albert Collins. He said Stevie was a wild child, more

Austin's Auditorium Shores, 7-15-81. *(Watt M. Casey Jr.)*

flamboyant than Jimmie—and loud! I finally saw him perform in February 1981 in San Antonio, where I was showcasing Son Seals at a college talent buyers convention. After a long, frustrating day— Gallagher busting watermelons onstage was the rage, and there were plenty of college boys wearing bedsheets as togas and pretending they were in *Animal House*—at 11:30 p.m., a kid said that he loved real blues and added, "You should go see Stevie Ray Vaughan at Skip Willy's tonight!" I ran around and told my like-minded friends, we packed up our display tables, ran out, hailed two cabs, and set out to find this raggedy-ass dive bar on the outskirts of town.

SHANNON: Skip Willy's was this big, horrendous, corrugated steel place outside of San Antonio that no one went to.

LAYTON: It looked like a warehouse, and it was on a two-lane road out in the middle of nowhere. The sign out front was one of those little marquees you pulled around in a trailer, and it said, "Saveeni Vaughan and the Double Troubles."

GILES: We arrived close to 1:00 a.m. and slopped through spilled beer just in time to hear a scrawny guitarist say, "Thank you very much. Good night!" Twenty people straggled past us, and there we were in an empty club, stranded by departed cabs.

I knocked on the dressing room door, it opened a crack, and Stevie, shirtless, skinny, and sweaty, said, "It's a girl!" I told him I was from Alligator Records and that I had agents from around the country with me. The door opened wide, Stevie grinned, shook my hand, turned to Chris and Tommy, and said, "Boys, put on your shirts; let's give this lady a show!" They lined up five chairs right in the middle of the beery concrete floor and with full house lights on, dead tired, played a riveting forty-minute set. Their show was full bore, no matter they had just played three sets. They played "Texas Flood," and I slowly turned my head and saw all my friends wide-eyed and speechless. My head was swirling by "Little Wing," and he sat on the edge of the two-foot-high stage as they closed with "Lenny." It was so beautiful I was crying. I called Bruce [Iglauer, Alligator founder] at 4:00 a.m. raving about Stevie and the band. Of course, I had woken him up out of a dead sleep, and he was pissed.

Four months later, Giles had a chance to introduce Vaughan and Iglauer, a meeting she hoped would lead to a signing. Double Trouble played *Musician* magazine's private party at the Chicago NAMM convention, opening for Albert Collins. Giles also arranged for Vaughan to play a second, more intimate showcase the next night at the tiny Tut's club, hoping that her boss would sign him to the country's leading blues label, which to that point had put out virtually no artists who were not African American Chicago club stalwarts. Stevie Ray was excited about the prospect of being on the same label as Albert Collins and Son Seals. It wasn't to be.

BRUCE IGLAUER, *founder and president, Alligator Records:* The first showcase was in some huge hall where I was a million miles away from him at a round table with bad hors d'oeuvres and overpriced drinks. I kept think-

Musician, Player & Listener
&
Bose
cordially invite you to a night of
Red Hot/Ice Cold Chicago Blues

featuring
Albert Collins
and the Icebreakers

plus guitar sensation
Stevie Vaughan

and Electric Stick virtuoso
Emmett Chapman

8:30 PM, Saturday, June 27
The Regency Ballroom
Hyatt Regency Hotel
East Wacker Drive,
Chicago, Illinois

Stevie opened for one of his heroes, Albert Collins at a Musician magazine party. It was supposed to be a showcase, but nothing happened.
(Courtesy Joe Priesnitz)

ing, "Boy, this is the loudest Albert King interpretation I've ever heard." I didn't get it as being special. The next night, Mindy arranged a showcase for Stevie in a very small bar right in my neighborhood. He set up in a booth where they removed a table, and mostly I remember that it was incredibly loud.

GILES: They were so powerful and loud, part of the presentation was rock-arena level, even in small clubs, but their dynamics were real, too. When

Tut's, Chicago, 6/28/81, showcase for Alligator
Records. *(Paul Natkin/ Photo Reserve Inc.)*

he would bring it way down on something like "Tin Pan Alley," I was
hanging on his whispered vocals. They weren't "just a blues band." But
they were blues.

SHANNON: Iglauer didn't like us.

LAYTON: Stevie was in kind of a tough place. His success, as meager as it
was, was based on his position within the Austin blues scene, bolstered
by the fact that he was Jimmie's brother. Playing anything other than
traditional blues was severely frowned upon by the people in that scene,
and Stevie had great respect for them all—even though his instincts
were telling him that he had to go beyond the confines.

IGLAUER: With my taste at that time, it was just way too rocked out for
me. I was very hard-core; blues is black music performed by black
people, and I didn't necessarily think that blues and rock and roll were
a natural mating.

LAYTON: Alligator's passing didn't seem to matter to Stevie. He didn't seem
too concerned about any of that. We were a band making our way
earning some sort of a living, and he wasn't going to change to get
signed, whether that meant going "more blues" for a label like Alligator or abandoning blues for a major label. He wanted to do his own
music.

Iglauer's dismissal represented a consistent problem Vaughan and the band faced; some blues purists rejected them as too rocked out, while a wider rock audience was not thought to be seeking a new blues/rock guitar hero. By then, however, Chesley was firmly stating that the band needed to be signed to a major label. He didn't want them tagged as a blues act and had a much bigger vision than a deal with a niche label. He instructed publicist Charles Comer to strenuously avoid having the band labeled as blues.

"We all kind of agreed with Chesley that we should be on a major label as opposed to just anyone who was willing to sign us," says Layton. "Yet I constantly wondered if we were ever going to have a record deal. I never doubted the greatness of what we were doing, but I certainly doubted whether it would ever succeed."

Some remnants of the old, sketchy business deals continued to haunt Stevie and presented challenges to Chesley. One was over the investment made on the John Dyer / Joe Gracey recording session in Nashville in 1979.

BRANDENBURG: We had a couple of shows at Al's Bamboo in Dallas [June 5–6, 1981], and Stevie seemed upset. I asked him why, and he said, "I can't believe you let those guys in the club." He pointed them out, and I went over to them, but they saw us talking and got up to leave. Stevie was upset because one of the guys had invested some cash in a studio recording [the Nashville sessions] and never got a return on his investment. There were some threats made to Stevie and Chesley about this tape being released, which Stevie didn't want 'cause it wasn't a good recording.

These goons would show up and bother Stevie, but we didn't think much more about it until the end of the show. James Arnold went to get the truck, came back a few minutes later, and said, "Cee, you ain't gonna believe this, but the van has four flats." All the tires had been slashed. As I was looking at the tires, there goes those goons, waving, smiling, and driving off. Man, did those flats hurt us at a time when we could not afford tires.

In December, the Double Trouble crew doubled when Brandenburg brought his old friend Donnie Opperman on board as Stevie's guitar tech. Opperman and Brandenburg had become close, working with Jo Jo Gunne and Ian Hunter. Their paths crossed in Albuquerque, New Mexico, when Stevie was opening for George Thorogood on December 8, 1981.

"We hung out before the show, and Stevie was real humble and soft-spoken," says Opperman. "I'd been around rock-and-roll guys for a long time, and he didn't strike me as that type of guy. I walked into the show, and from the first note, Stevie sounded just as powerful to me as Jimi Hendrix, who I had seen twice. I was floored. Cutter asked me to join, and I said, 'I'm in.' We were all paid the same; the money we made was split equally five ways, which never happens. That's how Stevie wanted it to be, which says a lot about how unusually generous a person he was."

Opperman's addition was another step toward professionalizing Double Trouble. He was fresh off the road with Joe Walsh, who was riding high on the Eagles' *Hotel California* peak and a thriving solo career based around songs like "Life's Been Good." Opperman brought Stevie some of his accumulated wisdom, including introducing him to Ibanez Tube Screamers, a pedal which would remain essential to the Vaughan arsenal throughout the rest of his career.

"Stevie had a very simple setup, just two Vibroverb amps and no pedals," says Opperman. "For the Hendrix stuff, Cutter would plug in a wah for the one tune. One of the first things I did was to show Stevie this trick I had picked up from Joe Walsh, who used a Tube Screamer in conjunction with his wah as a boost to make it sound more expressive, switching the Tube Screamer on and off as he saw fit. Later, we added an MXR A/B Box/looper to Stevie's setup, which allowed his guitar to bypass the pedals as he preferred. By using that, we created what is now common on pedals: true bypass. I made him a little pedalboard on a piece of scrap aluminum, just big enough to fit the pedals, switching box, and a stock Fender vibrato/tremolo switch."

11

A SWISS MISS

Early in 1982, several events conspired to give the band a feeling of momentum. "Stevie never failed to impress, and that finally started to pay off in a tangible way," Layton says. "It felt like some things were moving in our favor that promised to take us beyond the bars in Texas."

In February, Millikin gave a VHS tape of Double Trouble to the Rolling Stones' Mick Jagger, who was shopping for a horse at Manor Downs with his girlfriend, Jerry Hall.

On March 8, 1982, Double Trouble played the Continental Club, one of their monthly Monday shows there, scheduled, says Opperman, "as close as possible to the full moon." These shows were regularly sold out and so packed that Opperman had to set up his work station and Stevie's backup guitars in the alleyway, with people standing on the ledge all the way around the room as much as three hours prior to showtime. That performance was witnessed by Atlantic Records' Jerry Wexler, who had worked with Aretha Franklin, Otis Redding, the Allman Brothers Band, and many others, and was in town for the next night's record release party for Lou Ann Barton's *Old Enough,* which he coproduced with the Eagles' Glenn Frey. That night ended with a big jam featuring Stevie, Jimmie, Lou Ann, Doug Sahm, and others, but Wexler had already had his head turned by Double Trouble.

"Wexler was dancing to our music and told Chesley, 'This band is great

Continental Club calendar indicating the March 8, 1982
show witnessed by Atlantic Records executive Jerry Wexler.
(Courtesy Gary Oliver)

and should be playing the Montreux Jazz Festival. I know [festival founder] Claude Nobs. I'll call him,'" says Layton. "That got the ball rolling."

On April 22, 1982, Double Trouble flew to New York for a one-off gig at Danceteria, which was an audition for Rolling Stone Records. "Mick had seen the tape and been impressed, and Chesley said, 'You've really got to see these guys live,'" Layton says. "The next thing we knew, we were playing a private party for the Rolling Stones in New York. It was a gas."

Guests at the party included Jagger, Ronnie Wood, Johnny Winter, and

Andy Warhol. A postshow photo of a sweaty Stevie smoking a cigarette on a couch next to an elated-looking Jagger made it into *Rolling Stone*'s Random Notes section, and rumors swirled that the band would be signed to the Stones' record label.

LAYTON: It was a bizarre gig, not really a party. Danceteria had different bands and other things happening all night, with constant turnover. For one of those segments, we closed the club off and showcased for the Stones. There were only a few people there.

BRANDENBURG: Stevie and the guys pulled no punches, performing like they knew how important this was. They only had about forty minutes before the club would open to the public. Chesley fought with someone who was trying to shut it down while Mick and Ronnie were out in front dancin' and hollering. Some guy started pulling the curtain shut, and I pulled them open; Mick, Ronnie, and Chesley joined me in this tug-of-war.

OPPERMAN: As soon as Stevie started playing, Ron Wood grabbed a chair, straddling it right in front of Stevie. He stared at Stevie the entire time, *hypnotized*. During "Texas Flood," Stevie spun around, unbuttoned the guitar strap from the butt of the guitar, and swung the guitar behind his back. Doing that, he pulled the strap pin right out of the body and was struggling to get the guitar hooked on again. I ran out with part of an old guitar string, jammed it into the buttonhole, and screwed the strap button back in as fast as I could.

LAYTON: We played a short set, met them, the photographers took some shots, and then everyone was gone. It was like a drive-by showcase for Mick Jagger. Charles Comer made that photo happen. Jagger and Ron Wood came backstage, and photographers jumped in and began shooting. Then, just like that, it was over. It was exciting meeting Mick Jagger, and Charles got the shot published in *Rolling Stone,* which ended up getting us a lot of attention and spread rumors we were going to sign with their label.

STEELE: I ran into Stevie right after he got back from New York, and he said, "I've never seen so much cocaine in all my life. I think Ron Wood had cocaine in every one of his pockets. And it was some good shit—my heart was pounding!" He added, "Mick says he wants to sign us to Rolling Stone Records, and he's talking to Chesley about it, so let's see what happens."

LAYTON: The story goes that Mick Jagger told the guy running the label, "I like them, but everybody knows that blues doesn't sell." So they passed.

SHANNON: Still, it was cool that we were starting to get attention from people like Jerry Wexler and the Rolling Stones. We couldn't help but feel that something good was going to happen.

LAYTON: It seemed undeniable. We were playing Skip Willy's for four drunks, and all of a sudden Mick Jagger wanted us to play for him in New York. It seemed like there were too many heavy things going on for it to all mean nothing. This huge momentum seemed to be building.

The band's forward motion hit some turbulence when they opened the first of two shows by the Clash at Austin's Coliseum on June 8, 1982. The rough reception was indicative of how out of step with the contemporary music scene Stevie Ray Vaughan and Double Trouble were, even in their own hometown.

SHANNON: That was a nightmare. The audience was totally crazy. We were up there at home with people yelling, "Fuck you, Stevie Ray Vaughan! Get off!" It was horrible. We were supposed to play again the next night, but we said no.

LAYTON: It was traumatic! To walk out into the lights and see people throwing shit at us and shooting us the rod was awful. It was venomous. Stevie was like, "What is this shit?"

SHANNON: It wasn't the right bill for us, to say the least. Management was trying to get us in front of a large audience, but it was the wrong audience. The Austin punk scene was exploding, and we had never seen any of these people after years of living in town. We talked to the Clash backstage, and they were cool guys who thought we were great. We appreciated that.

LAYTON: Stevie thanked Joe [Strummer] and said, "I guess I don't understand your audience. We're not accustomed to this, and we can't do tomorrow night." Strummer was real apologetic, a great guy.

Any hard feelings or doubts the band may have harbored from the Clash fiasco didn't last long. Following up on Wexler's recommendation, Stevie Ray Vaughan and Double Trouble were booked to play the Montreux Jazz Festival on July 17, 1982, reportedly the first unsigned band to do so.

"Seeing [Stevie] at the Continental Club was almost an out-of-body experience," Wexler told *The Austin Chronicle*'s Raoul Hernandez in 2000. "I called Claude Nobs at Montreux the next morning [and] said, 'You gotta book this musician . . . I have no tapes, no videos, no nothing—just book him.' And he did."

EDI JOHNSON: For all the people who took credit for the Montreux gig, it would have never happened if Frances had not put up the money to get them there and back: airfares, hotel, ground transportation, per diems, et cetera. It was a tidy sum of money on top of an already large amount of debt.

LAYTON: Chesley had some brilliant insights into dreamer-type moves, and they often paid off. When he talked about playing free gigs in Switzerland, I was like, "Why would we do that when can make good money in clubs here?" He said, "I have a feeling that great things will happen," and sure enough . . .

SHANNON: I played Montreux in 1969 with Johnny Winter and remembered how great it was. I was really looking forward to it. It was like a magical thing.

OPPERMAN: We all felt like this was going to be something really big. Cutter told me they could only take one of us, and he wanted me to go because he thought Stevie would need me.

LAYTON: I had never been to Europe and thought it was pretty amazing that though we were pretty much broke, we were flying from Central Texas to Switzerland, basically just to do a single gig. We were booked on a night that was primarily acoustic music, and we came out highly amplified. It was like we had interrupted something, and some people starting booing.

SHANNON: We were so excited about this show, and suddenly, we thought we'd blown it. The truth is, there were really only about eight or nine people booing . . .

LAYTON: But it sounded like eight or nine hundred! It was bewildering. It was like, "God, we came all the way over here to get booed off the stage?"

OPPERMAN: The booing didn't seem so bad; people were dancing, and someone up in the balcony was waving a Texas flag. But it was hurtful.

SHANNON: The rest of the audience was just quiet, clapping politely. It wasn't an inspiring environment, but we played our best and didn't back down. As we walked off, Stevie turned around and said, "I don't think we sounded *that* bad. I don't think we deserved that!"

LAYTON: We walked back to our dressing room feeling dejected. We're sitting there real quiet, and someone from the fest came in and said, "David Bowie would like to meet you." We were, of course, excited, and met him downstairs and talked to him for quite a while. He was blown away by us and called Stevie the best urban blues player he'd ever heard. We all hung out in the musicians' bar for an hour, and he told Stevie that he was doing an R&B record and he'd love to have him take part in the recording sessions and have us as the opening band on the subsequent tour. Stevie said, "Sure, give me a call." Meanwhile, the next night, we were booked to play in that same bar, and we ended up jamming with Jackson Browne and his band all night.

BOB GLAUB, *Jackson Browne's bassist:* After we played our set, I was wandering around the casino and followed the sound of muffled music. I opened the double doors to the bar, and it was like a 747 jet engine going off in my face! They were playing an up-tempo song—a real fast double shuffle with incredible power, intensity, and volume—and I was mesmerized. I stood at the back of this small, dark room, with maybe a hundred people at tables until the end of the song, when I ran to the phone, called everyone in the band, and screamed, "You've *got* to get down here *right now!*"

Jackson Browne jamming with Double Trouble at the musician's bar in Montreux, Switzerland. This is where it all began. *(Donnie Opperman)*

RUSS KUNKEL, *drummer for Jackson Browne and countless others:* Bob goes, "You have come down to the bar immediately." I ask why, and he says, "I don't have time to explain. I have to call Jackson and everyone else. Just come!" So I go down, and there's a little club with a tiny corner stage that could barely fit a drum kit. Something very special was going on, and we all sat there with our chins on the floor, amazed at the sounds three people were making.

GLAUB: Almost everyone in Jackson's band came in one by one. They invited us all to sit in, and almost everyone did.

RICK VITO, *Jackson Browne's guitarist:* I may have been the only guy who didn't come. I was visiting with a friend when Bob called with great excitement and said this guy sounded like Hendrix. I said, "I don't want to hear another blues guitarist imitating Hendrix." What a mistake!

KUNKEL: Visually, Stevie was beautiful. He looked like an angel with a devil's smile, and he had this uncanny ability to deliver so much power with a light touch, a combination that made him so unique. He lit it up. I didn't play. I thought they were perfect and was yelling, "Play all night!" There were no frills, but Stevie's guitar playing was spot-on, and he had a great voice. It was just raw, beautiful All-American blues, and it was sensational.

GLAUB: Stevie had that incredibly powerful X factor and played with an intensity that I hadn't heard beyond guys like Albert King and Albert Collins. And the sound of the three-piece band was killing. I was with Chesley and Lenny, who could not have been nicer. On a break, I met

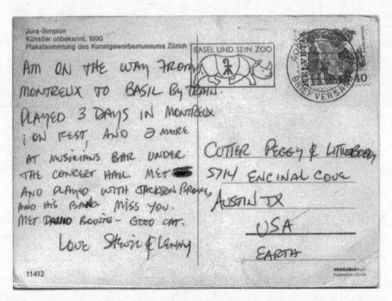

Montreux postcard from Stevie to Cutter.
(Courtesy Cutter Brandenburg Collection)

Stevie, Chris, and Tommy, and we immediately struck up a lifelong friendship.

LAYTON: We jammed until 7:00 a.m. When we were done, Jackson said that he had a studio in LA and we were welcome to come record tracks free of charge anytime.

RICHARD MULLEN, *producer/engineer of* Texas Flood, Couldn't Stand the Weather, *and* Soul to Soul: Chesley was dating Jackson's sister, which is how that came about.

VITO: Chesley knew Jackson. Before Montreux, we played a festival in Ireland, and afterwards, he and I were sitting in our bus when this guy came on and he and Jackson hugged, and Jackson introduced me to his old friend Chesley. He asked Chesley what he was up to, and he said, "I'm working with this brilliant Texas guitarist Stevie Vaughan—Jimmie's brother—but having trouble getting him a recording deal or into the studio." And Jackson said, "I have a loft studio in downtown LA, and if you're working with him and say he's good, he is welcome to use it for free." He had already made that offer.

LAYTON: The truth is that, after all the excitement of Montreux, we were back to square one, with no real prospects at all other than the offer from Jackson.

OPPERMAN: When we got back to the States, it was back to the grind.

12

CALIFORNIA DREAMING

Big Jim and Martha Vaughan see Stevie and Double Trouble off to Switzerland.
(Donnie Opperman)

Stevie Ray Vaughan and Double Trouble returned from Switzerland to Austin on July 23, 1982, and went back to grinding it out on the club scene. On September 23, they opened for the Fabulous Thunderbirds at Nick's Uptown in Dallas, earning a rave review from *The Dallas Morning News*. They played a triumphant twenty-ninth birthday show for Stevie at Antone's on October 2, going until 3:30 in the morning, and opened for Johnny Winter at the Austin Opera House a week later. They were firmly established as hometown heroes, but events in Montreux and over the previous year had provided at least a glimpse of the possibilities of something much larger.

"We needed to make something happen and thought, 'Why don't we take Jackson up on the offer and go to Los Angeles?'" Layton recalls. "I don't think Jackson expected us to do so, but Stevie called, and he agreed to give us seventy-two hours of free time over Thanksgiving weekend. Even though the studio time was free, we couldn't really afford the trip, so we had to set up gigs on the West Coast just to cover things."

Double Trouble drove the 1,500 miles from Austin to Los Angeles in a roundabout way, stopping for two shows in Santa Fe, New Mexico, and then heading north for a trio of gigs in the Bay Area—with John Lee Hooker and Elvin Bishop at the Keystone clubs in Palo Alto and Berkeley and with the Doors' Robby Krieger in San Francisco. They arrived in Los Angeles on November 22.

LAYTON: All of us and our gear crammed into our old milk truck that leaked oil, gas, coolant. Any kind of liquid that could leak, leaked.

SHANNON: The Sky King!

LAYTON: It was aptly named because we got airborne on the trip out there, when I hit an entrance ramp on I-20 a little too fast. We had a bed in there that we took turns sleeping on, which was suspended on this track . . .

SHANNON: Every time you hit the brakes, the bed would go flying forward. We had just enough money for gas to get to our gigs in California.

LAYTON: We had to play the gigs to survive. Two full days were set aside to record. We were just making tape, hoping that maybe it would result in a demo a real record company might actually listen to. We rolled into Jackson's Downtown Studio, and the guys working there were mildly annoyed because it was Thanksgiving weekend. We were like, "Hey, you guys got any tape?" We actually recorded over some of Jackson's demos for *Lawyers in Love*.

VITO: Jackson had just set up the studio for *Lawyers in Love*. The first thing we did there was "Somebody's Baby" for the *Fast Times at Ridgemont*

High movie, then the *Lawyers in Love* album. Then Stevie and the guys came in.

SHANNON: Downtown really was just a big warehouse with concrete floors and some rugs thrown down. We found a little corner, set up in a circle looking at and listening to each other, and played like a live band.

LAYTON: Jackson's engineer, Greg Ladanyi, was there to take care of us, but I don't think he really wanted to be there.

VITO: Greg didn't dig it. He thought it was just loud blues.

LAYTON: We'd brought in Richard Mullen, and the first thing that happened was that we almost came to blows! We said, "Hey, we brought our own engineer," and the reaction was, "Jackson sent me here to set this up for you guys, and I'm taking care of the studio."

SHANNON: That was within the first minutes of being there, and suddenly, it didn't seem like such a good idea after all.

LAYTON: We didn't want a big hassle; we just wanted to put some songs on tape.

Not wanting to ruffle any feathers and grateful for the free time, Vaughan had not objected when Browne and Ladanyi balked at having an outsider behind the console, but by the time they broke for dinner on the first night, the guitarist was vocally upset about the results.

"I was just standing in the corner with my hands in my pockets, and Stevie kept looking at me, like, 'Help!' He was not happy with the way things were going," recalls Mullen. A Texas musician and friend of the band who had been coming to their shows and running sound gratis, Mullen just happened to be in town, recording with singer Christopher Cross, who was working on his second record, *Another Page*.

Over dinner, Mullen urged the shy front man to exert his will, reminding him that this was his shot and his show. "I told him he was the only one with any clout, and he could do things if he wanted to," says Mullen.

Returning to the studio newly emboldened, they found that Ladanyi had left. In his place was James Geddes, Browne's second engineer, who Layton says did not think his job involved more than "pushing the Stop and Record buttons." So Mullen took over, tuned the drums, and dialed up the sounds he wanted to hear on Vaughan's and Shannon's amps. He also employed some sound baffles between the players to decrease leakage and allow cleaner tracks of each instrument without forcing the band to physically separate and lose the "live" vibe.

MULLEN: We had recorded one track and were listening back to it when Jackson walked in. He took one look at me and asked what was going on. After listening to what we'd done, he said, "Well, it sounds a hundred times better than when I left. You obviously know what you're doing, so the studio is yours for the next two days."

LAYTON: We'd spent about half a day going through this political stuff, so it was already late when we tried to get down to the business of recording.

SHANNON: By the time we'd gone through all of that, got Richard behind the board and got sounds, we only had time to cut two songs the first day. The second was the only one we used, and it was "Texas Flood."

LAYTON: The studio was a big warehouse, about twenty thousand square feet, and we set up in the middle like a gig, in close proximity, facing each other in a little triangle. Stevie and Tommy were only about six or seven feet away from me, and we just played, with bleed [microphone leakage between the instruments] all over the place.

MULLEN: I wanted the band's reality to be as close as possible to what they were used to playing live, so I didn't let them use headphones. I wanted them to play like it was a gig, with the same sense of abandon. If you give a musician the chance to think about what they are doing in the studio, they'll often mess up. I looked at their set list and said, "Let's go through the tunes just like a show."

LAYTON: Countless people have told me how much they loved Stevie's guitar tone on *Texas Flood*. There was literally nothing between the guitar and the amp. It was just his Number One Strat plugged into a Dumble amp called Mother Dumble, which was owned by Jackson Browne. The real tone just came from Stevie, and that whole recording was so pure; the whole experience couldn't have been more innocent or naïve. If we had known what was going to happen with it all, we might have screwed up. We just played. The magic was there, and it came through on the tape.

MULLEN: We were using one twenty-four-track machine, but I was really interested in doing it in a sixteen-track, two-inch format. This way, I could play the tape on my sixteen-track back home [at Riverside Sound] to record the vocals, which is what we ended up doing. Stevie's setup was so simple, so we only used fourteen tracks.

Moving through the greatest hits from their shows, the band cut "Texas Flood" on day one, "Tell Me" and "I'm Cryin'" on day two, and "Love Struck Baby," "Pride and Joy," "Testify," "Rude Mood," "Mary Had a Little Lamb," "Dirty Pool," and "Lenny" on day three, November 24, 1982.

SHANNON: On our second full day, we knew we had to get it on. During "Testify," Stevie broke a string halfway through. So we cued up the spot and punched in the whole band; I defy anyone to hear that punch-in.

LAYTON: It was the anti-record! We didn't do any of the things that usually happen when you make a record—hit the drums, go listen, play some guitar, go listen—because we didn't have any time, and this record proves that all of that stuff doesn't really matter. The only reason it's a record is because it was recorded. We cared, but it wasn't that big a deal. Afterwards, we did a few more dates and went home.

MONTHLY BAND SUMMARY SHEET	November 8, 1982 and November 19, 1982 thru January 1, 1983					STEVIE RAY VAUGHAN & DOUBLE TROUBLE		
Date of Engagement	Location	Guarantee/%	Gross	Comm. %	Rock Arts Fee	Date Paid	Amount Paid
11/8/82	Stubb's- Lubbock	$ 600.00	410.00	10	$ 41.00		
11/19/82	Keystone- Palo Alto	200.00	200.00	5	10.00		
11/20/82	Keystone- Berkley	200.00	200.00	5	10.00		
11/21/82	The Stone- San Francisco	200.00	200.00	5	10.00		
11/26/82	The Blue Lagoon- Marina Del	33%	120.00	5	6.00		
11/27/82	Cathey de Grande- Hollywood	$ 200.00	200.00	5	10.00		
12/ 3/82	Touch of Texas- Huntsville	500/100	500.00	10	50.00		
12/ 4/82	Touch of Texas- Huntsville	500/100	500.00	10	50.00		
12/ 9/82	The Cellar- Midland	750/ 80	984.00	10	98.40		
12/10-11/82	Fat Dawgs- Lubbock	2000/ 85	2000.00	10	200.00		
12/16/82	Golden Nugget- Baytown	600/ 90	600.00	10	60.00		
12/17/82	Fitzgeralds- Houston	800/ 80	1710.00	10	171.00		
12/18/82	Fitzgeralds- Houston	800/ 80	2514.00	10	251.40		
12/21-22/82	Nick's Uptown- Dallas	1500/ 75	1500.00	10	150.00		
12/31/82	Antone's- Austin	3000/ 90	3000.00	10	300.00		
1/ 1/83	Antone's- Austin	2000/ 90	1980.00	10	198.00		
				TOTAL	$ 1615.80		

November 1982–January 1, 1983 booking receipts, including the five shows in California before and after cutting *Texas Flood,* for which the band made $920 total.

(Courtesy Joe Priesnitz)

GLAUB: Right after they finished recording, they played a club called the Blue Lagoon Saloon in Venice, a little divey place where local bands played, and there were about ten people there. No one knew who the fuck he was.

BENTLEY: Stevie called and asked if I could get him another gig, saying they needed gas money to get back to Texas. I was booking bands at Cathey de Grande, in the basement of a Chinese restaurant. The owner said they had a band that night, but I told him how great Stevie was, and he said, "He can play first for $200."

They came into this little club, and he was loud as anything I had ever heard. He was just *unleashed* after a few days feeling constrained in the studio. It was one of the best times I ever saw him; he was on another planet in front of fifty to seventy-five people, most of them guitar players. He got his $200, and they left. I think they drove nonstop to Texas.

LAYTON: We drove straight through, twenty hours, stopping only for gas. Stevie and I may even have switched drivers without stopping once or twice, taking the wheel and stepping over each other. Ridiculous. The great opportunity was that we didn't have a pot to piss in and we got to record for free. We didn't sense that we had just gotten our big break.

13

SERIOUS MOONLIGHT

While Double Trouble was in Los Angeles, Vaughan received a call on the house phone in the apartment they were renting that would prove to be another momentous occurrence.

Recalls Layton, "The phone rang at three in the morning, and this quiet English voice said, 'Is Stevie Vaughan there?' I said, 'Damn, who is this?' 'This is David Bowie.' I'm thinking, 'You mean, the Thin White Duke? Ziggy Stardust? *That* David Bowie?' I paused and said, 'Oh, just one minute.'

"I ran into Stevie's room, shook him awake, and yelled, 'Get up, get up! David Bowie's on the phone!' They talked for a while, and then Stevie said that Bowie asked him if he wanted to cut some tracks in New York for his new record and maybe join his band for a world tour. Bowie had expressed interest in hiring Stevie the very first night he met him, but no one took it too seriously."

Adds Shannon, "Stevie was really excited about being asked to play on Bowie's next record. At that point, he also thought we were going to open the shows, because that's what Bowie told him."

Back in Austin, as Stevie made plans to go to New York and record with Bowie, the band and Mullen worked on the Browne tapes at Riverside Sound, where Vaughan recut most of the album's vocals.

MULLEN: I gave Stevie two tracks to work with, and he would cut the vocal part for each song twice. We would use either the best of the two tracks

Joe Priesnitz's booking calendar for Stevie,
January–May 1983. Note David Bowie sessions and
the next week, when Boz Scaggs was booked and
canceled. *(Courtesy Joe Priesnitz)*

or do a quick comp [*comping* tracks means to edit parts together from different takes]. Overall, there was no finagling of anything on *Texas Flood*; it was about as live and true to a performance as it could possibly be. When we were done, I did some mixes and ran off a cassette for Stevie.

LAYTON: The *Texas Flood* tapes were in someone's garage in South Austin. Necessity is the mother of invention, and we needed to get those recordings exposed. Cutter was the one who really made that point to us. Stevie was looking at a heavy commitment to Bowie, and interest in the tapes would have reminded him of where his heart lay and what he always wanted: to have his own band. It was not inconceivable that the tapes could have been forgotten, and we couldn't allow that.

Chesley Millikin, manager.
(Chris Layton)

Tommy, Cutter, and I conference-called Chesley to discuss this, and he said gruffly, "Don't bother me! Stevie's busy with David Bowie!" We asked him to take the tapes to somebody and see if we could get a deal. He said, "Well, that's not a bad idea." Expecting Stevie to get back in a milk truck after that run with Bowie seemed ridiculous, so we thought that we'd better up the ante and try for salvation.

Vaughan flew to New York in early January to join Bowie and producer Nile Rodgers at the Power Station studio. Most of the recording for what would become *Let's Dance* was already complete.

NILE RODGERS, *producer, David Bowie's* Let's Dance *and the Vaughan Brothers'* Family Style: Almost all the musicians and engineers on *Let's Dance* were mine. Bowie told me about this amazing new guitarist that he had heard in Montreux that he thought would be great for the album's solos. The first time I heard Stevie play was when he played my gold-plated hardware Fender Stratocaster, about twenty minutes before he heard "Let's Dance" in the Power Station Studio C control room.

CARMINE ROJAS, *bassist on* Let's Dance*:* There was talk about getting Albert King to play on "Let's Dance," because David was a genius at putting opposite forces at work and understanding what would work brilliantly. He heard that style of guitar on some of these songs from the start.

RODGERS: Carmine is getting the story a little mixed up. He's remembering me saying after hearing Stevie's first sparsely noted solo, "Why didn't we just get Albert King?" That was my first thought, but I regretted saying that almost instantly after realizing how carefully Stevie was listening and respecting the space. It didn't take me long to realize Stevie was something pretty special.

BOB CLEARMOUNTAIN, Let's Dance *engineer and mixer:* We did Stevie's guitar solos and a lot of David's final vocals after the band tracks were done. Stevie just had his Strat, a cord, and a Super Reverb amp, which stood out because so many guitar players at the time would bring in multiple racks and huge pedal boards. He made the most incredible sounds and was the sweetest guy.

ROJAS: I had finished my work and was back in the Power Station for another session, and I saw David and Nile and went in as they were recording Stevie Ray's guitar parts. I was astounded. He was set up playing crazy loud, but beautifully and with the best tone, and he was fully enveloped inside the music. He was amazing to watch.

RODGERS: Stevie was not one bit intimidated. Working with him was a breeze. He did all his solos in a day or two. He loved what he'd heard and knew it was important. He just listened down a few times and tore into each song.

CLEARMOUNTAIN: He worked incredibly fast, immediately cutting three solos on three songs, and what we used were mostly first takes. He listened once and then started playing. It was pretty incredible to witness.

ROJAS: He played the outro to "Let's Dance," and he just kept playing better and better. I used to go see Albert King and Hendrix at the Fillmore East, and Stevie was dishing out the same kind of soul, touch, and heart I heard from those guys. I was amazed that someone else had nailed something that seemed to be in the past, that I thought I'd never experience again.

RAY BENSON: I saw Stevie when he came back from the Bowie thing, which blew my mind. I asked him what he played, and he said, "I just sprayed Albert King all over the fucker."

CLEARMOUNTAIN: I think Stevie had only heard "China Girl" once before he started wailing away perfectly. At the end of the section, there's a chord change, and he lands on the wrong note, so it sounded a little dissonant. We played it in the control room, looked at each other and winced, and I said, "Let's fix that." But David said, "No. It's perfect." He liked dissonance, and he loved first takes.

RODGERS: Stevie actually went out of his way to make us comfortable by having ribs shipped up from Sam's Bar-B-Que. At the start of every session, I'd have someone take everyone's lunch order so it would be ready for a short break. Instead of ordering that day's lunch, he ordered the next day's lunch for all of us: amazing barbecue expressed from Austin. Everybody loved this Southern stranger from that moment on.

EDI JOHNSON: Stevie called me and said, "We need some real barbecue here. Go over to Sam's and send it up." They packed it in dried ice, and I drove it to the airport.

While in New York, Vaughan also cut a solo for bluesman Johnny Copeland's *Texas Twister* album and participated in *Texas Flood* mixing sessions. By the end of the month, he was back in Texas, playing a series of club dates with Double Trouble.

The Downtown tapes were in the hands of several record label A&R executives. The first to express interest in the band was John Hammond, the seventy-two-year-old Columbia Records executive who had signed Billie Holiday, Benny Goodman, Charlie Christian, Bob Dylan, Bruce Springsteen, and other icons.

GREGG GELLER, *Epic Records executive who had worked with Johnny Cash, Roy Orbison, Jeff Beck, Willie Nelson, Eric Clapton, and Merle Haggard, among others:* John came into my office in early 1983 with an acetate of *Texas Flood*, and he was very excited to put it out. I had some awareness to Stevie because I'd been hearing his name for some time. John Hammond had his own label, HME, that he wanted to release *Texas Flood* on, but he had run into financing issues. So he turned to me, and it didn't require a lot of genius to get behind signing Stevie to Epic. I was completely taken by what I heard. "Pride and Joy" was the first or second track, and I was won over immediately.

HARVEY LEEDS, *Epic Records head of album promotion:* By then, some people at the label thought of John as a pain in the ass, but I thought he was Godlike. I would call radio stations with him. Any radio programmer worth their salt would want to talk to the guy who signed

Stevie and producer John Hammond, who signed him to Epic Records.
(Don Hunstein © Sony Music Entertainment)

Billie, Bessie, Bruce, Bob, Aretha Franklin—and now Stevie Ray Vaughan!

AL STAEHALEY *Spirit bassist, Austin lawyer:* There were other labels interested, and I said, "Let us entertain other offers so we can get the best possible deal," but Chesley understood the power of being a John Hammond signing. As a lawyer, I was doing the right thing, but as a manager, he grasped that the significance of being John Hammond's last signing meant more than some extra bucks or points.

JIMMIE VAUGHAN: John Hammond had that history, and his track record was impeccable. He would champion people, and his endorsement was a huge stamp of legitimacy.

MULLEN: We felt we'd done a good job on the mixes, but it was viewed as a demo that would be used to try to get a deal. Hammond heard it and said, "This is great; let's just release this."

FREEMAN: It wasn't just me and my friends who thought Stevie was great; he was killing people for years, and it was hard to understand why people weren't jumping all over him. It took John Hammond to say, "Don't you hear this?"

GELLER: We were mired in dance/disco/electronic music. Stevie represented the type of music I'd always most believed in, and there was this gaping void for what he was doing. The audience for that music never dies; they just were not being provided with anything new that would appeal to them. Stevie was that thing, and I had absolutely no reservations about getting behind him.

LAYTON: Signing Stevie made sense, because he was on Bowie's next record, which they figured would blow up huge, and he was going to tour all over the world with him; there was our marketing right there. It was the perfect time to sign him for a modest advance and investment.

GELLER: I quickly became aware that there was an audience very ready to buy this release: the state of Texas. We had a great head of sales there, Jack Chase, who virtually guaranteed that we could sell eighty thousand records in Texas alone. Soon after hearing that acetate, Stevie, Chris, and Tommy came to New York, and the deal was made very quickly.

Stevie Ray Vaughan signed with Epic Records on March 15, 1983. They sent Jackson Browne a horse from Manor Downs as a thank-you. Millikin had always found Stevie's devotion to Layton and Shannon annoying at best. He still didn't think the band should be billed as Stevie Ray Vaughan and Double Trouble, seeing no need for a name that tied him to backing musicians he considered eminently replaceable, and he certainly did not think they should be partners in any deals.

EDI JOHNSON: It was very rare for the head guy to split everything with his band as Stevie did. He thought of the band as a unit, not just individuals with him as the star and them as the sidemen. Chris and Tommy were very lucky to be with him. Chesley thought it was ridiculous, but I thought it was a very kind gesture, and what was wrong with that? The money was the only way he could reward them and thank them for their loyalty.

LAYTON: We had a meeting about the Epic deal, and Stevie wanted us there in Chesley's office to learn what our part of the deal would be. Chesley said, "You are here because Stevie wanted you to be. I fucking disagree!" I actually appreciated that, because he wasn't saying one thing to our faces and something else behind our backs.

SHANNON: Later, Chesley really tried to separate Stevie from us. The three of us were very tight, and Whipper started to have questions about the finances. The normal business thing to do would be to get Stevie away from those dissenting voices. We were causing trouble.

LAYTON: He really wanted to get rid of me.

SHANNON: He'd point out bands and say, "Now, you need a fucking drummer like that in your band."

LAYTON: Stevie was better than anyone anyhow, so he might as well play with guys who loved him. We were like a family. And family doesn't just happen because you're paying someone.

STEVE JORDAN, *drummer/producer with Eric Clapton, Keith Richards, John Mayer, the Blues Brothers, and others:* I wasn't a huge Double Trouble fan. I didn't think they were heavily ensconced in the groove. I was super opinionated, but I've since come to appreciate the importance of chemistry and a family feeling in a band. Stevie and Eddie Van

Halen are very similar. They both carry the rhythm, melody, and lead and drive the band with the way they play the guitar.

KUNKEL: A lot of people overlook a key thing: that's the sound of three people not overplaying. Chris Layton is such a great, economical drummer. Stevie had all the motion and musical subdivisions: rhythm, lead, and vocals. Chris and Tommy held it down. Tommy on the bottom end with really basic blues parts and Chris with the deepest blues drumming. That's what made it so powerful; you could hear every single thing they did. The three of them weren't battling it out. They played as a unit.

COLONNA: When I was playing with Delbert McClinton, we shared the bill with Stevie. I stood there thinking how I would love to be playing with him again, and that I could make it sound better. My dad said, "Why don't you ask Stevie if you can play with him again?" so I did. And he said, "Well, I've already got a drummer, unless you know something that I don't!"

LOGAN: Doyle always said Chris was the right drummer for Stevie.

LAYTON: I heard other drummers play with Stevie who thought, "I can play things with everything he does!" It always sounded like a mess. I could have played other things than I did, but the music was telling me what I should be doing. Stevie was an absolute virtuoso, so it's easy to think everyone in the band should be the same. Tommy and I usually played pretty simple things because Stevie was doing so much, and that's what worked best.

JORDAN: The most important thing in a band is liking each other and having a brotherhood or sisterhood thing. And Stevie had that with Double Trouble. It's like Neil Young and Crazy Horse: they get on his back and *go*. They're like a family, and that kind of chemistry often translates to the audience more than expert musicianship does.

LAYTON: I took the *Texas Flood* demo tape on a visit to my family in Corpus Christi, looking forward to playing it for people, but they didn't hear it at all! They said, "It's good, but it's just shuffles and slow blues. Are people interested in that kind of music right now?" They couldn't hear what was special about Stevie's playing; blues was something Texans had heard for years.

MULLEN: Stevie had been kicking around Texas for a long time, and that tape sounded like him live, so people there may have shrugged. But people elsewhere heard a supertalented guy playing with aggression and soul, and it didn't matter if the form was familiar.

GIBBONS: The proficiency Stevie developed required very little in taking the style elsewhere. It simply got a little louder, a little faster, all with spot-on satisfaction. The importance Stevie carved for so many other aspiring guitarists is nearly immeasurable. The exacting delivery that appeared to be so effortless raised the bar and established the value of true dedication.

BRUCE: I remember a change in Stevie after the Bowie sessions. He came back from New York more confident. He was on his way to becoming a star.

LAYTON: Being validated by someone of Bowie's stature certainly had an impact. Stevie understood his talent, but how can you not doubt it when you're struggling to be noticed?

Just before signing with Epic, the group took another step toward becoming a national act when they dismissed Joe Priesnitz and Rock Arts as its booking agent and hired Alex Hodges and his Empire Agency, based in Marietta, Georgia. Hodges had worked closely with Capricorn Records' Phil Walden, booking Otis Redding, the Allman Brothers Band, and others. The first gig he booked for his new act was opening for Gregg Allman at Atlanta's Electric Ballroom on March 4.

ALEX HODGES, *Stevie's booking agent, 1983–1986; manager, 1986–1990:* I kept hearing about Stevie from Ray Benson and some folks around the Rolling Stones. When Chesley, whom I had known for a decade, asked me to work with him, I sent Rick Alter, who worked for me, to check him out, and he came back and said, "He is great. This is for you." I didn't realize just how great he was until I saw him.

BENSON: Alex was our agent, and he called and said, "I'm getting pitched on Stevie Vaughan," and I told him that Stevie was the best guitarist around and he was about blow up and that he should go for it.

PRIESNITZ: We got a letter from Chesley that they'd switched agencies and basically said, "And about that money we owe you . . ." It was rough. They were in debt to us for over $5,000 for commissions and were only paying us back $100 a month. Eventually, we sent a letter to Classic Management threatening to bring a suit against them for the owed monies. The matter was settled after months of haggling. Stevie had come by and said, "We're stepping it up." He was a good man.

HODGES: I think he had gained confidence and was entering a new phase. I met them all for the first time at the show in Atlanta, and my eyes were opened. The entire Gregg Allman Band was wide-eyed, which validated my own feelings. Gregg listened from his dressing room and said, "That guy's amazing." [Guitarist] Dan Toler was out front with most of the band, and he came back and said, "Alex, this is unbelievable." My whole team and I became instant believers, yet there was no album, no vehicle for advancement except booking him live. Chesley put a new requirement on me: no dates under $1,000. That sounds so little now, but when you're establishing yourself nationally on the club circuit, it's pretty difficult to achieve.

Let's Dance was released on April 14, 1983, and became Bowie's first platinum studio album in the United States. The title song was a number-one hit around the world, and for the first time, Bowie became an international superstar commensurate with his critical acclaim and influence. *Let's Dance* went on to sell seven million copies, making it by far his most successful album.

JIMMIE VAUGHAN: That was a great opportunity for Stevie. There he was playing his Albert King licks on the number-one record in the world. It was amazing! When they played the record in Texas, the DJs would always say, "And he's our own Stevie Ray Vaughan." For me, it was such a proud moment. It was an exciting *take that!* moment.

LAYTON: Using Stevie was a stroke of genius on Bowie's part. His guitar playing really jumped out and got people's attention. He hit everyone with something so strong it spun their head. Everyone has a story about the first time they heard Stevie, just as we do.

ERIC CLAPTON, *guitar legend:* I was driving, and "Let's Dance" came on the radio. I stopped my car and said, "I have to know who this guitar player is today. Not tomorrow, but today." That has only happened to me three or four times ever, and probably not for anyone in between Duane Allman and Stevie.

STEVE MILLER, *guitarist, rock star:* The first time I heard Stevie Ray Vaughan was seeing "Let's Dance" on MTV, and I was jumping out of my seat screaming, "Who the hell is playing guitar?"

GUS THORNTON: I was pretty hip to what Albert sounds like after playing with him for years, but Stevie got me! When I heard "Let's Dance," I thought, "Well, this is real nice. Albert with David Bowie!" Stevie is the only guitar player I've ever heard who could approach Albert's touch, tone, and attack. Hearing that sound on the radio was real cool.

JORDAN: The solo on "Let's Dance" is iconic. It's just a devastating, landmark moment in recorded history. It was pure greatness, a bolt of lightning screaming, "I'm here!" And you kept hearing it everywhere you went. It was a serious thing to walk into a club and hear that solo booming. And it sounded better every time!

Bowie's Serious Moonlight tour, which would kick off May 18 in Brussels, Belgium, and end in December in Hong Kong was set to be a huge sensation. Stevie and the Bowie band convened for rehearsals in Las Colinas, Texas, near Dallas in late April 1983. Guitarist Carlos Alomar, who had worked with Bowie for years, was the musical director.

ROJAS: Rehearsals went great because Carlos is one of the best on the planet. Stevie was phenomenal on the stuff he had recorded and on songs like "Jean Genie," but he struggled to find his place on some of the headier, more eccentric songs, because as musical as he was, that style just wasn't him. Carlos would just take over, and we worked around it.

CARLOS ALOMAR, *David Bowie's guitarist and bandleader:* I immediately realized the problems that I would have, cutting the first rehearsal short because Stevie Ray Vaughan does not read music and only knows basic blues chords. I can't tell him to play a minor seven flat five or ask him to do scale-wise progressions. Holy smokes, I can't even write him a dummy chart where you just get G, A, D. My job is just to make every guitarist sound great, and I got along with all of them. We're all guns for hire, and I needed Stevie to understand that he would be comfortable working with me, that he'd be able to dig in deep and improvise. His comfort was important, and after we shedded, he was able to bring his thing to the rehearsals. I was happy, he was happy, and David was happy.

ROJAS: The morale was really strong and got better every day. Stevie gravitated towards the more urban guys: me, Carlos, Tony Thompson [drums], and Lenny Pickett [sax], because that's who he was. You could have dropped Stevie in a ghetto anywhere and he'd get along just fine.

LAYTON: He felt black, culturally. He identified more with the black race than the white race. What that really meant to him is hard to say, but some of that could have started with things he said about growing up, being a scrawny little kid, pushed around a lot.

SHANNON: For a long time, he was honestly torn up that he wasn't black. He felt like he could have gotten closer to the music had he been.

ROJAS: We all understood each other, and we loved to jam during downtime, playing blues and "Mustang Sally" and just blowing.

SHANNON: There was a part of the show where Stevie was supposed to walk down a ramp, and they wanted him to do these choreographed moves, but he'd walk exactly the same normal way every time. They could never get him to do what they wanted, because Stevie was incapable of pretending to be something he wasn't.

ALOMAR: He was going to remain true to the blues, and we were going to work with him. I thought it was amazing to have a real blues player. One day, Stevie said he can't make a rehearsal because he was in mourning. I said, "I'm really sorry for your loss. Who died?'" "Muddy Waters." "Oh, did you know him?" "Not really."

At first, I said, "I understand mourning, but we've got a rehearsal to do." But no, no, no, brother, you do not tell a bluesman to just keep on walking when Muddy Waters died! That is a sacrilegious thought, so rehearsal was canceled, to Bowie's chagrin. I had to respectfully say, "You cannot make the man, a true bluesman, come, David. I'll cover

Stevie and Lenny.
(Courtesy Gary Wiley)

his parts, and we can rehearse without him, but you've got to leave him alone."

BRANDENBURG: He planned to go to Muddy's funeral, but he was really having a hard time with drugs and couldn't get it together. He always felt bad about that, but I know Muddy would have understood. He was a kind and loving, sweet man who called Stevie "my baby boy."

LAYTON: *The Dallas Morning News* ran a big story on Stevie, headlined DALLAS' FAVORITE SON on the front of the Entertainment section with a huge picture of Stevie and a little tiny shot of Bowie. Lenny felt that Stevie wasn't getting his due, and she went to the rehearsal with the paper, walked right up to Bowie, and threw it down at his feet. She said, "Look at that!" Lenny's intensity was not something Bowie would tolerate, and she and Stevie were doing a lot of drugs.

EDI JOHNSON: Lenny was causing a lot of problems, and someone called Chesley and said, "Get that woman out of here."

ALOMAR: Lenny disrupted things, but I think it was more of a buildup than one incident. Anyone's substance abuse problems are private—I don't care what you do if you play your ass off—but anything that disrupts rehearsal is disruptive. If you go to somebody's house, you don't put your feet on the table. If you smoke cigarettes, you don't ask to leave work to smoke every five minutes.

LAYTON: Bowie insisted that he orchestrate all press. He was turning the screw a little tighter, and Stevie hated to be controlled; it made him want to break out of jail, and things really started to become strained between Bowie and Stevie's management.

ALOMAR: There are many places where wives and children are not allowed, and anything interrupting the rehearsal will not be tolerated. I want everyone to be happy, but we cannot continue moving forward if you keep raising the threshold for our tolerance. It ain't gonna work, brother. When Lenny was asked not to attend, things got personal: "Anything that's an affront to my wife is an affront to me." As musicians, our sensitivities are much greater, and if you're in an altered state, then that awareness is distorted, and business decisions feel personal.

LAYTON: Tommy and I were just sitting here in Austin, on salary, wondering what would happen. David's original pitch was presented as, "Stevie should come and play on my record and world tour. It would be great if Double Trouble came, too, and opened the shows." But it was really an insinuation as opposed to a real invitation. It was a way to get Stevie interested in the record and tour. There wasn't any reneging, because it never was an actual offer.

BRANDENBURG: We were on salary under the impression that we were gonna open some shows, but we were a month or so away from the tour beginning, Stevie's rehearsing away, we have no dates, and no one from Bowie's camp is returning my calls. I called Stevie at Las Colinas and said, "I don't know what's goin' on, but I don't think it's gonna happen." I felt something was amiss and told Stevie that.

SHANNON: We weren't involved in any of these conversations, but I know that he was pissed off when he found out that they didn't really want us to open any shows. He didn't want to leave us in limbo for a year. Meanwhile, Chesley was pressuring Stevie tremendously: "Stevie, you've got to do this tour with Bowie!"

HODGES: There was talk about them opening shows and playing club dates late at night and on off days. Trying to figure out how to make that work with a different agent routing a major arena-level tour is pretty daunting. Having a parallel tour makes sense as a goal, but there are built-in conflicts, including logistical ones. What kind of access is he going to have to the press? How is he going to get from the arena to the club? Who is going to pull him out of the rhythm and schedule of the big tour? What if Bowie is traveling on an off day and you're trying to play a club in the last city? And how are you going to take care of Stevie's band and crew 24-7? I remember thinking, "I just hope this all works."

As tensions grew between Vaughan's and Bowie's camps, Epic was gearing up for the release of *Texas Flood*. Vaughan's camp and label were debating if it would serve the album better to have Stevie out promoting the record, or to be featured on a very high-visibility tour with Bowie. When Bowie's camp moved to New York, Epic set up two industry showcases with Bryan Adams at the Bottom Line on May 9 and 10.

Among those in attendance were Mick Jagger, John Hammond Jr., Johnny Winter, Cheap Trick's Rick Nielsen, and tennis player John McEnroe, ranked number one in the world and a huge star oft seen out on the town.

LEEDS: We wanted New York radio and press to see Stevie Ray, and my friends at A&M wanted to showcase Bryan Adams. Both projects were going to be attacking album radio, so I suggested doing a showcase together since we're trying to reach all the same people. A&M agreed but insisted that Bryan had to be the headliner. We were like, "Are you sure?"

BRANDENBURG: I met Mr. Hammond at the Bottom Line, and he said, "Stevie is a phenomenal artist and he's going to be an icon, and it's so obvious." I said, "I've kinda felt this way my whole life about Stevie," and he said, "Many artists struggle for years to become huge, and others are discovered overnight. I don't know why, but it's the obvious ones who seem to take longer."

JOHN McENROE, *tennis legend and guitarist:* Half the crowd was teenage girls there to see the new pop guy Bryan Adams, and the other half was music biz types or musicians who had heard about Stevie Ray. It was a totally bizarre, disparate group of people.

BRANDENBURG: Bryan Adams's crew was rude to us, providing very little stage room and no light gels, so Whipper and Tommy were in the shadows and I only had a white spotlight for Stevie, who wore a gold metal shirt that he had bought in a New Orleans secondhand shop. When the light came on, his shirt lit up like he was alive, and his performance was just as blinding.

LEEDS: Adams was very good and actually more suited to rock radio, but Stevie was a rock-and-roll guitar virtuoso. He went on first and was a total powerhouse, playing behind his head and with total commitment. He's Jimi Hendrix up there! It was like, "Follow that, mother-fucker!"

McENROE: Stevie blew the doors down. I remember wondering how it was possible for this guy to play for an hour and not miss a note. Stevie destroyed the place and when he was done, everyone left.

PAUL SHAFFER, *bandleader,* Late Night with David Letterman: There was a lot of excitement surrounding Stevie and a lot of people from MTV were there to see him play. His performance, which included a lot of Hendrix, was explosive.

McENROE: His level of intensity was unbelievable and so unexpected. I felt chills running down my spine. Seeing Stevie that first time was like seeing the Police at their peak or seeing a phenomenal Rolling Stones or Bruce Springsteen show. Stadium-level intensity and power in a small club.

GELLER: There was a big debate whether Stevie should do the tour with Bowie, which would elevate his profile but was at odds with him doing what was best for his own band.

ALOMAR: Stevie was at the pinnacle of his coming out; everything he had worked on for so long was about to happen, with his own album release riding the wave of *Let's Dance.* The thought was doing a David Bowie tour will heighten awareness, and I was very candid when he asked me about this. Anytime I'm with a musician, I feel that we're brothers, so I was just sharing information and experience. I told him man-to-man that the star here is David Bowie, and his fans *might* discover you and your new release, but history suggests they won't. Plus, dude! You only get one shot at your first album, and Bowie's management are not suddenly gonna put their press team at your disposal. You should know that we're about Bowie, the greatest superstar in the world.

HODGES: Stevie was doubting doing the Bowie tour, and I was backstage at the Bottom Line reassuring him that it would help set the stage for his career.

SHANNON: They gradually started taking things off the table. The idea of us opening some dates fell through. And then Stevie was told that he couldn't mention his own band or music in interviews.

ALOMAR: He had all these last-minute negotiations. There are many different things you can discuss, but the unspoken law is simple: if you enter into an agreement, honor it. You certainly don't hold everything up when everybody is downstairs getting ready to go to Brussels to do the first gig because you want to renegotiate your contract. That's like cold blackmail, and it's just bad management skills, but I never place things on management because the artist knows everything. So Bowie came to me and said, "I'm having problems." My reply to that is always the same: never create a problem where there is no problem. You want another guitar player, Slicky [Earl Slick] already knows half of the material, and he certainly can play blues. Given that, it was like, "Sorry, Stevie Ray, you're out."

BENTLEY: I sold a Stevie story to the *Los Angeles Times* to run when the Bowie tour came to LA. I did a really nice phone interview with Stevie, then he said, "I gotta run. I have to go quit this tour." I was like, "Are you kidding?" And he said, "No. I'm not a sideman. I have my own band and our own record."

LAYTON: Stevie said, "They wanted to try and control what I could say or not say about the record and about me." That's really crossing a line with Stevie Ray Vaughan, so he wanted to have a talk with David, and he was told David was on an island and couldn't be reached. Stevie asked, "Well, don't they have a phone on that island?" And they said, "David cannot be reached." Stevie said he told them, "Well, when you can get the word to him, tell him that Stevie Ray quit."

SHANNON: There weren't many people except us telling him that he'd made the right decision. Bailing out when he did was scandalous, but Stevie couldn't do what he couldn't put his heart into. Most guitarists would have played the game and worked their career. Stevie always came in the back door, never the front! That was his approach to life.

LAYTON: We were in New York doing stuff around the Epic deal and suddenly got word that Stevie's off the tour and we're going back to Texas. Tommy and I were very happy. I don't know exactly what happened, and neither does anyone else, but the big picture is Stevie had never been told what to do and he wasn't going to start right when he seemed on the cusp of getting somewhere with his own music.

BRANDENBURG: Stevie had worked his whole life to have his music out there. He was not about to blow that off to play on David's tour. Chesley was gung ho about that happening, and he thought it was a money problem, but it was not about money. Everything changed for him when he found out there were no opening shows.

J. MARSHALL CRAIG, *writer, confidant of Chesley Millikin:* Chesley felt like Stevie had really helped relaunch Bowie's career and they were disrespecting him, treating him just like another sideman. He thought he should be paid more than a backup singer. He wanted Stevie to be on the tour, but not for low pay, no opening shows, not allowed to talk about his own band. Chesley and Charlie Comer held a beef against David Bowie till the end.

The legend of the unknown Texas renegade quitting the rock superstar's tour made for an alluring story that boosted Stevie's image, but the reality is a lot more complicated. Lenny had made herself an unwanted presence at rehearsals, and Millikin was playing hardball with Bowie's managers, who grew irate about a sideman trying to dictate terms. Vaughan's departure came at the very last minute as the bus was loading up to take everyone to the airport for the start of the world tour.

ALOMAR: The bags are packed, and suddenly he ain't coming. I was in shock. I'm still in shock decades later! You just don't play that card to David Bowie. *Ungracious* is a word, but it doesn't tell you everything. *Ingratitude* is a word, but it doesn't tell you everything. We can facilitate a lot, but if you have your own agenda, then desperation makes for desperate moves. I asked him, "What do you think you're doing here?" I'm not ashamed of that conversation.

ROJAS: We were on the bus getting ready to fly to Europe, and I looked out the window and saw luggage on the ground and Stevie Ray standing against the hotel wall looking sad and saying goodbye to people. I asked Carlos what was going on in Spanish, which we used as code, and he replied in Spanish, "Stevie's manager was trying to get more money or have him open up, and they shot it down." Stevie brought a knife to a gunfight, going up against New York guys who make tours for the Rolling Stones. He hardballed the wrong people, and they weren't having it. And these guys just moved. We arrived at the airport, and Earl Slick was already there to replace him.

AL STAEHALEY: Stevie asked me to try and negotiate him back onto the tour, and I tried, but they already had Earl Slick on the payroll. Chesley spun a story: macho Texas guitar slinger tells poofed-up limey to fuck off. It wasn't really the way things went, but it was the right way for his career to be spun.

On May 21, 1983, the *Austin American-Statesman* wrote about Stevie leaving the Bowie tour. Writer Ed Ward quoted Bowie publicist Joe Dera as denying Millikin's claim that Vaughan's pay was supbar, adding, "We're disappointed that the people around Stevie Ray Vaughan have grabbed every opportunity for a publicity stunt." Still, Ward concluded, "Things may not have reached the end. . . . All concerned want him on the tour."

LAYTON: The advertising and advance on *Texas Flood* was *Let's Dance*, which stoked people's interest and curiosity about Stevie. People wanted to know who this unknown guitar player who told David Bowie to take a hike was. That was bigger news than if he'd done the tour.

JIMMIE VAUGHAN: Charlie Comer handled that situation like a genius, finding a way to capitalize on the story and play it to Stevie's advantage.

ELWELL: I came home to see Stevie and Lenny standing in front of my house holding a test pressing of *Texas Flood,* well before it was re-

Stevie Ray stays home

Contract tiff keeps Vaughan from Bowie tour

It's the number one single in the country, off of the number five album. David Bowie's "Let's Dance" is a certified hit. His tour, which opened Wednesday night in Brussels, is one of the most eagerly awaited tours of the year, but Austin's own Stevie Ray Vaughan, whose lead guitar work adorns the album and the single, won't be there.

Music

Ed Ward

ready rejected the first version of the contract when it was brought to them when they were rehearsing in Dallas at the Communications Center. He further maintains that Bowie's management has been asked by British music magazines for a copy

The *Austin American-Statesman* treated Stevie's departure from the Bowie tour as major news. *(Courtesy Joe Priesnitz)*

leased. He never had a stereo, and I had a good one, and we were all anxious to hear it. As we listened, Lenny and I were looking at each other, shaking our heads and saying, "We knew it! We knew it!" Stevie was up right on top of the speakers to hear every little pop. That was a magical moment. It was a wax pressing that you can only play about five times, and we wore it out quickly.

Texas Flood was not yet released and the band was back in their van touring clubs when they first saw the "Let's Dance" video, featuring Bowie miming Vaughan's guitar solo. He was none too pleased.

SHANNON: We saw it on the TV of a little club, and Stevie was furious.

LAYTON: Stevie was about to become world famous as the guy who played that solo, but the video really bothered him. Bowie's wearing white linen gloves, and Stevie said, "That motherfucker shouldn't be pretending to be playing shit he wasn't playing!" He couldn't understand why Bowie would do that.

14

TEXAS FLOOD

Texas Flood was released on June 13, 1983. Stevie Ray Vaughan was twenty-eight years old and had been grinding hard since he was sixteen. After all the hits and misses, the pieces finally fell into place, and at the center of his national arrival were the tapes he and everyone else thought were a demo, recorded in a couple of days at Jackson Browne's Los Angeles studio.

"We never made a record more honest than *Texas Flood*," says Layton. "It's like we walked out there naked and said, 'Here we are.'"

"There's a strong correlation between *Texas Flood* and *The Progressive Blues Experiment*, my first record with Johnny Winter," says Shannon. "Both are just raw blues played live by a trio recorded for virtually no money. I think *Texas Flood* sounds so powerful because it's so basic."

The album was launched with a release party in Dallas on June 16. Epic flew in many radio VIPs for the show, and they were duly impressed. A week later, Double Trouble launched a national tour in Bloomington, Indiana.

LAYTON: I don't think there's been a more *un*-thought-out record than *Texas Flood*! We were just making music—we weren't making a record for a record company to release.

SHANNON: I think of *Texas Flood* as a landmark album. What you hear is a kick-ass band contributing to the spirit and sound together as one.

Texas Flood represents the first time many people ever heard Stevie, and the two things that really set the record in a class by itself are that the performance is pure, honest, and right there, and it has the best guitar tone Stevie ever got on record.

LAYTON: One of my favorite tracks is "Mary Had a Little Lamb" because it's so tight. The way we all hit that one note together after Stevie says "*Tiskit*" always sounded so cool. And the guitar tone on the opening of "Pride and Joy" is as good as anything I've ever heard. It all speaks to the innocence and magic of those days.

SHANNON: I really like "Texas Flood" because I'd never heard anyone play a slow blues so intensely that it was like crossing over into something new. Some of his live solos on the song took my breath away. Every time we started it up, people would stand and scream. I never saw a slow song get that kind of reaction.

WARREN HAYNES: Stevie had the intensity of rock with the deep feeling of the blues. That was a lethal combination. Just like when Johnny Winter and Jeff Beck first came out playing blues that came across like something that no one had ever heard before. It was exciting and new.

DR. JOHN: "Texas Flood" became so ingrained in him. It's part of a Texas thing. It meant something totally different to this cat than it did to anyone else. He did the old Larry Davis song pretty straight, but certain things that came from other people became his thing in a very real way. That openness to other times and things that wasn't where music was hangin' at the minute, that's part of what made Stevie who he was.

MULLEN: You can hear every little nuance of Stevie's playing on the album, and his original songs are so strong: "Love Struck Baby," "Pride and Joy," "Rude Mood," and "Dirty Pool."

GRISSOM: It's hard to write a good blues song. Where do you go from Willie Dixon and Muddy Waters? Stevie wrote a bunch of really great songs for *Texas Flood,* all played with this simmering intensity and assuredness. There was a low-down, visceral quality to everything he did.

HODGES: Stevie had a vision, intellect, and artistic bent toward reinterpreting the blues. The label only pressed ten thousand units initially. They felt it was a John Hammond artistic commitment with not a prayer of commercial success.

Texas Flood was starting to take off, 3/26/83.
(Tracy Anne Hart)

LEEDS: There was a great independent promotion guy who could get any-thing played in Texas. We played him *Texas Flood,* and he said, "I'm not interested. Rock radio won't touch it." I was like, "Let me get this straight: I pay you a lot money to get music on Texas radio, and you're turning down a genuine Texas hero? If you pass on this project, you will never work for Epic Records again. You are so fucking wrong." It was surely different than anything that was out there, but it was fuck-ing great!

SHANNON: We could feel things changing on the road, the crowds slowly getting bigger and bigger. Stevie chose the milk truck over the chance to get in limos and fly all over the world because he really believed in

A page from Cutter's tour notebook. The *Texas Flood* tour was still seat-of-the-pants.
(Courtesy Cutter Brandenburg Collection)

what we were doing. Then we finally got a bus [on July 21]! It was a really shitty bus, but we were in heaven riding around in it.

LAYTON: We toured the whole country, selling out five hundred–seat clubs, with two hundred people standing outside trying to get in, and all of a sudden "Pride and Joy" was being played on MTV. It was just unreal to realize we could do all the things we'd dreamed about that represent a successful band on the road: get a bus, play some good gigs, and have decent food backstage. You take that stuff for granted pretty quickly, but it's hard to overstate what it meant to us at the time. Until that moment, we were still forced to think, "How long will I be fighting to keep the electricity and gas on?"

HODGES: A guitar player was the last thing any record label was looking for, but there are cycles and there's a world out there looking for a new spirit, and Stevie was that spirit. It started in Texas, but people everywhere caught on to Stevie Ray quickly when they had the opportunity, especially in New York City and Detroit and some other weathervane cities.

JACK RANDALL, *booking agent, former radio station program director:* I was working at an AOR radio station in Lansing, Michigan, and I went down to Detroit to interview Stevie on his bus before he played at St. Andrew's Hall, capacity one thousand. David Bowie was at Joe Louis Arena the same night—twenty times as many people almost across the street [July 30, 1983]. We shook hands, and he said, "I'm not going to say any derogatory shit about David Bowie." There were no other guidelines, and we did a great interview. Then we did a line of coke and walked onto stage together. I watched a ninety-minute set from behind the speakers and had my mind blown.

HODGES: We did a lot of shows around the Bowie tour. That began because we were trying to book club dates on off days when we thought Stevie would be with him.

Exactly a week before that July 30 Detroit show, the band had performed in Toronto at the packed El Mocambo club. The show was professionally filmed and released in 1991. The footage holds up as the ultimate capture of the band's magic on this coming-out tour.

SHANNON: We were on fire, and I was glad they were filming it, but that's the way we sounded! It's not like that was a much higher level than the night before or the night after.

BRANDENBURG: El Mocambo was a small but famous place, and Mr. Hammond had invited several people out to see Stevie. It was also a live radio and video feed, and they went full balls to the wall. Just before every show, we kind of hugged, and that night Stevie hugged me so hard, I thought he'd cracked my back. He said something like, "Buckle

SRV and DT followed David Bowie's *Let's Dance* tour around some of North America. They placed these flyers on cars in the parking lots of Bowie venues.
(Courtesy Cutter Brandenburg Collection)

your seat belt; I'm not stopping." And *boom,* he was like a racehorse out of the gate. A few times Chris or Tommy tried to pick up a drink after a song, but Stevie was starting again. I had goose bumps most of the night.

SHANNON: For me, personally, this success was a godsend. I went through all of those years of being in and out of jail and laying brick. To come out of that hell and actually get to an even bigger level than I had been at with Johnny was the greatest blessing I could imagine. My heart was full, and one of the real highs was when we went to Hollywood to play the Palace [on August 22]. We'd played there before to mediocre crowds, and we arrived to see a line going down the street and around the block. It was the first big indication that something was happening; it was a hallmark in the momentum of our career.

LAYTON: That fucker was sold out! And it was like that everywhere we went after that. We had gotten used to selling out the four hundred seaters, but the Palace held almost two thousand people. It was like we were getting ready to be stars.

SHANNON: All of a sudden, there was this big vibe going on about our record coming directly from the people, by word of mouth.

DICKEY BETTS, *Allman Brothers Band founding guitarist:* When I heard "Pride and Joy" on the radio, I said, "Hallelujah." Stevie Ray Vaughan single-handedly brought guitar- and blues-oriented music back to the marketplace. He was just so good and strong that he would not be denied. No one was interested in this stuff until they heard Stevie Ray, and I think it reminded them of what they had been missing.

BRAD WHITFORD, *Aerosmith guitarist:* There was a hole, a vacancy that most of us weren't even aware of until Stevie filled it in, completing the circle of greatness of Clapton, Hendrix, Bloomfield. It just made sense. It seemed like there was this big empty spot that his spirit filled. He came along at a time when we really needed him, and nobody knew it.

HUEY LEWIS, *musician, leader of the chart-topping News:* I followed the Fabulous Thunderbirds for years and thought Jimmie and Kim were terrific, so I was aware of Stevie Ray's existence. But I had not heard him until I got a copy of *Texas Flood* in the Record Plant [in San Francisco]. I put it on and lost my mind, so excited that I busted into a Jefferson Starship session, yelling, "You gotta hear this shit!" I stopped their session and put on *Texas Flood.* A couple of them flipped, and the other five guys stared at me, like, "What the fuck is this and what are you doing?"

We had these picture postcards to send back to fan club people, and I wrote one to Stevie saying, "Great record. Keep up the great work!" and sent it to an address on the back of the album. When I met him, he thanked me and said it was like his eighth fan letter he received.

GIBBONS: The underground awareness of this guy from Texas ran rampant through some lofty realms of an inner circle of players. It did not take long to become an immediate admirer of the sounds he was putting down. When it finally got committed to wax, it was over. There wasn't any denying that this guy Stevie Ray had arrived. The lid had been lifted, and the cat was out of the bag.

ANDREW LONG: I returned home to New York in the summer of '83 and heard the DJ on WPLJ announce a new song by this hot new guitar player from Texas. I couldn't believe "Pride and Joy" was blasting across the airwaves alongside Zeppelin, Allman Brothers, Springsteen, and Dire Straits. Here was this secret small local thing, the Antone's blues world, being discovered by the whole world. Suddenly, kids I grew up with were saying to me, "Have you ever heard of this guitar player Stevie Ray Vaughan? He's the best!" I just smiled and thought about all the times I watched him for hours on end from a few feet away.

MARK PROCT, *Fabulous Thunderbirds / Jimmie Vaughan road manager and manager, 1981–1998:* The T-Birds had been kings of the hill, touring all over with a great agent, with fans in Clapton, the Stones, Nick Lowe. Then *Texas Flood* took off, and Stevie became the big shot in town, surpassing the T-Birds, who had no label at the time.

Stevie and the band were invited to play Tennis Rock Expo, a benefit at New York's Pier 84 organized by John McEnroe and his tennis buddy Vitas Gerulaitis, on July 23, 1983. The event also featured Rush's Geddy Lee and Alex Lifeson, Buddy Guy, Bruce Springsteen's sax player, Clarence Clemons, and Aerosmith's Steven Tyler and Tom Hamilton. After the show, many of the artists, including Vaughan, Guy, and the tennis players, jammed in a studio.

"Stevie's playing that day was phenomenal, so consistent and precise, on as high a level as I have ever seen," McEnroe says. "We talked, and he asked what I thought about him leaving the Bowie tour. He said he was offered something like $500 a week, basically wondering why David Bowie was paying so little. But he still felt bad and worried that he might never make it after leaving such a big tour. I said, 'I think you should do your own thing,' because his brilliance was just so extraordinary."

On August 27, Double Trouble started a two-week European tour at England's Reading Festival. These would be Cutter Brandenburg's final shows with the band.

BRANDENBURG: I couldn't deal with us having worked as hard as we had just to see it all go down the hill for: drink that, snort this, smoke that. I also felt they were tired of me ragging on them, but I couldn't stop. I was becoming disenchanted because I just knew this band was headed for a brick wall, and I wasn't sure whether I could watch it happen.

LAYTON: Cutter was frustrated because people were drinking and doing drugs and the business was sideways, and there was all this stuff going on with Chesley and he wanted to go home. He freaked out in Germany. He could be unstable in his reaction to things, out of sheer frustration. He took some deli meat from a gig and shoved it in a hotel air-conditioning unit and almost got us kicked out. And we were like, "What is wrong with you?" And he's ranting, "This is bullshit! You guys are out of control."

BRANDENBURG: When we got to the last show in Amsterdam, I was down. I didn't want to go out at all, and Whipper told me to relax, that everything would be okay. But I knew it wasn't okay, and I wasn't relaxing. I was making a decision that I couldn't do it anymore. He thought that we needed to hug and make up and go on, but it was more than that; it was all about Stevie and Tommy continuing to get high and me not wanting to watch these guys die on the road. I had decided this was my last show, and I was going back to Texas to be a dad. It was one of the hardest decisions of my life, and also one of the easiest.

OPPERMAN: There was an incident involving Lenny that precipitated Cutter quitting. She got into Cutter's house while he was out on the road with the band, and started digging through his paperwork; she got it in her mind that Cutter was taking advantage of Stevie. It was ridiculous—that was the last thing Cutter would ever, ever do. When I first met Stevie, Cutter was supporting him financially, and he loved Stevie like his own son.

Lenny convinced Stevie to confront Cutter, whose response was, "If you think that is what's going on, then I quit."

BRANDENBURG: I was empty and out of gas. I cried through most of the Amsterdam show, thinking, "This is it." The next day at the airport, I told everyone with tears in my eyes, "It's time for me to quit. I'm not a yes-man, and I can't watch you guys kill yourselves." Chesley said, "Cutter, I am shocked, I am ashamed, and I am hurt." Stevie said, "It goes two ways. You've been a jerk, too." And I thought, "You're right," and let it go. On the plane, I told Chris and Tommy I was sorry that it worked out that way and that I hoped they'd still honor the pledge of points on the record if it took off, which I felt I had earned. Stevie was still very high from everything he had gotten in Amsterdam when he sat down next to me, and I said, "I'm sorry about the way things happened." He said, "Man, I am, too." I said, "It's time for me to go, Stevie, I want to be a dad, and I'm worried about you guys." He said, "Cee, I understand. I love you." And I said, "I love you, too."

LAYTON: We returned to America for three weeks of touring on the Eastern Seaboard. We landed at JFK, and as we were pulling up to the gate, I heard the stewardess yelling, "Sir, you have to be in your seat!" I look up and see Cutter coming down the aisle, his arms filled with everything from his briefcase, which he threw at me and said, "Here. I guess you're the new road manager." Pens and pencils and rulers and receipt books and itineraries fell on my lap. He got off the plane, and I didn't see him again for years.

BRANDENBURG: At the airport, everyone was running around without a road manager. I got in a cab and saw Chesley going in circles, Stevie carrying two guitars, Whipper dragging his cymbal bag, and Tommy and Byron [Barr, crew member] lugging all this luggage. Chesley was waving his arms around because they were going the wrong way. I looked back from my cab with tears in my eyes, seeing their confusion. Stevie and I never really spoke again. Many people would ask him where I was, and he would simply say, "He couldn't stand the weather." It has always been hard for me to listen to that song because it was about me.

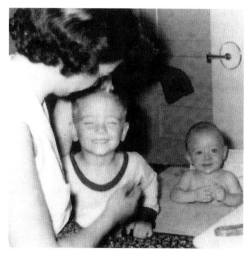

Five-month-old Stevie and four-year-old
Jimmie with their grandmother, Ruth Cook.
(Courtesy Gary Wiley)

The boys with their mother, Martha.
(Courtesy Jimmie Vaughan)

Jimmie, Stevie, and Martha in front of their Oak Cliff home.
(Courtesy Joe Allen Cook Family Collection)

Stevie, Big Jim, and Jimmie, 1963.
(Courtesy Jimmie Vaughan)

Family Style: Stevie on his first guitar, playing with Jimmie in the living room.
(Courtesy Jimmie Vaughan)

Vaughan family portrait.
(Courtesy Jimmie Vaughan)

Jimmie performing with his first band, the Swinging Pendulums. *(Courtesy Jimmie Vaughan)*

Stevie at ten, performing with his first band, the Chantones, at the Cockrell Hill Jubilee, June 26, 1965. *(Courtesy Gary Wiley)*

Stevie sits in with his big brother's band, 1965. *(Courtesy Joe Allen Cook Family Collection)*

Stevie's high school band, Liberation. *(Photo by Connie Foerster/Courtesy Larry Chapman)*

Stevie's school portrait. *(Courtesy Jimmie Vaughan)*

Stevie at twenty-two, on Christmas day, 1976. Left to right: Cousin Mark Wiley, Uncle Joe Cook, Stevie, Big Jim. *(Courtesy Gary Wiley)*

A teenage Stevie beams in the back seat. *(Courtesy Joe Allen Cook Family Collection)*

Performing with Paul Ray and the Cobras.
(Mary Beth Greenwood)

With the Cobras in 1975.
(Watt M. Casey Jr./www.wattcasey.com)

Original Larry Davis "Texas Flood" 45, borrowed by Stevie from Denny Freeman to learn the guitar licks and returned with a chip. *(Courtesy Denny Freeman)*

Stevie, April, 1978. Photo shoot for the *Austin Sun* cover story.
(© Ken Hoge/www.kenhoge.com)

Stevie and Jimmie, April, 1978. Photo shoot for the *Austin Sun* cover story.
(© *Ken Hoge/www.kenhoge.com*)

Triple Threat Revue singer Lou Ann Barton and Stevie, 1978.
(© Ken Hoge/www.kenhoge.com)

Triple Threat Revue, late 1977. Left to right: Stevie, W. C. Clark, Lou Ann Barton.
(© Ken Hoge/www.kenhoge.com)

Stevie and Lou Ann in California, backstage at the San Francisco Blues Festival, August 12, 1979. *(Mark Weber)*

Stevie songwriting in the van, California, 1979, Kools and Hendrix bio at the ready. "He did this all time," says Lou Ann Barton. *(Courtesy Lou Ann Barton)*

Double Trouble in California, August, 1979. *(Courtesy Lou Ann Barton)*

Double Trouble drummer Chris "Whipper" Layton and Stevie getting ready to take a dip. The chest tattoo was brand-new. *(Courtesy Diana Ray)*

Stevie promo portrait, June, 1980.
(Daniel Schaefer)

Early SRV and DT trio promo shot, 1980. *(Daniel Schaefer)*

Behind his head at Austin's Auditorium Shores, July 15, 1981.
(Watt M. Casey Jr./www.wattcasey.com)

Austin's Auditorium Shores, July 15, 1981.
(Watt M. Casey Jr./www.wattcasey.com)

Stevie Ray Vaughan and Double Trouble—Chris Layton and Tommy Shannon—at one of their favorite local haunts, Sam's Bar-B-Que, July 20, 1981.

(Watt M. Casey Jr./www.wattcasey.com)

Stevie and the band arrive in Europe, 1982. *(Donnie Opperman)*

Stevie Ray Vaughan and Double Trouble perform at the Montreux International Jazz Festival, July 17, 1982. *(Donnie Opperman)*

After the Montreux gig, from left, John Hammond Jr., Tommy Shannon, Chris Layton, and David Bowie, who asked Stevie to record with him that night, July 17, 1982. *(Donnie Opperman)*

Jackson Browne takes Stevie's hat and guitar for a spin during an all-night jam in the Musician's Bar, July 18, 1982. *(Donnie Opperman)*

Post-jam group shot, left to right: Bottom row: Danny "Kootch" Kortchmar, unidentified, Jackson Browne, Chris Layton; second row: Richard Mullen, Tommy Shannon, Stevie, Bob Glaub; in back: unidentified. *(Donnie Opperman)*

Texas Flood photo session, March, 1983. First publicity shoot for Epic Records.
(Don Hunstein © Sony Music Entertainment)

A couple of weeks later, I took all the money and receipts from Europe to Edi Johnson, who was shocked at what was going on. I was out of money, and she called Stevie, who told her to pay me for another couple of weeks. He was a great friend, kind enough to give me a month's severance pay. We were in a weird place, and I was not going to be able to watch them go where I saw them headed. It actually took longer than I thought it would for the drug and alcohol abuse to catch up with them.

OPPERMAN: I had quit working for them right before they recorded *Texas Flood* because Stevie kept getting worse, and after ten years of living that lifestyle, I did not want to go down that path again. I'd go check on him in the dressing room ten minutes before we hit, and he'd shut the door because he was waiting for his connection to show up. I watched the most humble, nice guy simply become a less nice person as he got deeper into drugs. We were all doing it, and I had to get away. We all loved each other like brothers and parted as good friends.

EDI JOHNSON: When he finally had some money, I took him to the bank to cash a check for $5,000 so he could buy his Caprice convertible. He asked me to stop on the way to pick up the car so he could grab a six-pack. We pulled into a shop, and he asked me for five dollars—with $5,000 in an envelope in his pocket!

After six months of rigorous touring behind *Texas Flood,* Stevie Ray Vaughan and Double Trouble joined the Moody Blues national tour, an odd billing that the group embraced. Starting October 17 at the Hartford Civic Center, they opened twenty-eight arena shows for the band, who were still riding high on their 1981 number one album, *Long Distance Voyager.*

HODGES: The Moody Blues tour was not an obvious move, and there was pushback at the label and from people doubting if Stevie could command a large stage, but Chesley was a creative thinker, and he and Stevie got it. I believed Stevie had a captivating magnetism that commanded attention and that the Moody Blues shared fans with Eric Clapton, who would be Stevie fans if they saw him. It was hard to see him walk onstage with a guitar and not know you were seeing something unique.

LAYTON: Alex said, "There's been an offer, and it's gonna seem strange, but don't be hasty." The Moody Blues felt all wrong, and he made the point that their fans weren't that different from ours in terms of age group and musical tastes, and he was right; their audience loved us!

SHANNON: We were playing big arenas full of people who didn't know who we were, and we just wiped them out. It was our first time to experience a big crowd and big stage together, and we kicked ass, getting standing ovations. *Glorious* is the best word to describe that tour, which was our introduction to working up a big stage show, and it fit like a glove. The sound rang through those big coliseums like a monster.

ANN WILEY: Martha and I were Steve and Jim's biggest fans, so we went together to see them play whenever we could. When Steve opened for the Moody Blues [November 4, 1983, Reunion Arena in Dallas], that was a big night for the family. Martha got so many of us together to go to that show—almost all of the Cooks were there, at least a dozen of us altogether. It was so exciting to see Steve playing a big show like that.

GARY WILEY: Stevie gave us free seats way up high, and before he started playing, he said, "My family's here tonight!" He asked us to stand, pointed up, and said, "That's my family!" They put the spotlight on us and everything.

We all loved Steve dearly, but we knew he had a drug problem. We went backstage, and he was in need of a fix. We were talking, just enjoying company, but he was not himself, looking very tired and worn out. Somebody came and visited him and brought him something to pep him up. I had to hold my brother Mark back, because we knew what was going on, and his instinct was to protect Steve. After that, Steve was "up" again. Our mothers and the older family members did not see it, but we did, and we were concerned.

BENSON: I went over to see Stevie in Travis Heights, where he and Lenny were living, and they were strung out really badly. I was kind of shocked because Stevie was saying shit that didn't make sense. We went to dinner with Lenny's mom and grandma at the Big Wheel Café, and every fifteen minutes they'd go into the bathroom and hit it up, and I was sitting there with Mom and Grandma, who knew something was off.

On December 4, 1983, at the Kabuki Theater in San Francisco, Stevie received three awards from *Guitar Player* magazine: Best New Talent, Best New Electric Blues Guitar Player, and Best Guitar Album. He flew from there to Hamilton, Ontario, to record the *In Session* TV show with Albert King. Stevie and Albert had continued their relationship since their first meeting. At least once, King was told that Stevie Ray Vaughan was in the house and would be sitting in, only to proclaim, "No he's not!" When Vaughan showed up and King saw him, King lit up, asking, "Why didn't you tell me it was Little Stevie?"

THORNTON: We never really rehearsed for the taping, but the night before, we met with the producer and discussed what we were going to do. Then we all went to the hotel to chill. Me and Tommy and Mike [Llorens, the brothers who played drums and keyboards] were drinking and playing cards, and there was a knock on the door. Stevie came in with a *Texas Flood* cassette and said, "Here, guys—we'll play a couple of these songs." We were good and buzzed up by then, pretty well blasted, so we put that tape on the bed and never did listen to it.

The next day, we just got up and started jamming. We listened to each other and played along. Stevie was very easy to play with. He was a good, experienced musician who knew when to play and when not to play. We were just listening to one another and complimenting each other. When you're zoned in like that, it's easy. We all were very happy for every opportunity to play with Stevie, definitely including Albert.

SHANNON: Stevie always said that 50 percent of learning how to play is learning how to really listen. He had a certain kind of awareness to music that is hard for a lot of people to get in touch with. He *really listened.*

O'BRIEN: A short time after the taping, I asked Albert about it, and he said, "Oh, man, that was great! Stevie played so good, but, you know . . . I had to step on him!"

A week after the session with King, Stevie and Double Trouble capped off a momentous year by recording their first performance on *Austin City Limits,* the public television show that was growing in national stature. It was a joint appearance with the Fabulous Thunderbirds that did not air until late the following year, as the final episode in the show's ninth season.

The show, which began in 1974, initially focused heavily on country, both the cosmic cowboys lighting up Austin—Willie Nelson was the very first performer—and classic Texas artists, including Bob Wills and the Texas Playboys. The scope slowly expanded, with featured artists including Lightnin' Hopkins, B. B. King, and Tom Waits.

LICKONA: I really liked Stevie and saw him all the time, and I wanted to have him on the show well before he finally made it on. His management thought of us as a local show and didn't want him treated him as a local act. They just weren't cooperating. Chesley came from a different world and had a different notion of what Stevie should do and not do.

LAYTON: I ran into Terry Lickona at a cafeteria right before the whole Montreux thing and said, "You ought to get us on *Austin City Limits*," and he goes, "Well, actually, I'm sorry to say that what y'all do is not the kind of thing we present on the show. We really can't do it." Then *Texas Flood* comes out, and they call and say, "Oh, we'd love to have Stevie Ray Vaughan and Double Trouble on the show!"

SHANNON: We were really excited about being on the show, and it came off real well.

LICKONA: Stevie was definitely in an altered state, which is how he spent much of his time back then. He was coked up, sweating, and almost paranoid; he kept going off the stage because he felt like he was such a mess. In reality, he *looked* like a mess, but his playing was terrific, and the people there were blown away. Every guitar player in America either saw the show or quickly became aware of it and begged us for repeats or copies. It became the stuff of legend, and we were flooded with requests.

Austin was a small town, and his lifestyle was common knowledge. Frankly, almost everyone else was doing the same thing; it was just part of the culture, and not only for musicians. For the most part, it didn't really impact Stevie's performance. It was just having a real bad effect on him personally as well as his decisions about his career and business. A lot of the issues were compounded once he started getting some acclaim outside of Austin and had some money coming in.

15

STORMY WEATHER

After eighteen months of nonstop touring, Stevie, Chris, and Tommy were a well-oiled musical machine when they entered the Power Station in New York City in January 1984 to cut their follow-up. Mullen was once again engineer and coproducer with the band. John Hammond was there as executive producer. The only problem was they lacked new material, having included the highlights of their club years on their debut.

One song fell into Stevie's lap when he went to San Antonio, where he was being recruited by Arrowhead Music Management, which hoped to sign him away from Chesley. Stevie's old Triple Threat bandmate Mike Kindred was working for Arrowhead and attended the courtship lunch, where he gave him a cassette of "Cold Shot," the song the pianist wrote and sang in their former band. "Stevie said, 'Oh, I had forgotten about this,'" Kindred recalls. "Arrowhead did not acquire management of Stevie, but I got 'Cold Shot' in there."

The band spent time in an Austin studio writing and making demos as they worked to come up with an album's worth of new material. "We hadn't had all of those songs floating around for most of the band's life as we did the first time," says Shannon. "We had to start from scratch."

The high volume of excellent outtakes from these sessions released in ensuing decades is indicative of both the band's strong playing and the fact that songwriting remained laborious. The extra tracks were mostly covers,

including "Little Wing," "Wham," "Close to You," "Come On (Part III),"
"Hideaway," "Look at Little Sister," and "Give Me Back My Wig."

MULLEN: We did three weeks of preproduction in an Austin studio, where
they wrote "Couldn't Stand the Weather," "Stang's Swang," "Honey
Bee," and "Scuttle Buttin'."

JIMMIE VAUGHAN: "Scuttle Buttin'" was like Lonnie Mack's "Chicken
Pickin'."

SHANNON: We had to come up with the songs pretty quickly. Stevie wasn't
a fluent songwriter; he'd spend a lot of time on a song, rewriting parts
and lyrics. "Couldn't Stand the Weather" came together over a period
of time. We worked through it in rehearsals and gradually put all of
the sections together.

MULLEN: It was really the first time they were going to a studio to make a
record, and it was a lot more difficult simply because they were unsure
about what they wanted to do. They had toured relentlessly since the
release of *Texas Flood* and only had pieces of songs written.

LAYTON: *Couldn't Stand the Weather* was our first real record, because
Texas Flood was a demo. It was a very exciting time. All of the great
opportunities that arose simply strengthened our belief in ourselves,
which was coming to bear on this record. Just being flown to New York
to stay at the Mayflower Hotel for six weeks was a big deal for six guys
from Texas, as was working at the Power Station, where Stevie had
worked with David Bowie. And to top it off, we were being produced
by John Hammond!

SHANNON: What an honor to work with that guy. Billie Holiday, Bruce
Springsteen, Bob Dylan . . .

LAYTON: Charlie Christian. He's one of the coolest guys ever in the history
of music.

SHANNON: In every generation, he found something spectacular. He just
knew.

LAYTON: He said that he hadn't heard anyone imbued with the blues spirit
like Stevie since Robert Johnson. He'd come in his tweed coat and bow
tie, bring his sack lunch and *New York Times,* sit down, read the pa-

per, and listen to what we were doing, then make a comment here and there about the groove or whatever.

MULLEN: John wanted to be involved, and though his ear was one of the best ever in terms of picking out talent, he was pretty unfamiliar with modern recording techniques. Every time the guys came in after recording a take, John would tell them a story, which seemed to be his whole reason for being there. He would also use a stopwatch to time all of the songs and tell you how long every take was. I didn't know what he was doing, but in the old days, tape machines didn't have timers, numbers, or Return-to-Zero buttons. I kept saying, "John, you don't really need to time this stuff."

LAYTON: On the very first day, Richard asked us to play something so he could get sounds, so I did the floor tom drumroll that starts "Tin Pan Alley," and Stevie and Tommy just fell in. When we were done, John hit the talkback mic and said, "You'll never get it better than that!" I said, "Y'all recorded that?" It was a warm-up, but he was right; that's the track we kept. He knew when something was really special and had an intuition into people's nature; when you played something that reflected your truest nature, he knew it immediately.

SHANNON: There's no telling how and when that magic is going to happen, and John had amazing ears and knew immediately when we'd captured the best take. We always thought he wasn't paying attention behind his *New York Times,* but he heard every note and offered valuable insight. His instincts were impeccable.

MULLEN: He was really sweet and had all of these great stories, but I think the guys felt on edge around him. It was like having your high school principal there because they had to conceal the drug activity.

LAYTON: We were like "Party down, man!" Big record budget, living at the Mayflower, drinking, snortin' cocaine . . . but we thought, "We can't do drugs in front of John Hammond!" So we'd go sneak off behind the Steinway piano or a sound baffle. But he knew what we were up to.

SHANNON: Why else would a whole group of guys go crouching down behind a piano together? We couldn't have been more obvious, really.

LAYTON: John is sitting in the control room reading the paper, which he closes, sets on his lap, then looks off, like he's going to be real reflective. He says, "Years ago, I worked with Gene Krupa. Fabulous drummer—incredible musician! One of the greatest. He had this thing, though, that he liked to do from time to time. He loved to smoke pot, marijuana. And when he did, his time went all to shit. He became something not like what he really was when he smoked that marijuana. Even since then, I just don't like drugs in my sessions." And he picked up his paper and started reading again! We were all speechless, but we got the message, even though all we did was try to hide it from him a little better.

MULLEN: There were probably five thousand different song lists. We joked that every time Stevie did a line [of cocaine], he'd come back with a different list; I was guilty of the same thing.

LAYTON: We were high on how cool it was to be recording in New York with a record company's backing, but we were real high, too; two distinctly different highs going on.

SHANNON: We were becoming successful, so dealers found us. The drug intake had increased dramatically, though the real negative effects hadn't taken over yet. We were feeling great, and the drugs were just a part of everything else.

LAYTON: Label people—A&R and marketing—wanted to come in to evaluate midstream. They had ideas about how to make a "great record," and Stevie didn't want them in the studio *at all*. He said, "Do you think we did pretty good on the first one?" They said, "Oh, it's wonderful," so he replied, "Then we don't need your help on the second one. Get out."

Stevie didn't want any music to get out of the studio till we were done, but a guy came in one night after we were gone and took some tracks. Stevie called and ripped him a new asshole. "Don't you ever steal my music again! I don't give a fuck if you're with the record company!"

MULLEN: Stevie knew he would benefit more from originals and left a lot of great covers off the album. "The Sky Is Crying" was one of my favorite songs that Stevie played, and I pushed him to record it. The version that was finally released [in 1991] is actually a comp: the instrumental track was recorded during *Soul to Soul,* but the vocal track was recorded during *Couldn't Stand the Weather.*

LAYTON: Jimmie played some amazing rhythm guitar on "The Things (That) I Used to Do" and "Couldn't Stand the Weather," with chord voicings that added so much. He really plays more like a keyboard player than a guitar player.

JIMMIE VAUGHAN: I put all the parts down in one afternoon. We'd gone over the tunes before, so it was a breeze.

SHANNON: I came up with the funky guitar/bass unison lick on the title song's intro, but I had the first note falling on "two" instead of "one," more like a horn line. Stevie suggested changing that first note to the "one."

LAYTON: The third time that lick is played, we wait two extra beats before we come back in, and that was something we'd never done in rehearsal. We were cutting the track, and when we reached that point, Stevie put his finger up to his lips like, "Shhh!" and then cued us to come back in.

SHANNON: That was actually Jimmie's suggestion.

LAYTON: I wasn't even certain that Stevie was interested in cutting "Cold Shot" until we recorded it. And he didn't sing even a scratch vocal, so I didn't really know the arrangement, and it was the first time we'd ever played the song beginning to end. Drummers have always asked me how I got that super-laid-back, in-the-pocket feel—well, I'd been awake for twenty hours, then finally fallen asleep, when Stevie woke me at 4:00 a.m. and said, "Whipper, come in and do 'Cold Shot'!" I got behind the drums, and we cut it in one take. I've always wondered if it would have been any better if I was really rested and had known the arrangement!

MULLEN: Stevie started relying more on his own instincts and didn't want to make the same kind of record, which led to cutting "Voodoo Chile." They'd been doing it live for a few years, and I pushed him to record it, because he brought a *life force* to the song that no one else possibly could.

SHANNON: I really had to talk Stevie into doing that track. He needed encouragement to help him pursue what was in his heart, and "Voodoo

Chile" was our point of departure into the future. It felt like breaking out of jail. Stevie played the song with so much soul and spirit. That take was live from beginning to end, seven minutes of pure guitar energy without a single miscue. It would be hard to find anyone that could play guitar *that way* without some sort of mistake, but he blew right through it.

LAYTON: I was unconscious on the couch again when it came time to do "Stang's Swang," so Stevie grabbed [Fabulous Thunderbirds' drummer] Fran Christina, and that's why he ended up on that track. Everyone in the T-Birds showed up in the studio with Jimmie and hung out for two days.

MULLEN: Stevie had more of a guitar collection by then, but he still favored Number One, which I was very vocal about him using, because he had the most authority and best sound on it. It always had a huge tone whether he slammed it or picked it gently. I got sick whenever I saw him live, standing on top of the guitar pulling on the neck. If I told him the guitar was a little out of tune, he'd just give the neck a *yank,* and it would be right back to pitch.

RENÉ MARTINEZ, *Stevie's guitar tech, 1985–1990:* Number One was always Stevie's primary guitar. There's been some debate about the year of the guitar, mostly because it was a "parts" guitar, put together with pieces from different years. Stevie always referred to the guitar as a '59. The truth is that the neck, which has a "veneer" fretboard, is stamped "1962," which is also handwritten inside the body cavity. One day, I asked Stevie why he referred to the guitar as a '59, and he said, "Well, if you look at the back of the pickups, '1959' is handwritten on there." Back in those days, it was the standard practice to handwrite the year on the back of the pickups. Ever since Stevie saw the '59 on there, he started calling it a '59.

SRV: Number One has a real unique sound, but I can't use it all the time, because, for some reason, it wants to rattle real bad. The low E will be this high, and it still rattles.

The neck has also been broken up by the headstock. Have you ever seen Jimmie throw his guitar? I learned this trick from him, except his guitar never broke! I was playing in Lubbock, back in '81, and

Stevie standing on Number One. His abuse of the guitar made others cringe.
(Donnie Opperman)

when I threw it, it hit this paneled wall, catching it up by the head-stock, snapping the wood. It laid there on the ground, and some of the strings went up, and some of them went down! It was doing all this "BLUBGBBNGBG!" by itself, and I was standing there, going, "Yeah!" It was during "Third Stone from the Sun," and it sounded fine, like it was supposed to be there! But then I cried later.

MULLEN: Chris's drums were in the big room, and Stevie's amps were in the larger iso [isolation] booth with a sliding glass door sometimes left open, though he played so loud the guitar sound bled into the drum mics. This wasn't a big problem, because most of his takes were keepers, and the bleed is only a factor if you have to drop a new track in. We had a twenty-four-track machine but were only using about twenty. The extra tracks were for additional takes, but Stevie was so good, we didn't need 'em. He'd either stand right next to his amps or with Chris. I think guitar players play better without headphones, which can get in the way of their relationship with the instrument; they start to over-pick because they aren't feeling it the same way. I always tried to allow Stevie to play without headphones so he would be just as animated in the studio as he was in his live performances. He danced around, sli-din' across the room on his toes, stuff like that.

LAYTON: We'd normally cut a tune three or four times and go on from there. If we didn't get it in a few takes, we'd try another tune.

MULLEN: Stevie was a piece of cake to record. Until he slipped a little because of drugs, he almost never missed a lick, virtual perfection. Most guitarists who play with that kind of intensity and aggression tend to rush, but Stevie's time was rock-solid. He was the band's met-ronome, which always amazed me.

GRISSOM: Stevie was the Time. In most bands, the drummer defines it, but Stevie was the one who defined where the "one" was, and where the groove was at all times. He *was* the groove.

MULLEN: That fact that he could pull everything off with such precision is the very thing that allowed us to make the albums how we did. Each take was based on Stevie's performance; if he exploded on the track, that's the one we used.

GIBBONS: Stevie took to the style with an intensity that led to a deep devo-tion. So deep that over time, the expert technical dexterity became sec-ond nature, and these mesmerizing riffs seemed to be so easy. Stevie got real, real good. And, of course, he had the feel. He swung!

MULLEN: If you got close enough to Stevie while he was doing his thing, it was like he was in a trance, like something else was playing *through* him. I was around Stevie all of the time, but I'd go to a show and hear him play things that he'd never done before, like he was tapped into a higher plane.

JIMMIE VAUGHAN: Stevie could get so deep into his playing, where you could feel that he was just in the *zone*. Flamenco guitar players have a name for it: it's called *duende*. Duende is the same thing that blues guys

Stevie, 1983, wearing a Tsingtao beer hat given
to him by David Bowie. *(Tracy Anne Hart)*

call *soul,* when you get so excited and wild, it evokes this magical feeling that takes you over. It's like a visitation from a spirit.

There is a legend of Mexican conjunto bands, where they are
playing a gig, and everyone is dancing and the whole place is going
crazy, and you go in the bathroom and there's this beautiful, handsome guy with a suit on, very sharp looking, and you look down and
he's got chicken feet! You know you are having a good gig when the
guy with the chicken feet shows up! There are legends about *visita-
tions* like these.

SHANNON: I don't think guitar playing was ever hard for him. I never saw
him struggle to learn a part. He'd never play a lick over and over, struggling to get it together, like every other musician I've ever known.

He'd go over something in his head until it was just how he wanted it, then he'd pick up the guitar and play it.

LAYTON: He'd already have it down by the time he picked up the guitar. He had one of the best ears ever! He was actually against copying things exactly, though. He was interested in getting into the spirit of how a song was played. Even with our own songs, he'd say, "We can't copy what we're doing. All we can do is try to get back to the same kind of spirit we put towards it."

SHANNON: One time, I asked him to teach me Jimi's "Castles Made of Sand." Then I asked him about his fantastic vibrato, and he said, "Here's how I do my vibrato. If you do it this way, you'll learn it. I only need to show you once." Most people cannot learn something from being shown one time, but Stevie didn't see it that way. He'd start at the first fret with one string, get the right vibrato going, go all the way up the neck, and then he'd move to the next string. The feel of the vibrato changes with each fret and each string, and he'd move the vibratos to every part of the fretboard.

MULLEN: On *Couldn't Stand the Weather,* Stevie was coming into his own and branching into things that were more ambitious than *Texas Flood*. During the *Weather* sessions, [mix engineer] Lincoln Clapp said to me, "You did such a great job on *Texas Flood*—everything is so consistent." And I laughed and said, "No wonder, because it took two hours to cut and not a knob was moved!"

SHANNON: Stevie was exploring the power of a three-piece band, which allowed him to venture into uncharted territory. I really felt that we kept the same "live" intensity on the records. We still all played at the same time. We didn't get into that click track and "you do your part and I'll do mine" thing. We did a few overdubs, but it was still pretty much a live album. That was the only way Stevie would do it, and I loved it.

On March 19, 1984, Stevie and Double Trouble performed at the CBS Records Convention in Honolulu, Hawaii. *Couldn't Stand the Weather* was completed but not yet released, and the appearance was in part to stir the enthusiasm of label staff, which was easily accomplished with a dynamic performance. Jeff Beck, one of Stevie's original guitar idols, also appeared, sitting in with Double Trouble, as did Jimmie, T-Birds drummer Fran Christina, and singer Angela Strehli.

LEEDS: Stevie was very cooperative, but Jeff was not. I wasn't sure if they didn't get along because Jeff was not really informed why he was jamming with this person or jealous that this young kid was going to pass him on the highway. I never knew what happened, but he was not a happy camper.

SHANNON: Hawaii was the first time they jammed, and Stevie felt really intimidated by Jeff, which is not something he felt very often.

STREHLI: Stevie and I were never close friends, so his inviting me was strictly musical respect, and I certainly appreciated that. He made this

Brothers backstage at the Austin Opry House, 1984. *(Tracy Anne Hart)*

breakthrough and brought a bunch of us along with him whenever and wherever he could.

LONG: As their careers blossomed, there was often talk about a rivalry between Stevie and Jimmie. I knew nothing about their sibling dynamics, but coming from a family of seven brothers myself, I had an inkling—misinterpretations, feeling overshadowed, different approaches, outside pressure, wanting to establish individuality. Fans always wanted to compare them. That was impossible.

16

IN THE OPEN

Released on May 15, 1984, *Couldn't Stand the Weather* solidified Stevie Ray's standing as a guitar icon and illuminated the band's breadth more clearly than their debut had. The album opened and closed with instrumentals, kicking off with the scorching "Scuttle Buttin'" and ending with the cool swing of "Stang's Swang," songs that highlighted his debts to Lonnie Mack and Wes Montgomery, respectively.

With covers of Jimi Hendrix's "Voodoo Chile (Slight Return)," Guitar Slim's "The Things (That) I Used to Do," and the blues standard "Tin Pan Alley," the album featured a limited amount of new original material, but the title track and "Cold Shot" underlined that the band was further developing their own sound and approach to blues-based music. As a composition, "Couldn't Stand the Weather" is much more rock-oriented than any of the *Texas Flood* material, revealing a range of influences, with a soul/R&B bass line, a distinctly Hendrix feel to the rhythm guitar part, and sharp Albert King–style soloing.

The album was an immediate hit, selling 250,000 copies in its first three weeks. The band simultaneously made videos for "Couldn't Stand the Weather" and "Cold Shot" with two directors, and Layton recalls running from a scene in one video to a scene in the other.

"After the release, we hit the road with all of these new, fresh songs that no one had ever heard, which was great," says Layton. "We were told we were selling fifty thousand albums a week, much of it in Texas, Arizona,

Oklahoma, and New Mexico, thanks to Jack Chase, who headed Sony's southwest branch and was a great record guy."

SHANNON: We didn't start out with an agenda. The music led us, and as we drew bigger crowds, the validation gave us more strength to take off to a higher level. We were growing from gig to gig, secure that we belonged on the big stages.

LAYTON: There was something particularly exciting about this time because it was the actualization of the things that I felt from the very first time I saw Stevie play and had a vision of where we could go. The three of us were so much on the same page, in terms of personal ethics and morals, social justice, politics, and how you treat other people, and that crossed over into the music. We shared a deep connection and chemistry. I think the audience got a reading of the type of relationship the three of us had, that they could feel it, and it had meaning to them.

CLARK: I've seen other white boys play up close, including Eric Clapton himself, but they didn't show me what I saw from Stevie. I saw that from him and him alone. Even my mama saw it. She saw us play and said, "That is a guitar-playing little man, isn't it?" and I said, "I am, too, Mom. Why don't you give me a compliment like that?" Jimmie heard that, laughed, and said, "Welcome to the boat, man."

SHANNON: I don't think Stevie ever knew how incredible he really was.

LAYTON: I only once heard Stevie acknowledge his talent. He and I had gone to Buddy Guy's club in Chicago, and someone shot a video of Stevie and Buddy jamming, which we took back to the hotel and popped in the VCR. There was a part where Stevie had the guitar up on his shoulder, like a violin, playing with one hand, and it was amazing—like Stevie Ray Hendrix. He looked at me, paused, and said, "I'm good." I thought that was cool because he was usually so self-effacing.

Concerned about replicating Jimmie's rhythm parts on "Couldn't Stand the Weather" and "The Things (That) I Used to Do" and about simultaneously covering his guitar and vocal parts, Stevie talked to guitarist Derek O'Brien about joining Double Trouble.

Doing that violin thing, Palace Theater, New Haven, CT, 11/14/85.
(Donna Johnston)

"He gave me a cassette of the record, and a week later, I was onstage at Antone's when someone said I had a phone call," says O'Brien. "I said, 'Tell them I'll call them back!' And the guy goes, 'It's Stevie!' I ran offstage and got the phone. He said, 'The time is now. Do you want to do this?'"

O'Brien and Angela Strehli joined Double Trouble for an eight-city Texas tour, starting July 10, 1984, in Amarillo and ending July 21 back home in Austin. The guest guitarist and singer would join the trio for a few songs midshow. Strehli says she has no recollection of actually discussing becoming a band member, but that was Stevie's pitch to O'Brien from the start. Millikin made his displeasure known before a note was played.

O'BRIEN: Before the first show, Chesley called and said, "I don't agree with this, and as far as I'm concerned, it's not going to happen. You can play these dates, but I don't know why Stevie wants you. This is one of the only trios left in the world, and it should stay a trio. He doesn't fucking need a fourth member in his band."

LAYTON: Stevie said he wasn't comfortable with how his playing sounded on some songs that were hard to sing over. He said, "Let's just get Derek to handle that," and kudos to Chesley for saying, "You can't have another fucking guitarist in this band." He was absolutely correct, and I think Stevie knew it.

O'BRIEN: After the final show [July 21, 1984, Palmer Auditorium, Austin], Stevie said, "Hey, man, is this something you really want to do? 'Cause I'm fixing to talk to Chesley about it," and I said, "Count me in." They went into a dressing room, and I was just hanging out backstage as everything got loaded out. I finally went outside into an empty parking lot. Chesley eventually came out, and I said good night to him. He didn't make any kind of greeting but just turned around and yelled from across the parking lot, "This ain't gonna fucking happen! Everybody is against this!" I heard from Tommy before the next run that I was not going to be along for the ride.

SHANNON: It went over like a lead balloon! Chesley said, "You're gonna fuckin' fire 'em, and you're gonna fire 'em right now!" Stevie actually saw that it wasn't working, so he apologized and let them go.

Stevie and Derek O'Brien, during the latter's brief run as Double Trouble's second guitarist, July, 1984. *(Watt M. Casey Jr)*

LAYTON: It was really a cop-out, Stevie being lazy. We love Derek, a great friend of ours for many years, but Stevie's idea to have someone else play a handful of guitar parts that were hard to do while singing didn't make sense, and he eventually agreed. It wasn't the solution Stevie was looking for.

GRISSOM: I saw Stevie at the Majestic Theatre in San Antonio [July 13, 1984], and they put his Dumble 4×12 cabinet in the basement and mic'ed it because it was *too loud* to be on the stage! I went down there and it was deafening, about 140 decibels. The only thing you could hear was his guitar, and there was nothing remotely close to a stumble or missed note in the twenty minutes I stood there. No drummer was needed, because the pocket and the groove were just impeccable. The groove of it all made a huge impression on me.

Isolated like that, his guitar playing took on another dimension. It was like this righteous freight train; the thread that ran through everything and tied it all together was this incredible groove. The whole room could have danced to the guitar by itself. It was *that strong*. In that moment, I realized that there was another level to this whole thing.

Vaughan's desire to add another trusted member was doubtlessly his way of saying he needed help. On the road, the drug and alcohol use was consistently escalating.

SHANNON: When we went back on the road, it got a little crazier still, and some people who knew us started noticing it, too, and tried to talk to Stevie.

LAYTON: After Cutter left, Jim Markham became our road manager. We were at Constitution Hall in Washington, D.C. [October 11, 1984], and after the show, Jim was sitting on the bus crying. Jim was a great guy, an experienced road manager, and he said, "I have to leave." He looked at Stevie and said, "You guys are killing yourselves. You seem to have some kind of romantic notion about doing drugs and playing music, that the drugs are the driver of your creativity. All that is a bunch of bullshit. I'm watching you guys kill yourselves, and I can't stay around and watch that happen. So I'm leaving."

When Double Trouble crossed paths with Eric Clapton on a 1986 tour of Australia, the elder statesman assessed Vaughan, watching the hungover guitarist sit at the bar and shakily down a few shots of Crown Royal. Understanding that he wasn't ready to be helped, he simply said, "Well, sometimes you have to go through that, don'tcha?"

Vaughan's mentor Albert King took a more direct approach when the two played a show together. "He walked backstage and said, 'We gonna have a little heart-to-heart,'" Vaughan told *Guitar World* in 1988. "'I been watching you wrestle with the bottle three, four times already. I tell you what, man: I like to drink a little bit when I'm home. But the gig ain't no time to get high.' He was trying to tell me to take care of business, give myself a break, but I did my usual deal of trying to act like I had it all together."

BUDDY GUY: I cussed Stevie out 'cause I saw him and Johnny Winter once and he didn't even know who I was. I got in his face about the drugs.

CLARK: We didn't get to see each other as much after Double Trouble took off. One night, he flew in from Hawaii and came straight to where I was playing, walked up on the bandstand, and hugged me, and he was trembling. Trembling! That really bothered me for a while.

LICKONA: Stevie worshipped W. C., revered him almost as a father figure. W. C.'s personality is so gentle, and he shows so much love towards people, and I think Stevie really needed that, especially during that tough time. When life started to getting more confusing with his success and figuring how to deal with it, W. C. provided great comfort and helped Stevie to cope with everything going on in his life.

CLARK: We had a real special friendship, and I think he came to me for some type of spiritual feeling. He didn't ask me for anything, and he didn't have to. He was seeking God and he knows I'm real religious, and I think he just needed to come around me. I gave him the guitar and got the bass, and we tore the house down for a while.

FREEMAN: As Stevie started to have success, he would rent nice places, but most of them looked like a tornado had hit them. He had nice houses that were big wrecks. He never established a real home.

EDI JOHNSON: That was not who Stevie was. He was not a nester. He wanted to play music, hear music, be around people in music, and work at music. He worked very hard at it. He loved going down to Antone's and jamming with whoever was playing for as long as they were allowed to play. If I had walked into Stevie's house and saw him on a couch watching TV, I probably would have asked him if he was feeling okay.

STEELE: The true Stevie was the one playing the guitar. I don't know if he played the guitar or it played him, because Stevie and his guitar became one unit. The expressions on his face—you could feel the passion he had.

EDI JOHNSON: He loved working and improving his talent and being on the road, which he was most of the time. During the first three years with Classic Management, they were probably playing three hundred days a year. They were the band that kept going, and they got better and better at what they did, and Stevie just took off. He seemed happiest when he succeeded playing his music the way he thought it should be heard. *That* was his living room.

Stevie at home, with kitty. *(Courtesy Tommy Shannon)*

LAYTON: We toured constantly. We'd only be home for a day or two here and there.

SHANNON: We were on the road forever! I didn't even have my own place to live. My "home" was the Imperial 400 motel! Or I'd stay with Stevie and Lenny.

LAYTON: Tom was like Howard Hughes! I'd go over to the Imperial 400, knock on the door, and he'd yell, "What?" "Hey, Tommy, it's me, Whipper." "Yeah, hang on." He'd unlock the door, and by the time I opened it, he'd already be back in bed. It would be like forty-eight degrees in there, the AC was blastin' so hard, with the windows completely blocked off so not a speck of sunlight could come through. He'd have a liter of vodka, and if we wanted something to eat, he'd call Roy's Taxi and say, "It's Tommy. Can I get a cab over here?" The cab wouldn't take Tommy anywhere; they'd just make stops to pick up food, cigarettes, and whatever else and bring it to him. Tommy had a system goin' over there!

SHANNON: I called it "Uncle Tom's Cabin."

Stevie playing "Texas Flood" with the song's composer, Larry Davis, circa 1985 at Antone's. Clifford Antone on bass. *(Andrew Long)*

LAYTON: We were happy with the success of the band, but we all had issues that we weren't looking straight in the face.

SHANNON: We were enjoying what we had, but our lives were getting complicated. *Happiness* is an elusive word.

LAYTON: We were working our asses off every single day. "Caught up in a whirlwind." It was like being in the center of a storm that you are having a great time being in. You wake up, fly here, TV station interview, radio station interview, sound check, do the gig, celebrities are showing up . . . "Hey, there's Matt Dillon!" "Mick Jagger's back!" You don't ask yourself if you're happy.

One night in '84, Stevie met Prince in Saint Paul, Minnesota, on the opening night of Bruce Springsteen's *Born In the U.S.A.* tour. Prince was sitting backstage with his bodyguard, Chick, a big ol' bald guy wearing a leopard-skin leotard thing. Stevie tried to lean around the guy, and he said to Prince, "Hey, man! My name is Stevie Ray!" Prince wouldn't look at him, but he leans over to his bodyguard and says,

"What did he say, Chick? Is he speaking to me?" So Stevie goes, louder, "I said, my name is Stevie Ray!" Prince goes, "I didn't hear him, Chick. What did he say?" Stevie got pissed and said, "You might be the Prince, motherfucker, but I'm the King Bee! Deal with it!"

Stevie and Double Trouble capped the *Couldn't Stand the Weather* tour in August with a run of sold-out arena dates opening for Huey Lewis and the News, who were riding high with the seven-times-platinum album *Sports,* which featured the hit songs "The Heart of Rock & Roll," "I Want a New Drug," and "If This Is It."

LAYTON: Right after *CSTW* had come out, we were back at New York's Mayflower Hotel doing press, and I stepped into the elevator and there was Huey Lewis and [News member] Johnny Colla. I said, "Huey!" And he goes, "Yeah, man—'Cold Shot'!" He starts singing the song, then says, "That's a rockin' record, man. I love you guys! We gotta do some playing together."

LEWIS: My agent said, "The *Sports* tour is all sold out. Who do you want to open? It doesn't matter." I said, "Get Stevie Ray Vaughan!" He called back and said, "The manager is crazy. He wants ten times what they're worth." I said, "Forget about it. Book them."

LAYTON: That tour was huge for us. It was all sold-out arenas, and that's when things really started taking off. We were still playing some smaller venues, but that tour pushed us to another level. While we were on tour with them, we started to get some really, really good offers.

LEWIS: The first night they were with us, I got there early to see them and walked right up to the edge of the stage, mesmerized by this long slow blues. I was just knocked out, and when it ended, the crowd just went . . . zip, nothing! Chants of "Huey! Huey! Huey!" I felt awful. It was one of those moments where you really hate your audience. I knocked on their bus door, walked to the back lounge where the whole band was sitting, despondent, and said, "Guys, you are fantastic. People are going to go home and say, 'Who the hell was that band that opened for Huey Lewis?' Then look you up and be blown away. That's all you're going to do here, but have fun doing it. Just play, be yourselves, and trust me. It's gonna be great." Stevie came out and jammed with us almost every night, and it was incredibly exciting for us and I'm sure for the audience. We were basically inseparable for two months.

JIMMY STRATTON, *photographer:* I saw Stevie and Double Trouble opening for Huey Lewis and the News and have often compared it to Jimi Hendrix opening for the Monkees.

On October 4, 1984, the day after his thirtieth birthday, Stevie Ray Vaughan and Double Trouble played New York's Carnegie Hall in a benefit for the T. J. Martell Foundation dedicated to using music to help find a cure for cancer. In his introduction, John Hammond called Vaughan "one of the great guitar players of all time."

They played a scorching set that included "Voodoo Chile (Slight Return)," after which Vaughan said with amazement and a slight snicker, "It's fun playing Hendrix in Carnegie Hall!" The second set featured an expanded ten-piece band featuring Jimmie Vaughan, the Roomful of Blues horn section, Dr. John, Angela Strehli, and drummer George Rains.

SHANNON: Stevie pushed hard to make that show happen. It was a dream for him to play Carnegie Hall. We went out and had special clothes made just for the gig, and we got all the guests. We were going to film it, but CBS backed out.

LAYTON: We went to all kinds of lengths for that show, partly in anticipation of it being filmed. Jimmie had the idea to have mariachi suits made, and we went to Nelda's Tailors and talked to the Mexican women there. We looked at all this material and their cool silver buttons and buckles hardware and picked out what we wanted for our pants and jackets, and Stevie decided to have two suits made, one blue and one red. We all rehearsed for three days on an Austin soundstage and had everybody fitted for their clothes.

EDI JOHNSON: They did an incredible rehearsal show at Caravan of Dreams in Fort Worth [on September 29]. I thought it was even better than the final show in New York.

BENSON: I went to the studio to watch them rehearse for the shows. Dr. John arrived, and Stevie was thrilled because he loved him. They start back up, and Stevie's playing everything he knows, as he often did, and all of a sudden Dr. John goes, "Hold on, hold on," and waves it all to a stop—like flagging down a train chugging down the tracks at seventy-five miles per hour, and Doc goes, "Stevie, what we need here is some *dynamicals*." Stevie goes, "Yeah, yeah, yeah," and they restart and he pulled back—he understood what Doc was saying—and it just sounded so great.

LAYTON: We had an elaborate stage set built and painted lapis-blue enamel with gold lamé striping. It was like a set for a television show. They shipped it to New York and set it up in a warehouse, where we did a dress rehearsal. The next day, it was broken down and reconstructed in Carnegie Hall. There was a horn riser and levels for the two drummers. At the very last minute, CBS pulled the plug on filming for budgetary reasons. Years later, I learned it was only $15,000. And it's a shame because it looked great, Stevie played his ass off, and the big band stuff is so special.

BENSON: Pulling that money from recording is so stupid, shortsighted, and shameful, because that was a fantastic performance.

JIMMIE VAUGHAN: I knew that was going to be a great record—we were at Carnegie Hall and all of our friends were there. On "Dirty Pool," I tried to come up with parts that would fit into the sound of the big band but also add something cool. Find a spot to throw some of your stuff in there. I approached it sort of like an organ player, which is something I have always enjoyed doing. It's all about how all of the parts fit together.

SHANNON: I don't think enough people have caught on to what a great performance that was. That's some of my favorite playing from him, ever. It was such a special event: it was his birthday, his mother was there, along with all of our families. It was a great, great night.

LAYTON: We had a bunch of stuff flown up from Sam's Barb-B-Que in Austin.

STREHLI: Even the rehearsal was joyous. It was just a ball seeing everybody together in one spot as was the amazing fact that we would be playing a blues concert at Carnegie Hall. Just walking onto that stage for a sound check fills you with humility and gratitude. Pulling that off was typical Stevie, as was sharing the spotlight. The T-Birds had taken blues to a wider audience after a very down period where even the all-time greats didn't have much work or interest. Stevie took it to the next level where the music got worldwide attention from people who had never cared: rock and rollers and guitar guys. His music just grabbed you, and Carnegie Hall was one of those new milestones he kept setting.

Another milestone happened six weeks later, on November 18, when Stevie won two W. C. Handy Awards, for Blues Instrumentalist of the Year and Entertainer of the Year. He was the first white artist to be awarded the latter, and it meant so much to him that he flew twenty-four hours back from a tour of New Zealand to Memphis to attend and perform "Cold Shot" and "Texas Flood." The concert at the Orpheum Theatre included three of Stevie's biggest heroes: Albert King, B. B. King, and Hubert Sumlin.

"Stevie was so honored by that because it was coming from the blues society," says Shannon. "On the big jam with B. B., Albert, and Hubert, we played 'Cold Shot' and 'Every Day I Have the Blues,' and it was an incredible night for us."

The next month, Stevie leapt at another opportunity to work with an idol, producing a comeback record for Lonnie Mack, whose "Wham!" was the first record he ever bought. Mack had signed with Alligator Records, the same label that four years earlier had rejected Stevie Ray as too white, too loud, and too derivative of Albert King.

It was a great opportunity for Mack, who had not released an album in seven years and who had at times drifted toward country music. Stevie and Alligator shared a passion for returning Mack to his hard-hitting early guitar sound, which included a Vaughan-Mack duet remake of "Wham!" renamed "Double Whammy."

IGLAUER: Stevie and I were united by our mutual admiration of Lonnie Mack, and Stevie volunteered to serve as producer of our *Strike Like Lightning* album, which we cut in Austin. Stevie really wanted to do something to bring his hero to the fore of the public eye. He was very

Lonnie Mack and Stevie, during the *Strike Like Lightning* sessions, 1985.
(Andrew Long)

conscious of using his budding good name to shine a light on Lonnie and his other heroes. Anytime someone told Stevie he was great, he would immediately say, "Have you heard Lonnie Mack? Have you heard Albert Collins? Have you heard Albert King?" He was constantly mentioning other musicians and pushing them on people and seemed very sincere in his love of those guys. It wasn't about him.

SHANNON: Stevie was so glad to work with Lonnie on that record.

IGLAUER: Stevie arrived at the studio straight off the road, went to Lonnie, and said, "So what do you want me to do?" At no time did he act like a producer; he left all the important decisions up to Lonnie—and a little bit to me. Calling himself *producer* was to put the SRV seal of approval on the album. He ended up playing on four or five songs. His rig was set up in a booth right next to the control room, and he was so loud that he kept leaking through, which made it very hard to monitor the performances in the control room, but he played fantastically.

LONG: During those Lonnie Mack sessions, I was sitting on a couch next to Stevie, who was out of it on a few intoxicants, playing an acoustic guitar with super high action. He was just killing time between takes, and he was astounding. I was convinced at that moment you could string baling wire on the wall and he'd still be better than 99.9 percent of guitarists out there.

IGLAUER: The talent he showed in this era was not apparent to me a few years earlier. Whether it was his growth or mine, I now understood what made him so special.

EDI JOHNSON: Stevie was so happy to be working with Lonnie, but Chesley didn't approve of the project, probably because he hadn't thought of it. So I went out to the studio as our representative.

IGLAUER: I was walking pretty cautiously around Stevie. We didn't know each other well at all, and of course, I was the record company guy, and all artists are suspicious of the record company guy. He was in a heavy drug period, doing a lot of coke and drinking Crown Royal, but he was very intense and focused in the studio, and he did a great job. He stayed up all night playing alternate takes of his solo on "Double Whammy." When Lonnie and I arrived in the morning, Stevie was sure that he didn't have one good enough to please Lonnie. He had saved two or three choices. They were all thrilling, and Lonnie picked the one that appeared on the album.

17

SOUL STIRRERS

By the time Double Trouble entered Dallas Sound Lab to begin recording their third album in March 1985, the band was feeling and showing the strains of drugs and alcohol abuse and a few years of relentless touring.

Soul to Soul marked the return of Vaughan's old friend, bandmate, and vocal inspiration Doyle Bramhall as a collaborator. The group recorded two of his songs, "Change It" and "Lookin' Out the Window."

"Doyle started trying to get sober way before any of us," says saxophonist Joe Sublett, who also played on the sessions. "He pulled off the whole scene and was gone for a while because he was serious about his sobriety. He was always sipping from a large cup with crushed ice and soda. He quit being in bars, then got slowly back into playing music on his own terms. Stevie needed songs and knew that Doyle had them. And he didn't just send them over; he was in the studio."

Bramhall's sobriety was very much still a work in progress at this time, and his son, Doyle Bramhall II, notes that participating in the *Soul to Soul* sessions was a setback. "I don't think that studio at that time was a place for sobriety," Bramhall II says.

The sessions also marked the addition of keyboardist Reese Wynans, a Jacksonville, Florida, native who had played keys in the 1968 jam sessions that led to the formation of the Allman Brothers Band; he was replaced by Gregg Allman. Wynans had played in the Jacksonville band Second

Coming with future ABB members Berry Oakley and Dickey Betts and by 1985 had been an active, touring musician and well-respected sideman for almost two decades.

Stevie Ray's decision to bring in old friends Bramhall and Sublett and to add Wynans were unspoken acknowledgments that Double Trouble needed some reinforcements.

LAYTON: There was a lot of stretching on that record, but it was getting more difficult. It was like trying to run a race when you're really tired. You might make it and even get a good time, but it feels like it's gonna kill you.

SHANNON: Things were getting pretty bad. We were paying for studio time and spending hours playing Ping-Pong waiting for cocaine to arrive before we'd play. You can kind of tell that we're a little out of sorts.

LAYTON: In the studio, you have to confront what you really sound like. You can't just walk off the stage. You're under a microscope. We were in a bit of a drug-and-alcohol frenzy, and *Soul to Soul* was difficult to make, which had a lot to do with inviting Reese to play. It was like, "We need some help here."

SUBLETT: They asked me to play on some tracks, and I came in late at night a couple of times. We cut "Look at Little Sister," then Stevie said, "I'd really like to have a keyboard on some of this stuff." I recommended Reese, who was in Delbert McClinton's band with me, and said, "As a matter of fact, he just gave his two-week notice."

REESE WYNANS, *Double Trouble keyboardist, 1985–1990:* Stevie called and said they wanted to add some keyboards. They wanted acoustic piano on "Look at Little Sister," but it didn't really work because the studio was set up like a live performance, with an entire PA, and it was screaming loud.

SUBLETT: Boy, was it loud in there. It was painful, and the loudness came from Stevie, who had a Frankenstein wall of amps. I was there with a little microphone, thinking, "This is all going to bleed." I played live for a few days, because that's what Stevie wanted, but Richard Mullen suggested he get me on a clean track separately. He had a lot of common sense.

WYNANS: You could not hear a piano, so I suggested that we try a Hammond organ, where I could isolate the cabinet. We played "Change It" and the instrumentals ["Say What" and "Gone Home"], and it went great. My organ playing surprised them a little, that I could bring that kind of energy to their material, and I think the way the B3 sounded with their songs is what cemented me in there. We recorded till seven in the morning, and they asked me to come back the next night.

SHANNON: "Say What!" had been a jam we'd been doing for a while, kind of like Hendrix's "Rainy Day, Dream Away." Stevie had the idea of breaking it down and singing, "Soul to soul!" Stevie uses a wah that had belonged to Jimi Hendrix on that track. [This was the wah pedal Jimmie got from Jimi Hendrix in 1968.]

Doyle came down to the studio and played "Lookin' Out the Window" and "Change It" for us, and we immediately decided to work them up and record them. "Ain't Gone 'n' Give Up on Love" was a new tune. Reese came up with that great walk-up part that we played on the bridge, which I thought was one of the coolest things about the

"Soul to Soul"—Tommy and Stevie, 6-7-85, Chicago Blues Festival. *(Kirk West)*

song. He was clearly adding more than just keyboard parts. We were all hanging out one night, high and drinking, and Stevie said to Reese, "Hey, man, want to join the band?" We never sat down and discussed it. It was just "Okay, that's settled."

WYNANS: I was as surprised as anyone. I was just happy to be a part of it. Being a Texas bluesman, getting to play with one of the best power trios ever was like a bucket list thing. The guys told me they were glad I came over because they had been having a hard time getting the project off the ground.

LAYTON: A lot of people were urging us to keep the trio thing, but we really needed a new perspective, which Stevie understood on some level when he tried to bring Derek in. We had been on an endless three-year tour punctuated by time in the studio, and we were getting burnt. We needed somebody else to help carry everything.

WYNANS: We kept some wild hours on those sessions; we'd get to the studio at about 8:00 p.m., start playing at 11:00 or 12:00, play till 5:00 or 6:00 in the morning, go home when the sun was coming up, sleep till about 3:00 in the afternoon, and start over.

With Wynans suddenly a member of Double Trouble, recording sessions continued, sometimes in fits and starts. Sessions could be delayed not only by the members waiting for drugs to arrive but by Vaughan's incessant search for new sounds.

MULLEN: As Stevie learned more about recording, he got more particular and wanted to try different things, which was sometimes more of a detriment than a help. During these sessions, he had me open up a snare drum and fill it with packing peanuts because he thought it would sound good. It didn't!

LAYTON: We called him "Modern Man" because he loved to fool around with electronics, take things apart and put them back together, and just try crazy stuff. For instance, on "Ain't Gone 'n' Give Up on Love," Stevie put paper matches under the bridge saddle of a six-string bass to muffle the sound, which is what you hear on the little strum on the downbeat. We would get crazy ideas after we had been up too long and our minds were racing. "I wonder what I would get if I put a half-cut Coke can under my bass drum pedal." Sometimes those things would actually work.

BRAMHALL II: Stevie secretly wanted to be an inventor. He showed me sketches and drafts of spaceships he wanted to build. He always had side hobbies like amplifiers with one knob that just read "Turn up or fuck off" or another that just had a plug and no knobs so when people running sound would ask him to turn it down, he could honestly say, "Sorry, I can't. It doesn't have any knobs."

SRV: I played drums on "Empty Arms." Me and Tommy were in the studio by ourselves, and we like to play bass and drums together. We were just messin' around. When we started it off, that song was *real slow,* slow enough where it's hard to keep going at the same speed. Then we sped it up 13.5 percent with the Varispeed and recorded the rest of the song to it.

SHANNON: Stevie was a great drummer, if he could last through the song! On a shuffle, his arms would get tired. The two of us were in the studio early one day, and he said, "Let's do 'Empty Arms' real slow!" He sat down behind the drums, and Richard [Mullen] didn't want to turn the tape machine on. Stevie's going, "Turn it on!" and Richard's going,

Stevie behind the drums during the *Soul to Soul* sessions.
(Courtesy Tommy Shannon)

"What for?" They had a little argument, then Richard turned it on, and that's the one we kept. Stevie knew exactly what he had in mind for that song.

WYNANS: What tune was it where one guy played hi-hat and snare, and another guy played the rest of the kit?

LAYTON: "Lookin' Out the Window." Doyle wrote the song, and instead of playing on two drum sets, he pulled up a stool and sat right next to me, and the two of us played one kit! I played the ride cymbal and the snare, and he played the hi-hat. So, there's a 4/4 thing going on the hi-hat, but a 6/8 thing with the ride and the bass drum. We tried to sit on the same drum throne, but we kept falling off! We really just wanted to be able to say that we played the same drum set at the same time.

Vaughan took a left turn with "Life Without You," a moving soul ballad written for and dedicated to Stevie's close friend, guitar maker Charley Wirz, who built Stevie's signature white Strat and who had died suddenly in February 1985. The song also reflects Vaughan's passion for soul singers like Curtis Mayfield and Donny Hathaway.

SHANNON: He was so scared to sing "Life Without You" because it was so personal, and he was afraid he wouldn't be able to do it right.

WYNANS: He brought it to us pretty much finished. The song had a lot of chord changes, and because Stevie wasn't about to explain it, we had to play along with him quite a number of times to get it together. It had two different bridges, which was a little confusing.

SHANNON: He had been moving down chromatically from the A chord to an F♯. I said, "That would sound better if it was a minor chord," so he switched it to F♯ minor. He did the walk-up from A to C♯, and then he wanted to do another walk-up from B to D, and then a walk-down from D to B. There were too many walks, so we took some of them out. For the solo, I said, "Stevie, it would sound cool if you did something like the 'Bold as Love' solo," with that slow *whine* in the beginning.

WYNANS: The first time we ever played the song all the way through, we got to the solo section, and, all of a sudden, the song became massive.

LAYTON: Business as usual.

RAY BENSON: Reese was subbing for us in Asleep at the Wheel, and he told me that he was joining Stevie Ray Vaughan and Double Trouble, and I said he might get bored playing limited changes, and he said, "Are you kidding me? Stevie tunes down a half step, and everything is in really challenging keys for me." He was a great addition to a great band.

SHANNON: Getting the pictures done for *Soul to Soul* was another ordeal.

WYNANS: We were out in some pecan grove somewhere, in Podunk, Texas . . .

SHANNON: Bugs, mosquitoes, summertime, 180 degrees . . . Christ!

LAYTON: We'd done the cover shot of Stevie at Anderson Mill. There were shots of all four of us, leaning against the wall together, but they decided not to use those and wanted to do more shots.

They had an idea about a location off of 290 on the way to Houston. The three of us went out there together because Stevie was going with someone else, and he was going to meet us. But Stevie never showed up! We stood out there for three hours, slapping bugs off us, saying, "Where the fuck is Stevie?!"

WYNANS: I was sitting up in this tree with bugs all over me, sweating and miserable.

SHANNON: I finally told the photographer, "This is all you're getting!" You can tell I'm pissed off by the look on my face in the picture they ended up using; I'm pouting like a little kid. I was bored and irritated.

LAYTON: We all look so unhappy in that picture—and that's how we felt, too.

STRATTON: I got to know Stevie after shooting him a few times, and he treated me like a friend and brother, and I photographed a bunch of shows. One was on a riverboat in New Orleans, and afterwards backstage, he rolled his face across a mirror, and the oil from his skin made an imprint of him looking at himself. He wanted that to be the *Soul to Soul* album cover and asked if I could reproduce it photographically. Of course I said yes!

A few nights later, I get a call from Lenny at about 10:00 p.m. They

Soul to Soul cover session outtake. *(Brittain Hill/
Courtesy Sony Music Entertainment)*

were all sitting around looking at Polaroids of the pictures that were shot on the porch for the cover of *Soul to Soul,* and no one liked them. Stevie got on the phone and asked if I could come to Dallas and do the photo we had talked about. I arrived two days later and spent a week just hanging out in the studio. Late one night, at about 3:00 a.m. after Stevie had been awake for a few days, he said, "Let's go do that," and we went back to the hotel room. I had him paint his face with black theater makeup, and we made some impressions on poster board, one of which he took and started finger painting Jesus from the image on the left. He said, "I'm looking at Jesus." He left me in the room and went down the hall to show the band. Afterwards, I didn't see him for a few days, and I never saw the board again!

On April 9, 1985, Vaughan was invited to play the national anthem for the Houston Astros' Opening Day, marking the twentieth anniversary of the Astrodome. Mickey Mantle, who hit the first home run in the stadium, was there, and he autographed the back of Stevie's Number One and Lenny guitars. Vaughan's solo slide guitar rendition of "The Star Spangled Banner" was not well received.

He had worked out the arrangement in the studio during the *Soul to Soul* sessions, but, as Shannon notes, he forgot it and was booed. It was a rare public performance stumble.

"The Houston paper ran a picture of him shrugging as he's being booed," says Layton. "That's what happens when you stay up for four days in a row."

The band returned to the road as a four-piece ensemble on April 21 in Dallas. "I initially thought I was just going to play on the songs I played on the record until the first show when Stevie told me I was playing on everything," says Wynans. "He didn't want to play rhythm all of the time so he could concentrate more on the singing. Chris, Tommy, and I focused more on the groove and forming a tight three-piece rhythm section. They were obviously a great band without me, and I just wanted to add to it."

Stevie and the band were proud to play a tribute to John Hammond at New York's Lincoln Center on June 25, 1985, during which George Benson sat in for "Couldn't Stand the Weather." The night before, Stevie played with Eric Clapton for the first time, in a jam session with *Late Night with David Letterman* band members Paul Shaffer and Steve Jordan.

SHAFFER: Steve and I were jamming with Clapton and [guitarist] Danny Kortchmar at Top Cat Studios. Eric didn't have his own guitar, so we rented him one, but he couldn't get comfortable with it.

JORDAN: He said, "I can't get a sound out of this piece of crap."

SHAFFER: We found out that Stevie was rehearsing in the next room. Someone invited him over, and he comes in and says hello to Clapton, who says, "Let's play." Stevie's got his own guitar, and Clapton says, "I see you've got your baby with you. I'm having trouble with this guitar." Stevie says, "Here, use mine. I'll use that one." Stevie handed Eric his Strat, and Clapton starts playing his ass off, but when Stevie came in for his solo on this rented guitar, he blew everyone away with his musicianship.

SHANNON: Stevie called at 3:00 a.m. and said, "Hey! C'mon down here!" I was in heaven playing with Clapton!

LAYTON: I walked in rubbing the sleep out of my eyes. We were playing a standard blues tune like "Green Onions," and I was surprised that Paul Shaffer didn't know the changes.

WYNANS: He knew the changes! It was the same deal that happened with almost every keyboard player. Stevie played with his guitar tuned down, leading to keys that are murder on a piano player. He wanted to play a blues in A♭, which is a bad jam key for a piano player. That's really how I got the gig; I told Stevie that I didn't mind playing in all of those weird keys, but I was lying. I hated it! I took me months to get those keys together, and my hands were all gnarly from the weird positions!

A two-week summer tour of Europe climaxed with a triumphant return to the Montreux Jazz Festival on July 15, a show that had special resonance for the band, coming almost exactly three years to the day after their debut.

"It was a chance to redeem not ourselves but a situation," says Layton. "We had two successful records and lots of touring under our belts. We were going to have fun and receive some kind of closure."

Adds Shannon, "It's not quite like Stevie felt a vendetta, but . . ."

The band flew Johnny Copeland, the Houston native known as the

Stevie and Tommy with bluesman Johnny Clyde Copeland, the Texas Twister.
(Courtesy Tommy Shannon)

Texas Twister and one of Stevie's favorite blues musicians, to Montreux as a special guest for four songs. That fall, Copeland, who died in 1997, and his band opened up a run of shows in the Midwest.

SHANNON: Stevie loved Johnny Copeland and gave him his highest compliment: that he "was real." When he said that, you knew exactly what he was talking about.

MIKE MERRITT, *bassist for Johnny Copeland:* Stevie told everyone in the band and the crew, "This is Johnny Copeland and his band. You treat them like you treat us." Needless to say, this is not how opening bands are normally treated. Stevie really respected and revered Johnny. One show in Missouri, we finished our opening set and were relaxing in the dressing room, and someone from Stevie's crew came running in looking for me and told me to come with him. Tommy had gotten sick and had to leave the stage. They were in the middle of a slow blues, and I'm suddenly playing Tommy's bass; I couldn't play mine because Stevie tuned down to E♭, and it took me a couple of seconds to catch that, during which Stevie turned around and gave me this "You got my back?" look. I nodded back, like, "I got it." And from then on it was a fantastic moment. Most nights I would go sit in the audience and watch them, and that's when I fully locked in on what a massive guitar player this guy was and what an influence guys like Johnny and Albert [Collins] were on him.

Stevie's birthday happened on that tour, on an off day in Iowa, and they were having a big celebration dinner with his band and crew, and they invited us all to join them—again, not normal for an opening band!

18

DROWNING ON DRY LAND

Soul to Soul, the band's third studio album in just over two years, was released on September 30, 1985. Of the album's ten originally released tracks, Vaughan composed four: the simmering, sultry slow blues "Ain't Gone 'n' Give Up on Love"; the somewhat discombobulated "Empty Arms," on which he plays drums as well as guitar; the deeply heartfelt closer "Life Without You"; and the mostly instrumental "Say What!" with its group vocal chant, "Soul to soul." It also included Bramhall's "Lookin' Out the Window" and "Change It," R&B star Hank Ballard's "Look at Little Sister," the Willie Dixon–penned Howlin' Wolf tune "You'll Be Mine," and New Orleans bluesman Earl King's "Come On (Part III)," which Jimi Hendrix had recorded on *Electric Ladyland*. Vaughan was also oddly credited with the swinging Eddie Harris instrumental "Gone Home."

The album reached #34 on the Billboard 200 chart, with the music video for "Change It" receiving heavy rotation on MTV. Stevie Ray Vaughan was a mainstream artist, but *Soul to Soul* would peter out, selling fewer copies than the first two albums had. His record label grew concerned with the drop-off, but more pressing problems were arising with Stevie and the band.

Stevie would introduce the new quartet by saying, "They're no longer Double Trouble; now they're Serious Trouble!" Whether or not he was making a sly joke, Vaughan was expressing a deeper truth than most fans realized. The drinking and drugging were out of control; Crown Royal and cocaine were the preferred substances, and Stevie and Tommy were the most serious abusers. The band's performances were becoming increasingly frenetic and chaotic. Stevie's relationship with Chesley Millikin was also growing more strained. Despite growing performance fees, the band's expenses were also rising, and they began to feel like they were on a hamster's wheel, increasingly working just to keep working.

LAYTON: We were spending too much money, and no one cared. It was, "This will be a great hotel." And I'd go, "Well, how much is it?" For years, it was me asking the questions, because Stevie thought the better we play and the more badass we are, the more things will fall in line, which was bullshit. We struggled over that because I wanted to see the bottom line and know how we were doing, and Chesley would say, "Chris is causing trouble over here." Stevie didn't like trouble, so he'd ask me what I was doing, and I'd say we needed to pay more attention to the business. He existed under the delusion that if what you do becomes more and more wonderful, then everything will fall in line and work out.

EDI JOHNSON: Stevie didn't care about or respect money, which was both a strength and a weakness. It was impossible to get him focused on that. Chris maybe didn't understand where the money was coming from or going to, but every dollar they earned was put into the band account, and we only took 10 percent, not the 15 percent of most managers. Stevie didn't file taxes for years before he was with us, and we knew it was going to be a problem when all the 1099s started coming in after *Texas Flood*.

WYNANS: Once I joined up and went on the road, I was shocked by what was going on with them business-wise—or not going on! It was so ramshackle. They were so successful as a band, I assumed that their business was in order, but they didn't even know how much money they had. They were all just getting weekly draws, and no one knew what was coming in or going out, if they had a lot of money or were bankrupt. Chesley would come by and hand out hundred-dollar bills, which was old-school Muddy Waters–Chess Records stuff. "Take a few hundred bucks and move along." I didn't think that was the way to do things in the '80s.

LAYTON: We were not dealing with a crook but someone who thought, "We're going to have fun and figure out a way to pay for it." I was saying, "No. We need to see how we're looking." Every successful business asks what something means and how it projects before they just do it. It's just nuts-and-bolts business. People often work under the illusion, "We're in the music business, man. We're just gonna groove and everything's gonna work out." No, it won't. Somebody has to keep their eye on the ball.

WYNANS: I started saying, "We need to get separate accounting about what comes in from the gigs, the merchandise, the recordings . . ." You can't throw it all in one pile because the percentages are different. My meddling was not appreciated, and Chesley certainly let me know that I was the new guy, he was the boss, and I needed to toe the line. It just didn't make any sense to me that a band of their stature was in the dark about their money. I was really looking out for my friends, not protecting myself. I didn't even expect to have a long-term gig with the band.

Even as these problems were percolating and building to a boil, Stevie was enjoying the perks of stardom. He realized a lifelong dream when he was asked to record with James Brown, adding a solo to "Living in America."

"I was in the back room at Antone's when Stevie came back from the James Brown sessions and proudly put a cassette of the song on," says David Grissom. "He had this huge smile on his face. It was James Brown! Stevie had that youthful, infectious enthusiasm and couldn't wait to play it for everybody."

At the end of 1985, Double Trouble was in New York to do press for *Soul to Soul* and collect platinum records for *Couldn't Stand the Weather*. Stevie was scheduled to meet at the Mayflower Hotel with Peter Afterman, the music coordinator for the Ron Howard movie *Gung Ho*. Fabulous Thunderbirds manager Mark Proct was sitting in. The T-Birds' album *Tuff*

Enuff was scheduled to come out in January 1986 on Epic, their first release after a three-year label-less hiatus. No one was more excited about this than Stevie, who told the coordinator he had to hear his brother's record and urged Proct to go get a copy. He ran to his room and returned with a cassette tape. Afterman featured "Tuff Enuff" in the movie, helping turn it into a hit and relaunch the Fabulous Thunderbirds' career.

Jimmie and the T-Birds would join Stevie Ray and Double Trouble for many of the shows throughout 1986. Stevie jumped at the chance to appear on national television to an audience of millions when they were asked to perform on *Saturday Night Live* on February 15. They had to go to extenuating lengths to follow through on this commitment, but it afforded them the chance to reconnect with their old friend and supporter from the early days, Mick Jagger.

LAYTON: We had a six-night stand at the Royal Oak Music Theatre near Detroit, Michigan, three shows one week and three the next [February 12–14; February 20–22]. After the first of the six shows, we flew to New York to rehearse for *Saturday Night Live,* then flew right back to play the next two nights.

WYNANS: That schedule was a mess—we were clearly fried.

LAYTON: The T-Birds were touring with us, so Jimmie flew back to New York and played "Change It" with us on the show.

SHANNON: We were loud as shit in rehearsal, and the crew kept saying, "Can you guys play any quieter than that?" Mick Jagger was there because his wife, Jerry Hall, was hosting the show.

LAYTON: Mick hung with us for most of the night in this real tiny dressing room and told Stevie that he wanted to sing "Little Red Rooster" with us. The Stones had broken up temporarily, and just before we went on, Mick said, "Maybe I better not do it, because Keith and I have this problem right now. Maybe I shouldn't appear by myself on national television, because it might piss Keith off." He was uncomfortable and decided not to do it.

It was exciting to play on *SNL,* but the truth is, I can't say whether it was really fun or even a good time because we were so burnt out and on edge. There was none of the peaceful contentment that normally goes along with achieving a career accomplishment like that because we were all too fucked up on drugs.

On March 8, Stevie and Double Trouble and Jimmie and the T-Birds embarked on an eighteen-day tour of New Zealand and Australia. Stevie had insisted on the T-Birds' inclusion. It would be the most time Jimmie and Stevie had spent together in decades. Tensions between Stevie and Chesley deepened throughout the blurry, drug-fueled tour of Oceania. Stevie also met Janna Lapidus in Wellington, New Zealand, the fourth stop on the tour. The tall brunette beauty, who would be his closest companion by the end of the year, was a month shy of turning seventeen. She and her parents had fled the Soviet Union and moved to Wellington in 1974 when she was five.

WYNANS: We were driving in from the airport in Wellington, and Stevie saw this beautiful woman and told the driver to stop and he would see us later. He had to meet her. He was immediately smitten.

JANNA LAPIDUS, *Stevie Ray Vaughan's girlfriend, 1986–1990:* I was familiar with him because I'd seen a few clips on TV, and he had a popular fan base in New Zealand. But I was listening to bands like the Clash and the Psychedelic Furs.

After we spoke for a while, Jimmie came out, and the three of us walked around town. When I had to leave, Stevie asked if I would come back before the show, but I already had plans with a friend so I was noncommittal. My friend and I walked over later and saw a long line of people waiting to go in. Jimmie saw me and asked where I'd been and said Stevie had been waiting for me. I was surprised and amused as we walked back into the lobby and Jimmie called up to Stevie and said we were there.

We went up and hung out with Stevie, then walked across the street to the show with him. I thought he was quite incredible, and after the show, Stevie took my jean jacket and gave me his black velvet cape so that I'd have to come back the next day. We met in the afternoon and talked for hours about life, feelings, relationships, and the marriage he was trying to make a break from. He was intrigued that my family had moved from Russia to seek freedom, and despite our differences in age and background, we realized a lot of similarities. I was just getting through a struggle with an eating disorder, and he was struggling with the control that drugs and alcohol had on his life and searching for serenity. Before I left, he asked me to come to Auckland the next day, and I said I'd see. The next morning, caution wrestled with a sense of intrigue and a true feeling of connection. I decided I had to go and made sure I had my own hotel room.

WYNANS: Janna joined us on tour. They seemed to have become immediate soul mates.

LAPIDUS: My dad just looked at me and said, "What are you doing?" They knew I was going to do what I was going to do, so they didn't fight too much. I was their only baby, but they knew that I had my wits about me, that I wasn't just coming from butterflies and fairyland. My parents had been through a lot; they were kids through World War II and left Russia for a better life. I had a sister who died there. They weren't easily scared.

PROCT: I never got the feeling that Stevie's attraction to Janna was about trying for a one-night stand. It was like a light bulb went off when he saw her, and we could all feel that. He loved talking to her and being with her. He could go off on these raps that didn't make much sense and were impossible to follow, but he was very clear about wanting to be with her. He wanted companionship and love, and he found someone he could really talk to and open up with.

In Auckland, Vaughan asked Lapidus to stay on the road and join them the next day when they would fly to Australia for a ten-day, five-city tour. She agreed again.

LAPIDUS: It was still cocaine and Crown Royal backstage and flying around Australia, they'd be drinking and getting into rowdy fights with flight attendants. It was a bit rude and unnecessary. Stevie had this element of badassery. He carried around a lot of anger, but he was so bloody honest and open with me. You could see a beautiful heart struggling.

All the Best of Life!
Don't Mess With Texas! Stevie Ray Vaughan 87

Stevie loved this guitar, which was stolen
in 1987 and never recovered.
(Agapito Sanchez)

PROCT: In Australia, everyone was way over the top, acting excessively. It was crazy over there; everyone in the bar in the middle of the afternoon knocking down shots of vodka and whiskey. We all felt like we were invincible, but Stevie hit it a lot harder than any of us. There was a show towards the end of that tour, which was the first time I had ever seen Stevie unable to play well. He was always great no matter what he was doing, but not this time, and the Double Trouble guys did not know what to do. At one of the airports, Jimmie was just out-of-control hungover, and Stevie got so frustrated that he took this metal walking stick and smashed it into a pillar. It was that kind of tour.

At the end of the tour, in Perth, March 27–29, 1986, Vaughan and Millikin had a heated meeting. Chesley continued to find it ridiculous that Chris and Tommy were making the same amount on the road as Stevie, a longtime point of tension, but he also didn't appreciate Layton questioning the finances. Layton had long been a voice calling for financial accountability and what he considered common-sense business practices.

LAYTON: Australia promised to be a good tour, and before we left, I asked Chesley for a business projection, which he didn't have, so I said, "I want to know clearly, are we going to lose money, yes or no?" He said, "You're not going to lose a penny." We got to the end of the tour and found out we were in the red, and I told Stevie, "This is bullshit. It's killing us. I'm not going to be around to watch us hit the wall, so either he goes or I'm leaving. We cannot operate like this and think we're ever going to make any real headway in our career or our music because it will drag us down. It's got to change." It's not just that we had more to lose. A lot more was being lost.

PROCT: Chris was trying to figure out how they could stop losing money, but it's hard to make money when it's all going up your nose, and that's the situation everyone was in. Stevie had also insisted on having the T-Birds along, though we weren't really a draw yet, and I'm sure that cost them a bunch of money. Chesley was trying to keep it on track, and he definitely believed in Stevie, but he was kind of a control freak, and I'm sure that grated.

HODGES: Chesley had a lot on his plate and was going 24-7. He had the ability to think big, but some of the other attention to details weren't maybe as keen as Stevie recognized they needed to be.

LAYTON: It was a scary moment for me because quitting the band was the last thing I wanted to do, but I really felt that continuing as we were was going to be the end of us anyway. You could see the handwriting on the wall; it had to change, or there would be a day of reckoning when we would be staring at a dead end, asking what happened. I couldn't stand by and watch that happen. The way things were going was heartbreaking, and I had to take that stand. I really don't know if Stevie fired him or Chesley quit, because I wasn't in the meeting, but

Tommy Shannon and Chesley Millikin in Australia, 1986, during the manager's final days with the band. *(Mark Proct)*

Stevie agreed that something had to change, and in short order, Chesley was gone.

The result of the meeting was an agreement that Classic Management would no longer represent the band as of June 1. They had two months to finalize the split. Stevie's two most intimate relationships—with Lenny and with Chesley—were both splitting apart.

EDI JOHNSON: I knew Stevie was going to leave, and it wasn't about money. Stevie wanted someone to take care of him, to be on the road every day and watch out for him. Stevie asked me to talk to Chesley, and I tried, but he wasn't getting it. Chesley was not a guy that was going to change. He did a tremendous job getting Stevie out into the world, but he wasn't tuned in to what Stevie needed—which was to feel taken care of.

HODGES: The kind of tender, loving care Stevie needed at that time was not necessarily Chesley's forte, and I somehow got into that role. I loved Stevie and knew how sensitive he was.

J. MARSHALL CRAIG: Chesley was hard on Stevie, who was probably ready for something different at that stage of his career. It was just time to part. Chesley always said that he wasn't fired.

EDI JOHNSON: Neither Stevie nor Frances liked confrontations, so there was grumbling, not fighting. But none of it would have ever happened without Frances's backing and the money she poured into the band.

BRANDENBURG: Frances Carr took a leap of faith and invested money into something because she and Edi and Chesley *felt* it.

WYNANS: When we got back and had a meeting, everyone was sort of shocked to find out how much money we had lost on that trip.

HODGES: It's a tough thing when a manager loses a client's enthusiasm, but it's not uncommon, and the manager who gets an artist's career moving is often not the right guy once they're established. Stevie asked me for help finding a new manager, and I set up tentative meetings with ten people, and he was not at all pleased with the results of the first few because he felt like these guys were trying to tell him what to do. Regardless of drug issues, Stevie Ray Vaughan was 100 percent clear about who he was as a person and a musician. He wanted support and guidance, not a new musical plan. After a few meetings, he was complaining about these guys, and he said, "If you'll be my manager, then it's a list of one because I don't think anyone else understands what I'm doing."

EDI JOHNSON: Chesley talked about Alex Hodges as his best friend, and I can't imagine how he felt about this.

HODGES: His mind was made up by the time he came and talked to me.

19

LIVE—AND BARELY ALIVE

Hodges left International Creative Management (ICM) to focus on his Atlanta-based management company, Strike Force. Gregg Allman was another client. Stevie and his crew's work-hard, play-hard ethos did not intimidate Hodges, who had worked for years with the Allman Brothers Band, Lynyrd Skynyrd, and other road-tough rockers. But once he began studying the band's finances, it became clear to him that the situation was dire.

Double Trouble was deep in debt to Classic Management from early loans and everyone steadily taking "draws" and was facing lawsuits from Cutter Brandenburg, Richard Mullen, and others who filed suit after mounting frustrations that they had not been paid what they felt had been promised.

"There were some muddy waters," Hodges says. "Stevie couldn't pay all the bills. They had a road manager who was making promises and dispensing money. He was cutting and dispersing the drugs, and the protocols of a road manager were not being met or honored."

Hodges says that he lent a sympathetic ear to Vaughan's desire to play less but quickly realized that the only financially responsible recommendation he could make was the opposite: the band had to play more shows to dig out of their hole. "I saw that the touring could be done differently, but it was an absolute necessity," says Hodges. "Stevie's health was the paramount concern, but the only sustainable income was from the road."

Says Layton, "When Alex took over management, our fees somehow doubled. A $25,000 gig became $50,000."

HODGES: When I was told everyone in the band and crew was on salary, I said, "Uh-oh," because they weren't making enough money to do that, and I had to tell them, "You can't write the checks, and you really are going to have to listen to me." There were outstanding debts to people who said they had been promised money. And tax issues arose pretty quickly. The amount of debt seemed staggering. We had to change everyone's thinking. And that's what Stevie did.

WYNANS: We suddenly had exact knowledge of what we had—and what we owed. Debt had piled up, and for the first time we knew exactly where we stood, and it was cold water in the face.

LAYTON: It was like we woke up one day and realized that our business wasn't being handled right, we were in debt to the IRS, we're high on drugs, we're gigging every single day, we're doing five interviews, we gotta catch a plane, we're checking in and out of hotels. All of this became a weight that got heavier every day; you're walking along, and soon you're not upright and almighty anymore. The weight gets heavier and heavier till you just can't bear it anymore, and you fall.

Buying gear on the road.

HODGES: No one could disagree that Stevie was in rough shape. It would be hard to exaggerate the situation. I went out with them a lot, then I hired a friend of Stevie's, Tim Duckworth, to go on the road, and I think Stevie and the band understood why that was necessary.

TIM DUCKWORTH, *Stevie's friend; on the road in 1986:* Stevie stayed with me whenever they were in Southern California, and I became so concerned that I went and told Alex, "I'm frightened for Stevie's life." I never told Stevie, "You can't do drugs anymore," and honestly at that point, I was still using with him, but I tried to help him put a little intelligence behind it. Stevie wasn't ready to stop, but he wasn't oblivious to his situation and how difficult it was getting to carry on.

HODGES: Stevie needed help, but you can't get where you need to go by telling the person they can't use anymore or that they can no longer perform. You have to find some balance that allows a person to feel that they are still whole. It never works to just say, "We're off the road until you get sober." I must have done a hundred interventions over twenty years with Gregg Allman, with the help of his mother, bandmates, and kids. We all tried to help Gregg work through his demons, but you can't take a guy like Gregg or Stevie off the road and expect a miracle. You can't deny them such a large part of what makes them whole.

WYNANS: The drugging was getting so bad that I was really scared for the guys' health. Stevie was just so worn down and obviously needed a rest,

Somewhere in Europe, 1986.
(Chris Layton)

but it's hard to stop working when you find out you're in big debt. So we stayed out there, and it got worse and worse, and probably reached sort of a low point at some of the shows we were recording for *Live Alive*.

SHANNON: Stevie had wanted to do a live record for a while, and for many different reasons, this seemed like a good time to do it.

WYNANS: Everyone had been asking for years for a live Stevie Ray Vaughan album. We also didn't have a lot of new material, so it was an easy way to come up with a new album. Or, I should say, we thought it would be easy!

LAYTON: Doing a live record was a cry for help, and it turned out to be the toughest live record to make, ever. We just weren't playing well enough.

SHANNON: Truthfully, I'm amazed how well we functioned musically during that time. The growth of our sound was gradual, and by 1984/85, the band had become very powerful. We could still get in touch with the pure spiritual connection, and the playing was still there. But our minds and bodies were going through tremendous trauma. Eventually, in the very last period when everything got real bad, we shut ourselves off from that source.

STEELE: I was having dinner at a Mexican restaurant with some friends that Stevie knew well. He walked in dressed in full regalia and acted like he didn't know us. He just stood there, looking all around the restaurant for someone, then he noticed us, said, "Gotta go," and split. He was jacked up and looking to score. Stevie had been a really good friend, and I was hurt and angry. That was not the Stevie that I knew.

MARK LOUGHNEY, *fan:* I saw him in a Rutgers gym [April 15, 1986], and it was a mess. His solos were long, noisy, and self-indulgent. I was fortunate enough to have seen him twice before, so I knew what he was capable of. Every song was really long and jammed out and not in a good way. In a venue with terrible acoustics, it was absolute cacophony. When he was done, he rambled on into the mic for five minutes. He sounded really drunk, and the whole thing was off-putting, especially after what I had seen him do before. It was obvious that something was really wrong.

OPPERMAN: I went to see them in Monroe, Louisiana [April 27, 1986], and it was clear Stevie's drug addiction was getting worse. Chris and Tommy actually walked off the stage. Stevie was up there ranting and raving on the mic, talking nonsense to the crowd.

WYNANS: Stevie and Tommy were just completely out of control, and it was getting scary. The first year I was in the band, I saw people who were abusing substances but also were on top of it musically, but that started to change. Things were getting illogical and crazy, and Stevie would sometimes play himself into corners and not know how the hell he was going to get out.

LAYTON: We really did begin to get closed off from the spiritual part of playing. That had been our constant pursuit. Over the years, the music grew naturally, and the result was a bigger, more powerful sound; the music kept getting better. But as time went on, things changed.

HODGES: It took multiple conversations to have a single cogent five-minute conversation with Stevie. You'd have to repeat things over a number of conversations.

SHANNON: I have to be honest: when I first started doing drugs, they worked great in terms of feeling totally connected to music. For a long time, I did speed, smoked pot, stayed up all night playing, and learned some really cool things. But by the mid-'70s, I lost everything because the drug use had become my whole life.

When I got a new start with Stevie, the drugs were back, too, and it worked again for a while. I felt that they helped me open up more, to drown out the pain that got in the way of reaching what I wanted to reach. We needed a certain amount of intake of drinks and cocaine to feel right. But that amount changes, until finally, no matter how much you do, you can't get back to that place. It doesn't work anymore.

As the drug use continued to escalate and Stevie became ever more fragile, his relationship with Lenny was becoming even more volatile. Things between them could explode anytime on the turn of a dime.

SHANNON: Stevie and Lenny loved each other very much, but the relationship got so sick because they both became irrational and paranoid due to cocaine and alcohol abuse. Anytime Stevie was afraid to go home, he'd pick me up, we'd go out there, and she'd start swearing at him, throwing shit, swinging at him, and I'd get between them. The relationship had become so volatile that anything could set them off. Had they been clean and sober, maybe they could have worked through their problems.

BRANDENBURG: Things got bad because they both were too high; it's a love that would have never died. She looked out for him and understood music and some of the realities better than he did, and I always thought they were meant for each other. When the drugs got involved, they were not able to find that love and hold on.

SHANNON: This went on so long because deep down inside they loved each other. The other side of Lenny being difficult is she was very protective of Stevie and would get irate if she thought someone was fucking him around, and she would jump on him for not defending himself. In spite of it all, I have nothing but good thoughts for Lenny.

EDI JOHNSON: Stevie would sometimes call me when he was troubled, maybe because I was more available than anyone else or he didn't want anyone else to know what was going on. This one time, I could hear Lenny screaming and making all this noise, and I asked what was going on and he goes, "She's breaking my record collection." I said, "Don't let her do that!" He had a record collection to die for, including 78s of blues greats, and he loved it so much. I said, "Stevie, you've got to stop her and get away from that. You can't have that kind of conflict in your life." How do you react when you see something like that happening to someone you care about? I couldn't get close to Lenny, who was causing Stevie so much pain.

OPPERMAN: The most disturbing times were when we'd pick Stevie up at his house and there'd be three or four cars there, Stevie's and Lenny's friends. When we came back a few days later, the cars would still be there, unmoved. Nothing was ever said, but it was the elephant in the room; all of those people had been in there doing drugs nonstop for days on end. It was clear as soon as we pulled up that Stevie was really unhappy to see that. He'd just grab his stuff and go in, without saying anything. My heart went out to him.

SHANNON: One day, Stevie, Lenny, and I were on our way back home from the airport when she blew a fuse over some little comment Stevie made. She was screaming, getting more and more mad, with both of us telling her to calm down. Finally, she started to crawl out the back window right in the middle of town! Stevie braked, and we were trying to grab her, but she squirmed out the window and was screamin' at the car, then took off running. Stevie and I started circling the block, looking for her, with me saying, "Stevie, the cops are going to come! We got to go." I had a little vial with some powder in it, which I threw away, but Stevie kept saying, "Let me try one more trip around."

Sure enough, cop cars came from four different sides with guns drawn. Someone probably called the police thinking we'd kidnapped her or something. A big, black cop found this little vial of cocaine on Stevie and took him into a park for a fatherly lecture: "What are you fuckin' up like this for? You got too many people looking up to you to be doing this!" He took the cocaine from Stevie and let us go.

DUCKWORTH: Stevie's deepening drug problems had a lot to do with his marital problems. He used a lot but was highly functional for years— and then he wasn't. It was all catching up with him, but he was also getting distressed about his marriage, becoming more emotionally fragile at the same time he was becoming more physically fragile. He was gone for months at a time, he and Lenny were both doing a lot of drugs and doing things married people shouldn't do. Every phone conversation became fraught and filled with screaming and yelling. There was a lot of fire in the air.

CONNIE VAUGHAN: He had been hitting everything hard for years, and I think his body just fell apart. I just know Stevie and Lenny were not getting along, and it's because they we're both so fucked up.

DUCKWORTH: On the road, Stevie asked me to take Lenny's calls and say he couldn't talk, and she got really angry. All of a sudden, Lenny wasn't my friend anymore and started saying horrible things about me because I wasn't letting her talk to her husband—because he was telling me he didn't want to. He told me he just couldn't do it anymore. He was getting really weak and couldn't deal with the fighting.

BENSON: I was really worried. He had the means to get all the coke he wanted, and that's dangerous. I just knew that eventually he would either get busted, go crazy, or die. And I cared a lot, because I loved the guy. He had such a great heart, which was always visible, even at his worst.

On June 2, Stevie sat in with Jimmie and the T-Birds at Austin's Riverfest. Michael Corcoran wrote in *The Dallas Observer* that Stevie "emerged gingerly from a big, black limo and used a silver-tipped cane to pick his way to the side of the stage. His thirty-one years had been multiplied like dog years and almost suddenly he was old, frail and out of breath. His skin was gray and one size too big. You didn't need a doctor to diagnose the obvious: Stevie Ray Vaughan was dying."

Corcoran went on to note that as shaky as Stevie looked, once the song kicked off, he seemed "almost miraculously . . . to come back to life." It was a tenuous way to approach performances, and recording a live album became a far more difficult proposition than anyone had imagined. Vaughan set up some special performances, starting at the Austin Opera House, July 17–18, 1986. Putting these shows under a microscope revealed some ugly truths.

FREEMAN: I was at the Opera House gigs and was very disturbed by what I saw. It was a musical mess; they would go into these chaotic jams with no control. I hadn't seen them in a while and didn't know what was going on, but I was concerned.

SUBLETT: I was very worried about him. I was supposed to play on these shows, and it was a complete debacle. I didn't even have a monitor, I couldn't hear a note I played, I'm like a fly on the ocean being tossed around, just completely winging it, and we're supposed to be recording a live album. It was insane and over the top, not a situation where you could go, "Hey, I'm a saxophone player, and I need to hear myself." That kind of thing was just clearly a waste of time. In retrospect, all of us could have been in better shape, but Stevie and Tommy were so far gone.

SHANNON: That was the period when the drug use really started to get to us. And it happened fast, like a cold northern air blowing in on a hot day, and we looked at each other and realized, "Something bad is wrong here." I remember sitting backstage telling Alex [Hodges], "Stevie and I are headed for a brick wall." We all saw it coming, because we were really getting pathetic, but neither of us could stop—and we tried.

WYNANS: There was a dark period and a light period of my time with Stevie. The shows at the Opera House were probably the darkest days.

FREEMAN: The music was starting to go off the rails anyhow. It had gotten to just being guitar, guitar, guitar without much focus, but this was a new level of out of control. Joe and I were united in being disturbed by what we were hearing.

SUBLETT: I felt like I'd lost Stevie. He was still alive, but the guy that I knew was gone; it was a shell that looked like him but wasn't him. I couldn't talk directly to him and be honest. Anyone in that state is very distracted. This was a guy who barely knows I'm here.

CLARK: The thing is, when you're out on the road, playing for hundreds of people, they're still strangers, and the routine of going from one gig to another, waking up in a hotel, and trying to figure out where you are and what you're gonna do, it puts a toll on a human being's spirit. And you're doing this just to play music. I think those things were getting to him.

"I had been trying to pull myself up by the bootstraps, but they were broken," Stevie told *Guitar World* in 1988. "I would wake up and guzzle something just to get rid of the pain I was feeling. Whiskey, beer, vodka, whatever was handy. It got to the point where if I tried to say hi to somebody, I would just fall apart crying. It was like solid doom."

The day after the Opera House shows, Double Trouble recorded their performance at Dallas's Starfest at the Park Central Amphitheater. Following the show, they attended a pre-opening VIP party at the Dallas Hard Rock Cafe, along with Dan Aykroyd and some other celebrities. Hard

Rock owner Isaac Tigrett had lured Stevie to the event with the promise of checking out Jimi Hendrix's Gibson Flying V.

Vaughan happily posed with the guitar, and, apparently mistaking the offer to use it on a future recording session for a gift, he asked for the case so he could take the guitar with him. He became incensed when he realized that the offer was to lend it to him in the future, not give it to him that night. "Stevie really thought it was a gift, and he was fuming," says Layton. "He gave the guitar back and split."

The next week, when the band began working on selecting tracks, mixing, and mastering the material from the Austin and Dallas shows at Los Angeles's Record Plant, they quickly had to face reality: the music was just not up to snuff. Stevie wanted to fix some vocals and guitar lines, but once they started doing punch-ins, they kept going. It became evident that a band long-renowned for its live performances was no longer capable of playing consistent shows—and often not even consistent-sounding songs within any given show. Listening intimately to the tapes forced them to confront these hard truths.

SRV: God, I wasn't in very good shape when we recorded that. At the time, I didn't realize how bad of shape I was in. There were more fix-it jobs done than I would have liked.

SHANNON: There were a lot of things we didn't like that we thought we could fix.

WYNANS: It started with trying to put in new vocals, then new guitars over existing tracks.

LAYTON: We hauled those tapes all over the country, working on them whenever and wherever we could, booking time in different studios to replace parts. It just got silly.

SHANNON: Stevie got creative and ended up getting carried away, trying to do too much. And there began the saga. We began redoing guitar tracks and vocals, then we got into redoing bass lines . . . and as these were live recordings, there was a lot of bleed between the tracks, which made it a nightmare!

LAYTON: The drum tracks sounded horrible, so we ended up at Stevie Wonder's LA studio [Wonderland] with me trying to overdub entirely new drum tracks. We took all the drums off the live tracks, so we had all of the tracks except the drums. Then I had to try to play along with these tracks. It sounded like horseshit.

WYNANS: It was ridiculous!

SHANNON: It was insanity.

WYNANS: It was a miracle that we ended up with anything listenable. We all really wanted that live record to be a winner, but it was not one of our finest hours.

LAYTON: We were just trudging along, wondering if we would make it until the afternoon. It was like being in the middle of the desert wondering if the next step would be the one where we just fell over and died.

FREEMAN: I happened to be recording my second album when they came into the same studio to record part of that so-called live album. I got word that Tommy stomped off after a big blowout with Stevie and became very concerned. It was an indicator that the thing was off the rails because they loved each other so much. Pals can have trouble, but it was obvious that there was something deeply, profoundly wrong, and everyone who cared about these guys was concerned.

LAYTON: Stevie got mad at me for saying in an interview after *Live Alive* was released that it was horrible, but it just wasn't very good—and it wasn't really live.

SHANNON: He was defensive about that record.

SRV: "Texas Flood" is good . . . that was from the [1985] Montreux Jazz Festival, when we felt good about what we were doing. Overall, there were some good nights and some good gigs, but [*Live Alive*] was more haphazard than we would have liked.

SHANNON: *Live Alive* is a good example of the drugs not working anymore. I can see that happening all through that record. The best tracks were from Montreux, which was a year earlier.

LAYTON: I just don't think it's a great record. We basically played live on our studio records anyhow. Part of it is just listening and thinking, "I know we can do better than that." At some point, you're chasing your tail. By the time of *Live Alive,* we were about as squashed as we could get.

SRV: Some of the gigs were okay, but some of them sound like they were the work of half-dead people. Of course, my thinking [at the time] was, "Boy, doesn't that sound good?" And there were some great notes that came out, but I just wasn't in control; nobody was. We were all exhausted.

Band portrait for *Texas Flood*. First official Double Trouble photo session for Epic Records. New York, 1983. *(Don Hunstein © Sony Music Entertainment)*

Stevie Ray Vaughan and John Hammond. New York, 1983.
(Don Hunstein © Sony Music Entertainment)

At ChicagoFest, on the Navy Pier, August 12, 1983.
(Paul Natkin/Photo Reserve Inc.)

Riding high on the *Texas Flood* tour. Double Trouble backstage at the Metro, Chicago, Illinois, July 3, 1983. *(Paul Natkin/Photo Reserve Inc.)*

Buddy Guy and Stevie at Antone's, circa 1983.
(Andrew Long/www.bluesmusicphotos.com)

Texas Flood album release show at Fitzgerald's, Houston, Texas, June 20, 1983.
(Tracy Anne Hart/www.theheightsgallery.com)

Embassy Ballroom, Chicago,
February 17, 1984. *(Paul Natkin/Photo
Reserve Inc.)*

The brothers on stage at Memorial Auditorium, Burlington, Vermont, November 18, 1985. *(Donna Johnston)*

Shooting the cover for *Couldn't Stand the Weather,* January 1984. *(Betto Friedman/Sony Music Entertainment)*

Stevie and Lenny on tour in Europe, circa 1985. *(Tommy Shannon)*

Look Ma, we won some Grammys. June 1985. *(Courtesy Tommy Shannon)*

In the studio recording *Soul to Soul,* with Doyle Bramhall and Joe Sublett. *(Courtesy Chris Layton)*

Catching some studio shut-eye during the *Soul to Soul* sessions. *(Courtesy Tommy Shannon)*

Another game of ping-pong during the *Soul to Soul* sessions. *(Courtesy Tommy Shannon)*

Soul to Soul. Recording group vocals for "Say What." *(Jimmy Stratton)*

Soul to Soul sessions—Stevie in control at Dallas Sound Lab. *(Jimmy Stratton)*

Soul to Soul album cover outtake.
(Brittain Hill/Courtesy Sony Music Entertainment)

Surrounded by his road essentials, 1985. *(Agapito Sanchez)*

Chicago Blues Fest, June 7, 1985. *(Kirk West)*

Stevie loved this headdress, which was a birthday gift from
Jimmie. November 23 or 24, 1986, Orpheum Theatre, Boston, MA.
(Donna Johnston)

Cover photo of *Live
Alive,* July 1986. *(John T.
Comeford/Courtesy Sony Music
Entertainment)*

During the final show of the Fire Meets the Fury tour with Jeff Beck, December 3, 1989, at the Oakland Coliseum, Oakland, CA. *(Jay Blakesberg)*

And the road goes on. . . . *(Courtesy Tommy Shannon)*

Author Andy Aledort and Stevie during the *In Step* interview, June 23, 1989, at Epic Records, NYC. *(Charles Comer)*

U2's Bono and Edge dropped in on Stevie and Jimmie at Antone's following their Joshua Tree show at the Frank Erwin Center, November 22, 1987. Chris Layton on drums, Sarah Brown on bass. *(Andrew Long/www.bluesmusicphotos.com)*

In Step Sony band portrait, 1989. *(Alan Messer/Sony Music Entertainment)*

Sam Houston Arena, Houston, Texas, November 24, 1989.
(Tracy Anne Hart/www.theheightsgallery.com)

Stevie and Janna filmed a commercial together in New Zealand in 1988.
(Rob Pearson/Courtesy Geoff Dixon)

When love comes to town: Stevie and Janna after show at the Jones Beach Theater, NY.
(Michele Sugg/Courtesy Janna Lapidus)

At St. Catherine's racetrack outside Toronto. "After we got clean, we started doing things on the road," says Chris Layton. *(Chris Layton)*

Brothers, 1990. *(Andrew Long)*

Alpine Valley, Wisconsin, August 25, 1990. The next-to-last night.
(Paul Natkin/Photo Reserve Inc.)

Guitar World cover shoot, Colgate College, Hamilton, NY, April 29, 1988. "We sat at a table in a darkened, deserted cafeteria, drank coffee, talked about getting clean, music, and life," says photographer Jonnie Miles. "It was the most enjoyable photo shoot I've ever done." *(Jonnie Miles)*

20

WALKING THE TIGHTROPE

Despite their increasingly frazzled state, Stevie Ray Vaughan and Double Trouble continued to tour relentlessly even as they were attempting to finish recording, mixing, and mastering *Live Alive*. The strain was showing on Stevie, which anyone who was really paying attention was sure to notice.

"Stevie did things that would kill a normal person, and there was no secret about it," says Austin singer and songwriter Bill Carter.

Stevie did little to hide his increasing drug use. When Bill Bentley interviewed him in a Los Angeles hotel room, Stevie looked like he had been up for a few days. He poured himself a full glass of Crown Royal and then dissolved a package of cocaine in it and drank it all down. When Bentley asked him what he was doing, he said, "I'm having trouble with my nose, and I want to get high."

Stevie began to have stomach problems, likely caused by drinking cocaine, though, as Layton notes, "It's not like Stevie went to a doctor who told him he had an ulcer from drinking cocaine. But he thought that he could get the high he felt he needed by dropping a gram into a shot of Crown Royal. He said he got the idea from George Jones. Talk about mentorship!"

In the midst of this madness, Stevie walked offstage at the Saratoga (NY) Performing Arts Center on August 24 and learned that his father, who had been in declining health, had collapsed and was in a Dallas hospital. He flew back to be with his family.

On August 26, Stevie and the band flew to Memphis to perform at the Orpheum Theatre as part of the *American Caravan* TV show with Lonnie Mack, a show he felt obligated to make. Vaughan performed well, particularly with Mack, but appeared gaunt, his eyes sometimes looking blankly out over the crowd. During his regular rap in the middle of "Life Without You," he appeared to be on the verge of tears. He said, in part, "You know, it's a very strong day today . . . a very good day for all of us to remember a few things . . . You better pass around as much love as you can in your lifetime. That's all we really have to give or accept."

The next day, August 27, 1986, Jimmie Lee "Big Jim" Vaughan died at age sixty-four from complications of asbestosis. He also had Parkinson's disease and had been using a wheelchair for some time. Stevie flew home from Memphis to join his family. Jimmie, Connie, and Stevie spent the night before the funeral in their childhood home together with Martha.

On August 29, Mr. Vaughan was buried in Dallas, and immediately after the funeral, Stevie and the band went straight to the airport and boarded a Learjet to fly to Montreal for a show at Montreal's Jarry Park, where he played a two-hour show without mentioning his father until the encore, when he simply said, "This one's for you, Dad."

"There are no words for the mood backstage that day," says James Rowen, a Canadian A&R representative. "I saw Stevie well over twenty times, and I may have seen him play better, but I don't know if he ever came close emotionally. He was playing for Dad, and I don't think he even knew that the crowd was there. He was deep into himself on guitar, stretching out. And although he always had plenty of emotion in his playing, this was an entirely different level. This is hard to imagine, but true. It was an evening I will never forget and I still get a similar feeling just thinking about it."

Two weeks later, on September 12, 1986, the band started a European tour in Copenhagen. The bottom was about to fall out, starting on September 24, the second of two nights at L'Olympia in Paris.

WYNANS: Paris was a low point.

SHANNON: We'd really reached bottom. We played "Tin Pan Alley" for like fifteen minutes . . .

LAYTON: And Reese got up and walked off.

SHANNON: Stevie got stuck in the wrong key and just kept playing. I was thinking, *God, that is not like Stevie at all.* People in the audience were getting pissed off.

LAYTON: Stevie was playing perfectly in time on the wrong beat. He drifted off, and I couldn't figure out what was going on.

On September 28, four days after the show in Paris, Double Trouble performed in Ludwigshafen, Germany.

LAYTON: After the show, Stevie and I left the hotel together to get a drink, but everything was closed. We were walking around looking for a place, and he said, "Goddamn, I need a fucking drink." I said, "No, you don't," because he was feeling sick to his stomach. He started to throw up, and blood came up. And he still kept saying that he needed a drink. I told him he shouldn't, and he yelled at me, "Goddamn it! I don't need a fucking drink, but I need a fucking drink!" I said, "Man, let's go back to the hotel." He laid down on his bed, and I called Tommy.

SHANNON: Stevie and I always had adjoining rooms and left the door open so it was like one big room. I was lying on my bed sick as a dog and could see Stevie rolling around on his bed, mumbling shit and sticking his head over the side and vomiting blood onto the floor and himself, too weak to get up and walk to the bathroom. There wasn't much I could to do to help him because I was so sick myself, but I went over and he was gray, and the throw-up all over; his chest was a big pile of blood. We were very scared.

LAYTON: I looked into his eyes, and it was like looking into the eye of a dead deer on the side of the road. He eyes were almost dry, with no life in them. I got scared shitless.

SHANNON: He started shaking, trembling, sweating . . .

LAYTON: All of a sudden, the life came back into his eyes, and he very weakly said, "I need help." I took that as the moment where he realized that things had to change. Not like, "I need to get better so I can go back to doing what I've been doing," but, "Everything has to change."

We called an ambulance, and all of these guys showed up in white trench coats yelling in German. They pulled out IVs, and we were screaming, "What the hell's going on?" They spoke not a word of English, and we know no German. They determined that he was suffering from near-death dehydration and took him to the hospital with us yelling, "Where are you taking him? How will we find him?"

SHANNON: It was a very sad time.

LAYTON: He went to the hospital, and the next day we went to Zurich, Switzerland, for a show [September 29, 1986]. I had never heard him sound weaker. He was playing in time, but he was about two beats behind the rest of the band. He was just fully drained, physically and spiritually. We were headed to London with a couple days off, and I called Alex and said, "We've got to do something."

HODGES: The situation was very scary, and Stevie wasn't going to fight anymore. Someone suggested finding the doctor who helped Clapton, and I made some calls and found Dr. Victor Bloom. I called him and explained the situation and that it all had to go down really fast. There was total understanding, and he agreed to see Stevie immediately, and he didn't mince words after the meeting. He said, "First, send Stevie's mother over because he needs her. And he's been talking about Janna Lapidus. I think you want to get her to London." I said, "I've got several flight reservations myself." He said, "That's not what I want you to do." Of course, my first inclination was to be there, but he said, "He trusts you, so stay where you are and take care of business. I'm in charge here, and you'll be in charge there." He told me to use my resources to come up with my first and second recommendations for rehab centers.

LAPIDUS: Stevie hadn't called me in months, after calling all the time at all hours of day and night. I was frankly heartbroken but decided that whatever we had was over and decided to move on. I applied to an exchange program in Italy and made plans to go in December. Then he called and said, "I'm in London in really bad shape, and I want you here." I hung up, thought it through, and decided I was going if I could

get there. We hadn't even been intimate, but I had invested enough emotionally, and there was something magical there. I was just following
the heart.

CONNIE VAUGHAN: He called me from a phone booth and said he needed
help and sounded so weak. I didn't have a passport and didn't know
what to do.

LAYTON: Eric Clapton visited him at the clinic. Stevie said he was very encouraging. He told Stevie that he'd been through something similar and
wanted to encourage him to get better. He said Clapton was a kind soul.

DUCKWORTH: Stevie broke down with Dr. Bloom. It was in that moment he
grasped it was time to change.

After two days in Bloom's clinic, Stevie and the band returned to the
stage at London's Hammersmith Palais on October 2, the day before Stevie's thirty-second birthday. Martha Vaughan was in the audience. Janna
Lapidus was en route.

BOB GLAUB: I was at the show in London. He had that gray pallor, the skin
color of someone who's unhealthy. We were all hitting it pretty hard
at that point. Tommy asked me if I wanted to sit in for the encore, but
it never happened.

SHANNON: We were walking offstage at the end of the set, and there was a
very narrow ramp—really just a board—and the lights turned off just
as he got to it.

WYNANS: It was complete, pitch blackness.

HODGES: Stevie was wearing his American Indian headdress, and he told
me that as he looked down at the narrow gangplank, the weight of
the headdress shifted forward and over his eyes, thus resulting in the
misstep.

LAYTON: There was a gangplank leading off the stage, and he stepped off
the edge and scraped his leg up. The headlines in the English press said
VAUGHAN COLLAPSES ON LONDON STAGE and VAUGHAN FALLS OFF
STAGE, but that wasn't true.

SHANNON: He was totally sober when that happened—and he never fell
off the stage.

Stevie loved this headdress, a gift from brother Jimmie. *(Tracy Anne Hart)*

LAYTON: When Stevie fell off that gangplank, that was the straw that broke the camel's back. He thought, "That's it. I'm beat, and I'm done."

The band canceled thirteen remaining shows on their European tour. Stevie spent the next ten days receiving care from Dr. Bloom while Lapidus, Duckworth, and Martha Vaughan kept him company and tried to keep him steady and occupied. The rest of the band and crew returned home.

LAYTON: I thought, "The whirlwind has finally stopped. And we're alive."

WYNANS: Something had to give, and what gave was Stevie. He had a breakdown, and it was a huge relief knowing that he was going to get help. The guy was a priceless jewel, and we just loved playing with him. It sucked that he had let his health deteriorate to such an extreme, and it was heartening to think he could recover.

LAPIDUS: I just got a ticket and figured I would stay at the YWCA. While I was in transit, Stevie called again and spoke to my mom, who told him I was on my way. When I landed, Timothy Duckworth was waiting for me, and he took me to a hotel where Stevie's mother was staying.

These were intense days, as he was detoxing and fighting to overcome the urge to drink, which he'd been doing since he was a little boy stealing from his parents' liquor cabinet. We went to cafés, walked through parks, shopped at vintage stores, did some sightseeing at Windsor Castle and other places, and he checked in with the doctor daily. We were driving around with his mum, with Stevie saying, "I need a drink. I need a drink." We all understood and it would pass, but he was really fragile.

On October 13, Vaughan, his mother, and Duckworth flew to Atlanta, and Stevie checked into the Peachford Hospital while Lapidus flew back to New Zealand. Shannon, already back in Austin, entered rehab there at Charter Lane. On the plane from London, Stevie penned a four-page letter to Janna, thanking her for coming to London, expressing his undying love and gratitude, writing "you are responsible for much of the progress I have made in my life." He also confessed to a "fall in [his] character" that occurred early in the flight.

At Windsor Castle, with Timothy Duckworth, Martha Vaughan, and Janna Lapidus,
October, 1986, while Stevie was receiving treatment from Dr. Victor Bloom.
(Courtesy Janna Lapidus)

LAPIDUS: He wrote that he had a drink on the plane and was so ashamed. He had never flown without a drink. It was his last one.

SHANNON: I had to change my life, too. I saw Stevie hit bottom, and I had nothing to hang on to anymore, either. I was basically in the same place he was. My liver was all swollen up, and I was in bad shape. Sure enough, we hit the brick wall we had seen coming. We had really wanted to go to rehab together and were upset when they said that wasn't possible, but I get that now.

LAPIDUS: Stevie was struggling for a long time. And he got that big wake-up call. It's like he always said, you have a couple of choices left: you either die, you end up in jail, or you get sober. It's pretty clear.

JIMMIE VAUGHAN: Stevie finally realized that if he didn't stop drinking and using, he was going to die. It's a fortunate thing to realize before it's too late. We've got a lot of friends that didn't get that opportunity, didn't get to that place.

SHANNON: We both felt real gung ho about treatment but didn't know shit about what it would be like. It was all brand-new, but we'd made it over twenty-four hours without a drink or drug, and we knew it was the only thing we could do. After about ten days I was allowed to talk to Stevie for the first time.

HODGES: I spoke to him on the phone when they said I could. Everyone in rehab thinks they're ready to leave, and he made those intimations a few times, but he stayed the course. You just had to listen and say, "Call me tomorrow, and if we need to, we'll make a reservation. In the meantime, listen to the people there." And he had the good sense to look at the circumstances and add a little bit of patience to his life. I visited him, and we went out to Stone Mountain one day and played baseball with his niece and my son with a pine cone and a stick. We tried to have a couple of normal afternoons, but we had business meetings, too.

LAYTON: While Stevie and Tommy were in rehab, Reese and I went out to LA to master *Live Alive*. We would call Stevie on the phone from the mastering facility, which was so bizarre, because we had always done everything together. It was virtually impossible to master with Stevie on the phone. It was like, "Well, you can't really hear it, but . . ."

SHANNON: Our twenty-eight days were just the beginning of the day-to-day process.

EDI JOHNSON: When I was picking health plans for them, I rejected any that didn't cover rehab. Tommy thanked me for that later on.

LAYTON: We were all lucky to have someone like Edi watching out for us. I visited Tommy and sat in circles and held hands, so I was involved in his recovery. I figured they would both do their thirty days, but beyond that, who could say?

JIMMIE VAUGHAN: It didn't even occur to me that Stevie would really go clean. I figured that he'd do his thirty days to get everyone off his back, then go back to it. But he was serious and dedicated, and he showed the way for me and for a lot of other people.

RAITT: I was playing in Atlanta towards the end of his rehab stay, and he came to see me, and I invited him onstage, as we would always do for one another [November 12 at the Center Stage]. I found out later that he was really nervous because it was his first time playing sober, but he played great, and there went my last excuse for not getting sober. Because he didn't get any less funky, any less passionate or fiery or great as a musician. So a few months later, I checked myself into rehab and started over. It was without a doubt thanks to Stevie's inspiration.

WYNANS: Stevie was real worried about playing after he'd gotten sober. He'd never really been sober and didn't know what it would be like. He worried about whether he still had anything to offer.

SHANNON: He wondered if he had lost it.

SRV: I know that everything is better now, and I do mean *everything*. My whole life is better. It was hard for me to see that when everything is better, that includes the music, too. There's no reason why it shouldn't. I'm not saying that it's automatic; I have to work at these things harder than ever. And that's fine. I'm glad I do. It has to do with progression, and there's healthy and unhealthy sides to it. The balance is the thing to try to find.

OPPERMAN: After you go down that path for too long, you realize, this is leading me to *nowhere*. And when you get sober, you try to help other people not go down that same road, and that's exactly what Stevie ultimately did. That comes with the emotional healing of getting sober.

LAYTON: Stevie was the leader. He had led everyone with his incredible musicianship, he led everyone with his massive capacity for substance abuse, and he led us all in sobriety, too.

21

THE THINGS I USED TO DO

Throughout his monthlong rehab stay in Atlanta, Stevie and Janna Lapidus engaged in a steady, passionate correspondence. Stevie wrote her daily, sometimes two or three times a day, and sent her a steady stream of Polaroids of himself. After checking out November 13, he immediately flew to New Zealand to visit her. "We just wanted to be together," she says.

Seeing his new love meant leaving Atlanta at 3:30 in the afternoon on Thursday, November 13, flying to Los Angeles, changing flights to Auckland, crossing the international date line, switching planes again, and flying to Wellington, where he would arrive at 9:55 a.m., Saturday, November 15. Adding to the burden of this grueling travel, these would be his first sober flights ever—his last drink had been on his last flight, from London—and he could only stay for a few days. The first clean-and-sober Double Trouble show was November 22 at Towson State University in Maryland.

LAPIDUS: He met my parents for the first time, and they loved him. He was a beautiful, pure soul and so kind and sincere with them. I felt embarrassed bringing him to our little apartment. I was making excuses, and the irony is when I went to Stevie's mom's place, I saw the exact same thing in a very different location.

DUCKWORTH: I questioned that trip, but when Stevie did something, he gave it everything he had. He stayed at my house when he came back from his trip to Australia, where he and Janna had met, and talked a lot about how wonderful she was, and once she came to see him in London, that was it. He gave everything he had to her. He was vulnerable and in bad shape, and she gave him so much love, which he needed. He let Janna know before he left London how he felt, and I don't think he ever doubted it.

HODGES: Janna was very young, but I just felt like she was uniquely stable, grounded, beautiful, and smart—and tremendously in love with Stevie. What else can you ask for?

WYNANS: His relationships had their ups and downs, and we liked it when Janna was around, because he was very peaceful around her. He wasn't as prone to be so wild when she was with him.

LAPIDUS: He told me that he wanted to break the cycle of addiction because he came from that. He knew he had to be the one to break it. It's why he

Stevie and Janna Lapidus at Antone's, 1988. *(J.P. Whitefield)*

had never had children. He told me, "I never wanted to bring love into a place where there wasn't love that you could depend on." He understood that he had gotten a second chance. He said, "I was bleeding internally. I could have died. I'm getting a second chance, and I better not fuck it up." He was finding some kind of clarity, maybe just, "Life is good." A big thing for recovering addicts is to realize life is okay without numbing your emotions.

SRV: I learned all that stuff—the guilt and the shame—when I was a little kid; I didn't realize how deeply that was embedded in me. Without someone else doing it, I do it to myself, because I'm familiar with that, you know? It's a shame.

LAYTON: Sometimes when we had issues in the band and it led to some sort of confrontation, he would just shut down and be quiet, and it was frustrating and I didn't understand it. Eventually, I realized that it stemmed from his childhood.

LAPIDUS: A few times when we had arguments—and they weren't big, screaming fights—he would just break down. He said it reminded him of bad scenes in his childhood, holding on to his father's leg, asking him to stop.

SHANNON: Stevie and I spoke for hours about this stuff, and he told me things he never told anyone. I'm taking most of it with me to my grave, but he experienced some really tough stuff as a kid.

SRV: I'm just now learning how to let go of some of that, and I can't always do it. Sometimes, I can put the club down. And other times, I pick it right back up and go to flogging myself.

LAPIDUS: The steps he was taking gave him the strength to feel like he had something to hang on to. And hopefully, you also have love. You just can't mess with what your heart feels, so when you open yourself up to that, and it's reciprocated, you can show each other the way forward. I learned from him as much as he hopefully did from me.

HODGES: His inner constitution carried him through a lot of this. We were supportive, and I couldn't have been happier or prouder of what we did together, but nothing would have happened without Stevie's willingness and commitment.

SRV: A lot of times, our fears keep us from seeing what's really there. I realized the other day that, without my fears, without my guilt and my shame—without that club to beat myself over the head with—I got a glimpse of what life would be like without that. It was just for a couple of minutes, and I realized that without that stuff . . . I never realized how much those feelings and those emotions permeate everything. I got a glimpse of how I felt without all of that, and I felt a lot better about everything and everybody. It was a real neat deal. I was just talking to somebody, and they said something that sparked it. It was like being in a completely smoke-filled room—like a cloud—and then somebody turned on a vent and all the smoke was gone for a minute.

Live Alive was released on November 17, 1986, while Stevie was in New Zealand.

"It was a cruel irony that *Live Alive* came out right when Tommy and Stevie got out of treatment," says Layton. "One of the first times we got together again was to make a video for 'Superstition.' Stevie and Tommy were clean and fresh, and everyone was clearheaded and healthy, and we were trying to play along to this dope-and-booze-laden tune. It was like, 'God, can't we cut this song again?' It was a weird contrast, but it was a great feeling to have everyone really into it again, ready to put the whole thing back together and get back to work. That alone made it a great experience. It was the start of something real good."

As they prepared to return to the road, Alex Hodges put together a more professional crew around Vaughan. Not only had Vaughan and Shannon gone through rehab but so had guitar tech René Martinez and drum tech Bill Mounsey. With four people in the program, attending daily meetings became an important part of life on the road. The new tour manager was the calm, capable Skip Rickert.

LAYTON: Alex said, "You guys are sober. You need someone new," because our road managers had been guys getting us dope and finding us afterhours places to drink. Jim Markham didn't want to do that stuff and left. Alex understood that we needed a new clean-living guy, and he also brought in a new accounting firm, who looked over everything, straightened out our taxes, got our finances in order.

SKIP RICKERT, *Double Trouble tour manager, 1986–1990:* During the interview process, Alex explained that Stevie was just coming out of rehab and was going to be extremely fragile. So I boned up on the newly recovered, which was not something I had a lot of experience with. I just approached it with empathy and a very big, open heart. Stevie was fragile, there's no question. We maintained a rigorous touring schedule, and in my early days, he needed a lot of attention.

SHANNON: In sobriety, Stevie became more dedicated to the spiritual pursuits that he'd always been interested in. For the first time, he knew what he had to do, and he got the chance to help other people, something he had always wanted to do. He didn't become Superman, though; we were both struggling. He was like a baby taking its first steps.

JOE PERRY, *Aerosmith guitarist:* I saw him at the Orpheum Theatre [Boston, November 23–24, 1986], and he sounded absolutely phenomenal. Brad [Whitford] and I were in the fifth row right in front of his amps—the Dumble, the Marshalls, and the Fenders—with the plexiglass wall in front of them. I was blown away. I knew right then that he was going to go down in history.

ANDY ALEDORT, *coauthor:* The first time I met Stevie was to interview him before his December 2, 1986, show at the Mid-Hudson Civic Center in Poughkeepsie, New York. I had no knowledge of the severe drug and alcohol addiction that nearly took his life; it had been kept very quiet. It had only been two weeks since Stevie left the Charter Peachford rehabilitation facility in Atlanta. The Poughkeepsie performance was Stevie's eighth dry show.

The backstage vibe was very tense, which was very confusing at the time. Skip Rickert was barking orders at everyone. When I sat down with Stevie, he was generally in good spirits, though his energy level was very low. He was extremely pale and did not look well. But once we got going, and played some guitars together, he brightened up and became more comfortable. He was quiet and thoughtful and, at times, startlingly candid.

During the *In Step* interview, 6-23-89, at Epic Records, NYC. *(Andy Aledort)*

WYNANS: When we got back together, I was surprised and very happy that he held the AA thing so closely and that things had changed as much as they did. He became completely immersed in the program, and he loved it. He read the twelve-step book every day on the bus, along with Tom, Bill, and René. Every night, he would either go to a group meeting in the town we were in, or there would be a meeting backstage. He felt that he had found the answer. He was completely comfortable with the program and with having people around that he could talk about these issues with. He was very inspired and motivated.

LAYTON: We had a lot of resources and people helping us in our sobriety. They did not do things *for* us; they helped us do those things for ourselves. They gave us the hand we needed to make sense of everything, and there was a lot of work to be done. A lot of reconciling and cleaning up wreckage, and making amends.

KIRK WEST, *photographer, Allman Brothers Band's "Tour Mystic":* I was on the road shooting pictures of the Gregg Allman Band when they did two weeks opening for Stevie [June 7–21, 1987]. I was in the program, as was Bud Snyder, Gregg's soundman, and Gregg was trying hard at the time. We were really happy to have daily meetings with Stevie, Tommy, and several of their crew guys. Stevie's dedication was impossible to miss and felt totally sincere. Gregg came to five or six of the meetings and seemed, for the time, inspired by Stevie's example.

GREGG ALLMAN, *Allman Brothers Band founding singer, keyboard player; died 2017:* Stevie was a dear friend of mine. We had the same manager for a while and did many tours together and became real close. I'm surprised we never recorded together and wish we had. He was very insecure about his singing, and I told him, "Just walk out in the woods, point your head up towards the gods, and sing to them. And fuck anybody who don't like it!" It must have took because he sang pretty damn good.

WARREN HAYNES: I saw Stevie with Gregg and also with the T-Birds and B. B. King. The promoter wanted Stevie to close, but he said, "B. B. King is closing the show." Seeing Stevie live was a visual enhancement of what I'd been hearing on his records. The intensity in his whole body resonated with what he was feeling and playing. He never slacked off for a moment.

SHANNON: There was an unspoken rule that when we got onstage, everyone would put every ounce of life into what we were doing. Nothing less was acceptable. To slack off after all that we had been through would have been like spitting on God!

RICKERT: Things getting better for them has to be largely attributed to Stevie getting clean and everyone changing their lifestyle. Chris and Tommy were his best friends. They were more like a family than a band. These guys slept on each other's couches when they were coming up, and it was such a pleasure to watch them interact with each other and with anyone from that close group of twenty to thirty Austin musicians.

HARVEY LEEDS: After he cleaned up, he was a 100 percent different person. Everyone in recovery is different. Some people don't have a problem if there's alcohol at a table, but Stevie wasn't like that. I did a radio dinner with him at an Italian restaurant in Boston, and someone ordered rum cake for dessert, and I went over and said, "No alcohol allowed. Pick another dessert." That's how meticulous Stevie was. He was very, very serious about his rehab. Stevie carried around two book bags like a doctor would carry, filled with his recovery books.

WYNANS: Everything changed. They got rid of all the nonsense and any distractions, and it became a completely different thing. We weren't about the party as much as we were about the music. It was fun to play again!

RICKERT: There simply is a lot of mayhem and chaos that comes with being drunk or high. When I arrived, there wasn't any of that. Everyone changed their lifestyle. I was a new person, and I was very organized and things were done well. We were running on time and schedule. It has a lot do with Alex, too; he demanded it be run up to his specifications, and he laid out how he wanted things done. Stevie and I got pretty darn close quickly, and he was delightful.

DR. JOHN: Even at his worst, you'd see a glimmer of hipness coming through Stevie. It started really shining steady after he got clean. He got downright amazing.

RAITT: He was probably the most fierce of the bluesmen I've ever heard. He had a furnace in his heart, and was the epitome of all that is dark and sexy, brooding and passionate. The most extreme emotions of the blues and of life were in every breath he took. And to find out that he could maintain that while sober was just a revelation. If anything, he was covering *more* emotions. He was playing as if his life depended on it, and it did.

PERRY: Like Hendrix, Stevie was a great technical player who took it to an entirely different level. He played with so much assuredness that it was impossible to imagine him *not* playing on that incredibly high level. It's like he was born with the guitar in his hand. He had an aura of complete control at all times. Stevie had that coolness and self-confidence; you could tell by just the way he moved that he was totally immersed in playing, which is a really rare quality.

WYNANS: Stevie was real nervous about playing sober, but we hit the stage and it was just magical. Within a few nights, he completely hit his stride and was playing better than any of us had ever heard him. He was playing the way he always wanted to and was just ecstatic. Every song was exciting, and ideas were constantly popping up and flowering everywhere. The shows became more cohesive and more energized and gained momentum. They just got better and better with time.

RAITT: Having gone through the process, I understand how it feels to realize that the ecstatic, transcendent feelings music brings you have nothing to do with being loaded—which is what you think when you are loaded all the time. To realize that it is in fact the music which gives you that feeling is revelatory. The other twenty-two hours a day can be really difficult, but the time onstage just gets better and better.

SRV: The music has become really important [since being sober]. Music is a way to reach out and hold on to one another in a really healthy way. It's helped me to open up more and take a chance on loving people. It's a whole new world for me. Left to my own devices, I would have killed myself, however slowly or whatever. But for some reason, I'm not dead.

WYNANS: He had every bit as much fire, and the direction was more true. Before, he was searching for the place to go, and now he knew just where to go and how to get there. We realized that things could have gone a lot worse, and it felt like a privilege that we survived and were still making music together. We all appreciated every note on every night.

HODGES: The things we did to keep Stevie clean were going to happen regardless, but it was easier having at least three people in the program. We just didn't need to have booze around—and regardless of what they might have called themselves, we didn't need people whose first or second jobs were selling drugs. They could be local crew, the photographer you see at every show, or the guy you don't know what he does but he keeps popping up. All those people went away. You're not always sure where the danger lurks, but when we weren't buying, the whole scene changed.

RICHARD LUCKETT, *SRV merchandise manager, 1989–90:* Stevie said, "I never want to see a pre-rehab image of me on a piece of merchandise. You just tell your art director that I forbid it."

HODGES: He has a cigarette in his mouth on the cover of *Soul to Soul.* When we did a songbook deal, we had them take that cigarette out because it really bothered him. Stevie was very aware of his sobriety and the image he projected—and it wasn't a dangling cigarette. He was very conscious of his good health.

LAYTON: We filmed those nights at the Opera House where we were trying to record *Live Alive*—a four-camera, one-inch video shoot. When Stevie saw it after he'd become sober, he said, "Oh, God, I look like shit!"

SHANNON: I was feeling really good in sobriety for about four and a half months, when I was suddenly confronted with clinical depression, which became another mountain to climb. Ironically, it was actually much worse than anything I experienced from drug and alcohol abuse. There I was, clean and sober, thinking, "Wait a minute! This isn't supposed to happen!"

LAYTON: We played at a place in Phoenix with a revolving stage [Celebrity Theater, May 22, 1987], and Tommy was hiding behind the dressing room door. It was time to go on, and we were going, "Where's Tommy?"

SHANNON: I looked out through the curtains, saw thousands of people out there, and freaked out!

LAYTON: He said, "I'm too afraid to go out there." This gets to the profound fear at the root of the problem: the dysfunction that's only been exacerbated by drug addiction and alcohol abuse for all those years. Fear of life itself. The illness is talking to you, saying, "You're no good anymore." Drugs and alcohol can initially help release your inhibitions, and it's really fun . . . until it's horrendous. You reach an incomprehensible demoralization. A black hole of existence. If you survive, which is a real gift, you recognize when the day of reckoning is upon you. You just cannot live another day using drugs.

SRV: The hardest thing to deal with isn't what I thought it would be. I thought the hardest thing would be, "Oh, God, now I'm straight—can I still play?" That had nothing to do with it. The hardest part is trying to keep things in perspective. I found out that the biggest problem that I had was self-centeredness and ego. That's really what addiction seems to boil down to. To keep that part of yourself under control while everybody's telling you how great you are is quite a task.

RICKERT: I never saw a guy work a program as hard as Stevie did. He had notes and little sayings that he would jot down falling out of his pockets, and his big book was tattered and highlighted and yellowed. I probably went to a hundred meetings with him on tour. We had a directory and references, and we took advantage of all of them and found meetings all over the country. We'd call them to assure the time, get cabs, or walk over. He was very dedicated to it. After a while, he would take care of it himself; he'd just ask me to help get a cab, and off he'd go.

WYNANS: He and Tommy and the other people who had straightened up would have long conversations about the different steps.

SRV: Finding some kind of perspective is the hardest part, because I want to stay alive, and I want to stay as healthy as possible and grow in that way. My best thinking just about killed me, okay? Now, more so than ever, if I don't play the best that I possibly can—and really try to play better than I think I can—then I've wasted it. 'Cause I'm playing on borrowed time. Now I have a new chance.

HUEY LEWIS: Stevie's music was far more important than whatever substances he was taking. He was gonna play guitar and sing and write, so when it got to the point where that shit was interfering, the music had to win out. He was a true artist and a tough, disciplined guy, which you have to be to get that good. He was a star, and I had to believe he had enough sense of himself to withstand all that—and he did.

LEEDS: Even when Stevie had his issues, there was never any drama. He seemed like a guy who wanted to be left alone. He was quiet and shy offstage, then would walk out and become a full-on guitar hero, only to go back into his shell afterwards. He was sweet and easy to deal with but not really there with you. He was always the guy behind shades, with the hat on. Now, all of a sudden, the hat's off, the glasses are off, he's awake, and it's like, "Wow, I never met this guy before." There was now a guy smiling and talking to you. It was like meeting someone for the first time after knowing him for years.

WYNANS: A lot of people talked about getting Stevie back, but I never knew him another way, so it was like meeting an entirely different person—a more quiet, introspective guy, but one who was just as passionate and fired up about music. Maybe even more so.

SRV: It is getting a lot easier, in some ways. However, every time I think I've learned something, I realize that I've just uncovered a big hole! A big empty spot, or one that's going, "ARGHHH!"

LAPIDUS: There was such a dramatic transition. Some of that angry person was gone, but he would still stand up for what he believed in. I think that's a really important part of his personality. He was so sweet and kind, but he also maintained his integrity. If he heard someone make a racist joke, he'd call them on it, and I heard him do it more than once. He'd always say, "I can't respect anyone if they don't respect me."

FREEMAN: I was at one of his first gigs after he got sober, and it was the most cohesive, enjoyable show I had ever seen him perform. It was just night and day compared to that thing at the Opera House the previous year. That gig was really, really good, and I was really happy for him and excited to see what he would do next.

DR. JOHN: I saw an absolutely phenomenal consistency in his playing after he got clean. It was so pure and flowing, like water through an open tap.

B. B. KING: The ideas continuously flowed through Stevie. I don't have that, and not many people do. But Stevie had it, in a way that reminded me of Charlie Parker or Charlie Christian. Most of us play maybe twelve original bars when we solo, then it's all repeats, but not with him. The more he played, the better he'd get. And his execution was flawless, but no matter how fast he played, he never lost that feel. I would say you could feel his soul in his playing. I know I did. His guitar was his means of speech, and he spoke beautifully.

CLARK: Music came through the top of his head, and he just played it.

SUBLETT: We weren't the kind of guys to blow smoke up each other's butt. It was understood that we could play, so we didn't praise each other all the time. But one night, he just killed me, and I asked him how he can keep playing solo after solo and never run out of ideas, and he said, "Joe, every time I play guitar, it's like I'm breaking out of jail." He was saying that there are no half measures. A lot of people never reach that point where they are beyond being analytical.

EDI JOHNSON: When you saw Stevie onstage, that was the real Stevie.

SRV: One thing I've noticed [after getting sober] is that songs I used to sing *at* people, I should have been singing at myself. At least I think that way. I hear the words more now, and different songs mean different things than I used to think they meant, too. To put it mildly, a lot of blues tunes have to do with resentments, big-time!

Take "Cold Shot." I used to sing that at certain women that I've been involved with over the years. Even though I didn't write it, I had in my head the way I related to it. Since I sobered up, I realized that *I* left; *I* was the one who gave the cold shot. And it hurts when you realize that you've hurt somebody, as opposed to, all this time, you've been telling yourself how bad they'd hurt you. A lot of times, if I stop and look at it, those words could really be telling me that I hurt myself. There are also other songs that are *kinder* than I thought. They make me feel better than I knew.

LAYTON: After Stevie nearly died, through our instincts, our willpower, and the fact that we all had shaped up, we were able to put our lives back together in a more structured way that allowed us to open up again. Once again, we could grab ahold of that spiritual well to draw from. Following the ordeal of '86, we were headed towards great places again and coming back to the place where inspiration would fill our lives. We had come through hell, and we were finally back to our fighting weight. We were rested, energized, in shape, and ready to play better than ever. At that point, we discovered that some things were better than they had *ever* been.

WYNANS: We'd get on the bus after a gig and unwind and sometimes listen to the show and discuss how it was. Then Stevie would often want to put on a video of a legend like Albert Collins or Muddy Waters. That part wasn't that different than before, but there was so much more clarity. And in the morning, he would be up reading his twelve-step book. He was still passionate about the music, but now he was also passionate about sobriety, about Janna, and about his relationship with his brother and his family. I think he became even more of a family guy.

In December 1986, during a short break from the road, Stevie met Janna in Florence, Italy, where she was studying on an exchange program. He toured the sites in a full-length fur coat, wearing his trademark black hat and carrying a black walking stick.

"It was something I had planned during the time he quit calling and I was moving on," says Lapidus. "He called and asked if he could meet me there. I was in an exchange program and got in some trouble for blowing off the itinerary as we took off on our own and stayed in hotels. It was amazing. I came home and repacked before heading to Dallas. We just knew we were going to be together."

Stevie filed for divorce from Lenny, from whom he had been estranged, on January 13, 1987, and Lapidus, who was not yet eighteen, moved to Dallas shortly after.

SHANNON: It was a very painful time for Stevie. He and Lenny had a drug-inflicted relationship, which caused extreme behavior, but they truly loved each other, though I think they both knew it was over. They hadn't resembled a married couple for a while, but it took a long time to get resolved. They both knew that it was the best thing, but the process was painful for him. The damage had been done.

LAPIDUS: It was just gut-wrenching to watch him go through this. He'd come back from proceedings heartbroken and disgruntled and shocked that money was being fought over so much. He didn't have much money and was just starting to understand more about it. He cared about people; he cared about his crew and band and keeping anyone he could on retainer, and his naïveté about money was being turned on him.

Janna and Stevie moved in with his mother at 2557 Glenfield Avenue, staying in his childhood room, before renting a house in Dallas together and moving in on May 3.

LAPIDUS: We stayed in his old room for a few months, and it was a great, sweet time. Having that opportunity to be there together, to experience his life and his relationship with his mother as they got closer was amazing. It was part of why he moved to Dallas, along with seeing who his real friends were.

CIDNEY COOK AYOTTE: Stevie was crazy about his mom. He bought her a telephone that had a little picture screen on it so they could do video calls, which was the latest, greatest technology. She was so proud of it.

He was very affectionate, a really loving, caring son. He was that way towards my dad, too.

LAPIDUS: He also got one of those video phones for my parents. He loved that thing and all gadgets! At the same time, he was going through grueling divorce proceedings and talking to Alex, saying, "My schedule needs to be calmer. I need days off on the road." He was saying, "I need to do this my way more." As much as he was on the road, he also needed to be alive.

RICKERT: Stevie developed a life. He was *living,* not just waiting to go back on tour or into the studio as he had before and as so many musicians do. He had a girlfriend that he was very happy with. He would spend his off time doing things. As the years went by, he became happier and happier and had more and more of a full life.

SUBLETT: He seemed to be crazy about Janna, really smitten. It seemed to me that for the first time in his life, he had a healthy relationship, that he wasn't always in pain and agony over doubting the situation, that he finally had a mature relationship, where two people were equally crazy about each other and wanted to be together. I just know he wanted to be with her, and they were making arrangements for the future.

WYNANS: I really had the sense that he was all in with Janna. Their romance grew quickly, he loved being around her, and they would have long conversations on the phone.

CONNIE VAUGHAN: When Stevie fell in love, he fell hard. He was a romantic, and he wanted one person in his life.

JORDAN: I was walking down Park Ave in New York and I saw Stevie in a hotel restaurant, and we waved and I went in. He was with [Janna], and he was so sweet. We had a cool, little mellow meeting, and it was so chill. He was reinventing himself, and it was just great to see and left me feeling so hopeful. I remember thinking, "He's not gonna burn out. We're going to have him for a while."

BENSON: I was running through the DFW airport when I heard someone call my name, and there was Stevie standing with his beautiful gal. He introduced me to Janna, and they seemed so happy. Lenny and him had become such a mess because of the dope, and to see him radiating a feeling of serenity and happiness was just great. I ran off to catch my plane feeling so good about where he was.

BRAMHALL II: When Stevie was living in Dallas, his house was close to Poor David's, a little blues club, and when he was home, he'd go over there and jam with my dad or a friend like Anson Funderburgh and invite me to join him. It would just be informal, fun jamming.

SRV: Sometimes I'll go to a small club and jam with Doyle Senior and Doyle Junior. I love to say, "On drums, Doyle Bramhall . . . on guitar, Doyle Bramhall!"

BRAMHALL II: He liked to get me onstage and say my name as often as possible, which was part of him taking me under his wing. He did the same for Colin James and some others. He was always looking to shine a light and help people.

RAY WYLIE HUBBARD, *acclaimed Texas singer/songwriter, best known for "Up Against the Wall, Redneck Mother":* In November '87, I was a

Doyle and Stevie at Mama's Pizza, Fort Worth, 12-20-1987, at a surprise party for Doyle's stepson, Chris Hunter. *(Logan Hunter Thompson)*

blackout drunk who thought cocaine was the answer to my drinking problem. It just gave my booze legs so I could go on longer. I was a garbage head who would put anything in my body. A girl I was going with finally got me to go to an AA meeting, and there was Stevie. Afterwards, I sat with him and his sponsor and we talked, and he did what he was supposed to do: he shared experience, strength, and hope. Everyone else I knew who got sober ended up on *The 700 Club* [Christian-faith television show], and I thought of myself as an edgy guy. Stevie was the first cat who got sober and was still cool!

LAPIDUS: Stevie always had that open heart. Rehab and the program gave him language and lingo to use to express what he always felt, and it gave him something to hold on to. Very importantly, it also gave him strength in numbers, knowing he was not alone, knowing he was taking baby steps and feeling every day, "I can do this."

HUBBARD: The thought of going an hour without a beer was unbearable, much less a day, much less the rest of my life. I asked Stevie, "What happens? What goes on when you're sober?" He said after about five or six months, it was like he took off a pair of boxing gloves that had always been on his hands and he could finally play guitar. I told him that he had always been great, and he said, "No, once I got sober, there was nothing between me and my music." That was the first thing that gave me hope and it finally clicked, and I started going to meetings and got a sponsor. I thought my life was over: "If I can't drink a beer, I'm doomed." I had no way of knowing that it was just beginning. I'm not sure anyone other than Stevie could have put me on that road.

RONNIE EARL: Stevie came in and sat in with me whenever he could, which was a blessing and an honor itself, but there was one night at Lupo's in Providence, Rhode Island, that changed my life. I was high and pretty messed up when Stevie walked in, and I noticed a sticker on his guitar case that said, "Say No to Drugs." Those simple words hit me like a ton of bricks—because it was Stevie, not someone preaching. It was a signpost on my road to getting sober, which I finally did six months later. Stevie didn't say a word to me about this, but he showed me the way. He had gotten sober, and I took note of the fact that he was still playing so beautifully, with just as much power but even more focus and clarity. What a beautiful man.

SCOTT PHARES: Stevie was a huge, positive influence on my getting sober. He spoke at several AA meetings I attended. He was a role model for sobriety just as he had been as a musician and guitarist when we were teenagers.

LAYTON: Stevie was frustrated, because he felt he couldn't meet people as "Stevie Ray, regular guy." It was always, "Oh, Stevie Ray Vaughan!" He'd say, "I'd like to meet someone that has no idea who I am or what I do so I can just talk to them and they won't be fawning all over me." Now that he was sober, it was really important for him to be able to speak to people just as a human being without all the trappings of his fame.

Stevie with Otis Rush, one of his heroes, backstage at Antone's, 1988. *(J.P. Whitefield)*

SHANNON: He refused to sign autographs at meetings. He didn't think it was appropriate. He'd say, "Not here." One of the cool things about getting sober was that he now had a fellowship of people who simply saw him as a human being. He was surrounded by more people like that, and he got more honest feedback. The things we talked about in meetings were very deep, personal things. You could say anything that you wanted in there. He regained a lot of that innocence, as it were, and that made him very happy.

On November 22, 1987, U2 played the Frank Erwin Center as part of their massive *Joshua Tree* tour. Afterward, Bono and the Edge came to Antone's and joined Stevie and Jimmie onstage. They were nearing the end of an eight-month tour that had sold over two million tickets, and Antone's was packed in anticipation of the world's largest rock stars joining the city's brightest lights.

LAYTON: The place was packed, and they came in the side fire door; it had all been arranged beforehand. They came up onstage, and the cameras were there. They filmed the entire jam, because they were making their documentary, *Rattle and Hum.*

ANDREW LONG, *photographer:* Truth be told, Stevie and Jimmie were ripping it up prior to Bono and the Edge joining. I love U2, but they were so far out of their element, I couldn't wait for them to get offstage.

LAYTON: Bono was up there singing the blues and improvising the lyrics, like, "I'm down here at Antone's, and I got the blues, and I walked in the door." Just a bunch of whatever. It was really cheesy. We did a twelve-bar blues, and he was singing with his foot up on the monitor— real rock-star, posturing stuff. After there had been enough solos and verses, he goes, "All right! All right! Let's go!" and I thought he was ending the song. I did this big ending hit on the drums, and everyone else stopped, too. Bono yelled, "Hey, c'mon, let's keep goin'! I didn't really want to stop!" Then he just dropped the mic and walked out the door, and their whole entourage split.

22

IN STEP

Throughout the summer and fall of 1988, Stevie and Double Trouble were preparing to record their first studio album since 1985's *Soul to Soul*, after releasing three in just over two years to launch their career. It would be Vaughan's first sober effort, and he had to overcome some of the same fears that had haunted him before performing his first clean shows.

"It took four years," Vaughan said in 1989. "I guess the world had to turn around a few times, and so did I."

"It took a little time for him build up the confidence to go in sober, and to earn a little money to right the financial ship," says Hodges. "I also think he was a little hesitant about writing and didn't have a songbook of stuff ready to go. We had all exhausted a lot of energy on this fresh start and on the live album. It took a while to be ready."

Vaughan was searching for a producer, and Carlos Santana recommended Jim Gaines, a veteran engineer who had also worked with Van Morrison, Steve Miller, Huey Lewis, and Albert King. "I flew down to LA to meet the band, and one of the first things Stevie asked me was whether I was willing to try and record ten amps at once," says Gaines. "That is, of course, an engineering nightmare, but I told him I used six with Ronnie Montrose and three or four with Santana and that ten sounded like a fun challenge."

Gaines and Vaughan visited many studios, sometimes joined by

Hodges, Layton, and Shannon, including Allman Brothers' drummer Butch Trucks's brand-new Pegasus in Tallahassee, Florida, but none of them seemed quite right. They finally booked six weeks at New York's Power Station. By the time they arrived there to start sessions in January 1989, Stevie and Doyle had met for a few songwriting sessions, and it was clear that the intense process of getting sober and immersing themselves in the twelve-step program would be reflected in the album's songs.

BRAMHALL: Stevie and I got together to write songs and did what we always did: spend a few days just hanging out talking and catching up, which would point us in the direction we were going to head. We had both sobered up and knew that was something we had to deal with. It was important for us to write about our experiences with addiction. We wanted to directly confront the issues that surrounded our drug-and-alcohol days, which led to songs like "Wall of Denial" and "Tightrope."

BRAMHALL II: Stevie and my dad became even closer; they became partners in life with their sobriety. I think that a lot of people wanted something from Stevie, and it was really nice for him to have someone he could confide in and trust absolutely. He knew that my dad loved him, and they could bond in sobriety. Stevie had looked up to my dad since they first met, someone who was his mentor in the same way that Stevie was my mentor when I was younger. I think they felt safe with each other to confront difficult personal life topics and use that to inspire other people.

HODGES: "Wall of Denial" and "Tightrope" are really program songs.

SRV: "Tightrope" and "Wall of Denial" are a lot different musically, but lyrically, they are almost the same song, but just different phases of it. I really don't want to sound preachy, and I was afraid that I'd turn people off, but somewhere along the way, that quit mattering. It seems real important to me to write about that stuff. I spent so long with this image of "I'm cooler than so-and-so because I get higher than he does." I really believed it for a long time, but it's just not true. And I'd just as soon spend the rest of these years making it clear that it's not true.

LAPIDUS: Stevie was undergoing a big evolution. He was digging deep, struggling to figure out just what he wanted to say. He went, "Who am I

Guitar World cover shoot, Colgate University, April, 1988. *(Jonnie Miles)*

now? I'm different from who I was, but I'm still me, and musically, I'm still true to what I feel in my heart."

BRAMHALL: It never was a situation where I went in with all the words or he came in with all the music. I play very little guitar, but I would have ideas or a riff and sometimes Stevie would have some words, and we'd put them together. We'd always just take a few days to talk about what was going with us, then we would get together and write for five days, ten or twelve hours at a time. It got to the point where we grew confident that something good would happen.

SRV: I went back and forth between feeling really strongly about it and wondering if anybody really wants to hear this shit or not. With what I was trying to say, if they got turned off, it'd only be for a temporary time. I've been there before, when somebody would try to tell me that I had a problem. I'd go, "Of course I do! Goddamn it, don't you think I know that?" I just had to come to grips with it.

WYNANS: Chris and Tommy and I would get together and try to write songs, and we got Bill Carter and his wife, Ruth [Ellsworth], who had written "Willie the Wimp," to come over and play guitar because Stevie was out writing with Doyle. We were a little frustrated because he didn't really want to write with us. "Crossfire" started off with a bass riff Tommy had come up with, thinking it would be a Sam-and-Dave-type soul song.

BILL CARTER, *guitarist/singer/songwriter/cowriter of "Crossfire":* We just started jamming on Tommy's riff, with me playing guitar and muttering a vocal melody. Ruth sat there with a tape recorder, then went home and wrote the lyrics. They just happened to fit with the themes Stevie and Doyle were also writing about.

WYNANS: Ruth is an incredible lyricist. I don't think Stevie really wanted to do it, but he worked it up, and the response the first couple of times we played it was great. I was so happy that we had actually put something together that Stevie liked and that it worked so well.

CARTER: I did a run of shows opening for them in spring 1988, and we had just written the song. Stevie didn't know the words yet, so he called me out to sing it a few times.

HODGES: Stevie worked to make "Crossfire" what it became. I mentioned he could take a writing credit, too, and he said, "It's their song. I helped make it as good as I can, and they help me make my songs as good as they can."

CARTER: It wasn't changed much other than adding Stevie's incredible guitar playing, which made it great. I was, of course, happy that he liked it and recorded it and proud that it became his only number one hit. ["Crossfire" went to the top of the mainstream rock charts.]

JIM GAINES, In Step *producer:* Stevie was very nervous, wondering, "Can I do this without a little enhancement?" I have never done drugs, which probably helped me get the job; they didn't want anyone around who could be a distraction or temptation in that regard.

We went to New York planning to record at the Power Station, but it just didn't work out. Stevie and I didn't like the sounds, and the iso room was too small to take the amps Stevie wanted to run. We were booked there for six weeks, and they were not happy about us leaving after three days of rehearsal. We moved to Kiva Studios in Memphis.

LAYTON: It was very tedious at first. There was some trepidation because we knew it was our proving ground, that we had to show that we could make good records without anyone being high. Stevie felt the doubt and spent endless hours getting sounds.

SRV: It was kind of a difficult record to make. We had fun, but we started and stopped a lot of times because of the amp problems I was having. There were amps that I had to send back and forth to California to get worked on, because we couldn't get ahold of the right schematics for them. I had to go through a lot of speakers to find some that I really liked [EVs], and we ended up *spraying* every amp with these speakers.

GAINES: I was the first outsider to produce him, and we didn't know what our roles were going to be, so there was a little tension feeling each other out. And this whole record was a step away from what he had been doing. It wasn't easy. I view my role as enhancing what an artist does, not making demands to change, and I tried to push him to his best performances.

LAYTON: I think these sessions ended up producing the tightest band performances of our career, and we really worked at it.

GAINES: We cut for live. Some of the rhythms are overdubbed, but 90 percent of the solos are live, so everything had to be sounding good, and everyone had to be in sync before we started recording.

SRV: Most of the time, the whole band played together live. For some reason, in the room we were in, a lot of things sounded darker, tone-wise. The rooms were all wood. I was having a hard time getting amps to hold up: I'd turn 'em on, set 'em to a real good sound, turn 'em off to let 'em cool down, and when it was time to play and I'd turn 'em back on, one of 'em would die or start going, "ACKHHKHK" or "BLLPPPP."

LAYTON: Stevie spent an ungodly amount of time messing around with his guitars and amps. It took him six or seven hours to get started some days, which seemed crazy, but I think was symbolic of him being nervous and getting ready in whatever way he had to. It was like standing on top of a huge mountain going, "If I'm going to ski down this, first I have to make sure my boots are tight, and my skis are waxed . . ."

SRV: I'd hit a couple of notes, and it would start making bad, horrible noises. The setup changed from day to day. The amps were dying like flies. This sounds crazy, but I took thirty-two amps with me. I thought, if worst comes to worst, there'll always be something I can pull out of a road case. I'm glad I took so many amps, because we ended up having only about three or four that worked. In fact, I bought an old '59 Fender Bassman and used it on the same settings for the whole session. I loved it! It was the one amp that stayed right the whole time. All these newfangled custom amps kept falling apart.

WYNANS: Stevie's old routine when recording was to get high before every song, and this was the first time he had not done that. The sessions were a chore because we would play stuff over and over, and there was always something that Stevie wanted to try differently, mostly with his own rig. We had never had that kind of difficulty making a record before. It felt like he was projecting his anxiety onto all these things. None of us got frustrated about it in front of him. I recall sitting in a bar on Beale Street, telling the bartender, "I think I need one more." We had some rough days. We must have played the same song fourteen times, but we tried to never let our frustrations show to Stevie. We all knew what he was going through, and he really stepped up to bat. We made a great record, and his playing was fantastic.

SRV: I usually record the rhythm track first and then the solo. I was thinking about getting [rockabilly guitarist] Paul Burlison to play on the record, but he never came back into town! We'd talked about it a little bit. He was telling us about how he got the sounds on the old records:

he'd drop his amp, break a tube! But he never came back, so he's not on the record.

GAINES: Stevie wanted to set up his full live rig in the studio, as he told me when we met. Every other producer said, "No way." But he was doing a lot of experimenting with sounds, running all these amps on-stage, and he wanted that in the studio. We had eight to ten amps running all the time. We called it the Wall of Doom, and he kept blowing up amps. Stevie would spend hours getting the sounds he wanted, then an amp would blow. César Diaz was fixing them constantly.

WYNANS: At least they weren't in the room with us. He would go in there when he was playing, and it was so loud that it must have been like going to work at the airport. I don't know how he did it, but he just loved that power and volume as guitar players often do. That's what moved him.

GAINES: Away from the Wall of Doom, I had a Fender Vibratone and a stereo Gibson amp, two teeny amps, which would have gotten eaten up in the big room.

SRV: Usually, I had one Dumble, one Marshall, the Bassman, and a Super Reverb. I ran them all at the same time, but they were mic'ed differently and set differently. Sometimes, I ran the effects through them—when I say *effects,* I'm not talking about space stations, I'm talking about a Fuzz Face, a Tube Screamer, or a wah-wah pedal.

For the "Wall of Denial" solo, I used a Leslie, but it was noisy on the slow speed. So I took a Variac, lowered the voltage, and then put the Leslie on the fast speed, making the Leslie go a little slower than fast, without making any clunking noises as it went around. That was a new trick that I learned.

HODGES: Stevie liked Kiva, but he said, "It's got a buzz, a little hum that we have to figure out." The report at first was no one else could hear it, so you started to think he was nervous and making stuff up, but they brought in a sound tester, and it was there, though audible only to him.

GAINES: Because of all these amps running at once, we had some sort of weird magnetic hum. I tried everything to eliminate it and ended up building a chicken-wire cage to break up the frequency, and he played standing half in there. It was crazy, but it worked.

SRV: The weirdest part was that we had to build this thing that looked like a square baseball backstop, made out of chicken wire. There was either a radio station or some kind of microwave stuff that came through the studio—you'd be playing along, and all of a sudden, there'd be these weird clicks and buzzes coming out of the amps—but if I stood inside this *cage* that they made, it wouldn't happen. They caged me!

SHANNON: Stevie would do anything to get new, different, or better sounds, and he seemed to spend a lot of time messing with stuff on *In Step*. But his actual playing just flowed once he got down to it.

SRV: We got an idea of how we wanted "Tightrope" to go, and that was one of the songs that I just played rhythm on when we first cut it. I didn't like the tone I had when I was putting down the rhythm track, so when it came up to the solo point, I decided just to groove! It wasn't intentional. Then I went back and played the whole song again, with the old track a little bit in one side of the headphones, and I played the solo where I was supposed to the first time. We ended up using both tracks together. We might overdub, but we just do it by saying, "Okay, roll the tape!" The only other song with a rhythm track [behind the solo] is "Scratch-N-Sniff." When I was doing that solo, I hated everything I played. I went, "Hmm, let me try this one more time," and I turned on all the gadgets I had, including the wah.

LAYTON: Albert King showed up several times while we were recording. He kept picking on Stevie, and he asked if he could borrow some money. Stevie said, "How much do you need, Albert?" "About $3,000." Stevie said, "$3,000? Well, okay." Stevie loaned him the money pretty early on in the process, and six weeks later as we were finishing, Stevie said, "Hey, Albert, um . . . do you have that money?" And Albert goes, "What money is that?" Stevie says, "That money that I loaned you." "That money you loaned me?" "Yeah," said Stevie, "I lent you $3,000." And Albert goes, "Haw haw haw! Now, come on, Stevie! You know you owe me!"

SHANNON: Albert would punch the talkback mic right in the middle of a song. "Yo, Stevie!" We'd stop, and he'd say, "When you come around to that one part, you should do so-and-so." Stevie was very patient. We weren't going to tell him to quit it, but he was really . . .

WYNANS: He was messin' with the groove! We'd be 90 percent done with a great-feeling track, and he'd bust in and say, "You're gonna have to turn that tom-tom mic down."

LAYTON: Bon Jovi was coming to town, and Albert says, "Hey, Stevie! I got the Bon Jovis callin' me. Are they big?"

Stevie said, "Yeah, Albert. They're a huge band."

Albert says, "They want me to come out and play with them, but I'm gonna go over to Arkansas and play cards with my girlfriend."

SRV: The record took a while to do because of the amp problems and also because, when I write songs, sometimes they have to grow for a while. We can rehearse, rehearse, rehearse, and it just sounds like we chopped, chopped, chopped.

LAYTON: Stevie said, "There's something I need to do. I want to record 'Riviera Paradise' because I need to make amends. This is the time. Let's turn the lights off." We turned all of the lights off so we were in total darkness. I couldn't see anyone. The engineers weren't even ready for the take, because the cue mix in the headphones was all wrong. He began to play just as they started the tape. It was really an instinctual thing, because the arrangement hadn't been discussed.

GAINES: Stevie told me he had an instrumental called "Riviera Paradise" he wanted to try, and I said that I only had nine minutes of tape left. He said, "Don't worry. It's only four minutes long." We dimmed the lights, and they started playing this gorgeous song, which went on to six minutes, seven minutes, seven and a half . . .

The song is absolutely incredible, totally inspired, dripping with emotion, and we are about to run out of tape! I was jumping up and down waving my arms, but everyone was so wrapped up in their playing that no one was paying me any mind. I finally got Chris's attention and emphatically gave him the cut sign. He started trying to flag down Stevie, but he was hunched over his guitar with his head bent down in a dark room. Finally, he looked up, and they brought the song down just in time. It ended, and a few seconds later, the tape finished, and the studio was silent except for the sound of the empty reel spinning around.

We cut the song a few more times, but it sounded like Muzak compared to that first, magical version.

SHANNON: I don't recall ever having played "Riviera Paradise" as a band before that.

WYNANS: Stevie looked at "Riviera Paradise" as a movie soundtrack, a beautiful, soulful tune that could be thought of as backing up some touching love story. That song supplied such a pleasurable moment during the live shows. After all of the turbulent rock songs and powerful blues songs, it offered a meditative moment that was very touching.

LAYTON: Stevie described it as "praying through the guitar." It was great to be able to play a song with so much dimension to it. With that song, you feel so relaxed, calm, and smooth.

SHANNON: Stevie always played what he was feeling inside, as opposed to "with feeling." There is a big difference.

SRV: I wrote "Riviera Paradise" about four or five years ago. "Travis Walk" we've been doing for about three months. "Love Me Darlin'" I've been doing since I was about three—or at least ten years. "Wall Of Denial" we played in the warehouse; that's all. I never learned how to sing it quite right before we did it for the record. "Tightrope" we'd done at two gigs. "Scratch-N-Sniff" we tried to do at one or two gigs. "House Is Rockin'" we'd done at two gigs. It was mostly new tunes.

GAINES: I think the place where I might have pushed him the most was the vocals, where I wouldn't let him get by with just anything. We paid more attention to it than he usually had, and I think it paid off. He hated singing, so he didn't want to spend any more time with vocals than he had to, which is not uncommon amongst the great guitar players.

There were times that he was in the studio by himself, lights down after midnight, and he would start playing Hendrix and you would swear that Jimi was in the building. It's a different side of the blues, and he could duplicate it amazingly well. I felt privileged to make this record with Stevie.

The final sessions, which included vocal overdubs, some guitar parts, and horns for "Crossfire" and "Love Me Darlin'" played and arranged by old friend Joe Sublett, were cut at Los Angeles' Sound Castle studios.

They also recorded the solo acoustic version of "Life by the Drop," written by Bramhall and his wife, Barbara Logan. It was left off the record, and released on 1991's *The Sky Is Crying*.

GAINES: Stevie told me in Memphis that he had a song he wanted to play solo acoustic and that he didn't see the need to do it with everyone standing around watching, that we could do it alone later. We just used some excellent Neumann mics and cut it. I thought it fit perfectly with the rest of the material, but they made the decision not to include it on *In Step*.

BARBARA LOGAN: It wasn't really about alcoholism, as most people take it. It was really about Doyle watching Stevie's success, seeing him attain those dreams they had talked about together for so long. It's more about taking it one step at a time and it all ties together if you know the suffering of the dry drunk.

Doyle had started writing "Life by the Drop" before the *In Step* writing sessions and played a bit of it for Stevie, who loved it and kept asking him about "that Drop song" but he had not finished it. Doyle came home one night and told me this and played the song, and the last verse just came to me. That's all I can tell you. I am not a singer or a musician but it just came out. He took it to Stevie, who loved it—but never even told Doyle he recorded it!

SRV: I did record one song [for *In Step*] with the twelve-string acoustic—just me. I recorded it that way because it sounded more personal. However, the more we worked on it—I did several takes—the more the producer and myself heard it as a band song.

HODGES: We left "Life by the Drop" off the album with the thought that he might do it differently. The power of the song was immediately clear.

The biggest debate was sequencing. An album should flow to listeners' emotions. I've seen some bands be haphazard with sequencing, but Stevie really got the importance, as did Gregg Allman and Otis Redding—artists who had grown up changing their sets as they watched the audience react and were attuned to the way people heard and felt their music.

LAYTON: Stevie's ear was incredible. When we were mixing "Scratch-N-Sniff," Stevie left the room, and the engineer changed this tiny thing.

There are three very similar rhythm guitar parts, which were all treated a bit differently with reverbs and EQs. One of the parts was buried, and the engineer barely changed its reverb. Stevie walked back in and asked, "What did y'all change? You changed something on one of the guitars." No one else would have noticed this.

SUBLETT: Stevie called and asked me to put together a horn section. He had wanted us to play on five or six songs, but Jim Gaines was like, "Oh, we have a lot to do," so it ended up being two.

GAINES: We were mixing and doing vocal and guitar overdubs and had a busy schedule, but I also thought it was a bad idea to put horns on too many songs unless he wanted to take a horn section on the road.

SUBLETT: I brought in [trumpeter] Darrell Leonard, played tenor, and overdubbed a baritone. It was a real pleasure because there was no drama. It was all civilized, and the music was so good, and it was the first time I had seen him since those awful Opera House shows. Stevie pulled me aside and said, "Come out to the car; I want to play you some stuff," and he started playing me different songs on the cassette player. We could have listened on the giant speakers in the studio, but it's the old-school thing that you test songs by hearing them how people really listen.

But he also wanted to speak privately. It was the making-amends thing from the twelve-step program. I did not feel like he had to make amends to me at all, so when he started with, "If I offended you or disrespected you . . ." I said, "No, you haven't, and you don't have to do this." But he said, "You have to let me do this," so I did, and then we hugged. He was probably 150 pounds, but when he'd hug me, I'd feel like my frame was going to break because he was so strong and so sincere. It was a very sweet moment. I was just so happy to have him back.

BRANDENBURG: When they reached the making-amends step, Tommy called and said getting sober saved his and Stevie's life. A few days later, I got a similar call from Whipper, and they both said Stevie would be calling. I came home to an answering machine message that simply said, "Cee, this is Stevie. I need to talk with you, and I will call you back. I love you, man, and thanks for always loving me. Talk to ya later. Love ya. Bye."

HODGES: We sat in a studio trying to come up with a name, and Stevie wanted to get the word *step* or *steps* in there, because of the twelve steps and the saying, "When the elevator's broken, take the steps."

HUBBARD: Stevie and I were in different groups and didn't see each other that often. On November 13, 1988, I got my one-year chip, and after the meeting, about ten of us went to a Mexican restaurant to celebrate, and Stevie Ray and his mom walked in. I went over and showed him the chip, and he hugged me and introduced me to his mom: "This is Ray Wylie. He's got a year." It meant the world to me. He was a big star, but he came over, sat down, and talked to everyone in my group.

He truly cared about other people's sobriety. We were getting ready to leave, and he came over and asked if I was working the steps. I said I had finished nine and was working on ten, eleven, and twelve, and he said, "Well, there ain't no elevators. You got to take the steps." He knew the book. He would walk the walk, not just talk the talk. He lived on spiritual principles.

RICKERT: Stevie never consciously tried to court an audience of sober people, but of course, people in that world gravitated towards him, saying, "I'm going to try because he did it." He showed that it could be done and that you could be bigger and better than ever on the other side. It wasn't easy. He put in the work and deserves any praise he gets for that.

BRAMHALL II: Stevie was very involved in my sobriety. One time, he heard I was going through a hard time and he called the house, and my dad handed me the phone and said, "Stevie wants to talk to you." He was really concerned about me and just talked about life and being healthy emotionally and physically. He wanted me to know that he was there to help me with anything that I was going through. He would always go out of his way to make sure to connect to whoever he was speaking with in the most genuine and deep way.

23

CHANGE IT

In Step was released on June 6, 1989, representing the recorded rebirth of a new, clean, and happy Stevie Ray Vaughan. It was the first time in a very long time that anyone could apply that last adjective to Stevie, and the album's success confirmed everyone's positive feelings, as it spawned a series of hit singles, including the powerful Stax-influenced chart-topper "Crossfire" and the hard-swinging "Tightrope." Lyrically, both songs addressed the travails and pressures of life as a star musician as well as a commitment to spiritual revelation and growth.

Stevie wrote or cowrote with Doyle Bramhall six of the album's ten tracks, which were rounded out by such blues staples as Buddy Guy's "Leave My Little Girl Alone," Howlin' Wolf's "Love Me Darlin'," and Willie Dixon's "Let Me Love You Baby." The disc closes with the Stevie-penned instrumental masterpiece "Riviera Paradise."

WYNANS: Everyone was so excited. Every track seemed to jump off the record. Radio picked up a song or two. We knew we created the music that everyone in the public and even in the band had been waiting to hear. We thought it was a step up, grounded in the blues but not as traditional and more accessible without being calculating at all. I thought there was some really good songwriting on *In Step* as well. It was probably our masterpiece.

SHANNON: Back on the road, Stevie was so great, it was just frightening.

LAYTON: Everyone even quit smoking, and it was quite a switch from just a couple of years earlier. Things were starting to get really good.

RICKERT: We had a surge in attendance. *In Step* was fresh and new, and the label was putting money into marketing and advertising. We did interviews, promotions, radio station stops—all the things that one did to break a record, and we put a lot of effort into it. We also started adding a lot of college towns with fresh audiences. Stevie never failed to impress.

SUBLETT: I had Stevie back. He was sweet and could be the goofiest guy in the world. He wasn't the serious guy with the hat. He was that guy onstage, but the Stevie you hung out with was this really fun, silly guy. He took his music seriously, but he didn't take himself seriously. That guy had vanished, and I felt like I had him back.

BRAMHALL II: Stevie was like a big brother to me, and he would always make me feel special and welcome. As his success escalated, there might be twenty thousand people at a show and a crazy scene with a lot of demands on him—photographs, interviews, meet and greets, autograph signings—but he would always make sure to make me feel special. He'd take me back to the bus and play me a bootleg or Jimi Hendrix demo that only a few people had ever heard. No matter what else was going in his life, he was always the same person to me: gracious, kind, sweet, and open.

RICKERT: One time, we had a day off in Philadelphia, near where I grew up. My sister called and said she was going to get the whole family together since I hadn't seen many of them in a long time. Wonderful! So I asked Stevie if it was okay for me to be gone most of the day, saying that I would grab a cab to go see my family. He looks at me, serious, sad, and a little angry, so I asked what was wrong, and he says, "So, I'm like chopped liver?"

I said, "Stevie, this is my family, dude! I can't vouch for them." But he really wanted to come, so I invited everyone. We packed the bus, stopped at a grocery store and loaded it up, and piled out at this suburban home in Levittown. I had blue-haired aunts and uncles who had never seen a tour bus and had no idea who Stevie was or why he was wearing cowboy boots, and younger cousins and nieces and nephews, telling them, "He's as big as Bob Hope or Johnny Carson." And they're

Salmon fishing in Alaska with Skip Rickert, 1990. *(Courtesy Skip Rickert)*

like, "That guy with long hair?" Stevie rolled right into the kitchen and started chopping up stuff and making salsa and going out and flipping burgers, and everyone loved him and we all had a ball. Stevie was so happy to immerse himself in a family.

GARY WILEY: Steve was very much a family person. He came to every family get-together he possibly could and would pick some tunes with Uncle

John. The fame that he achieved did not go to his head. It was just like when we were kids; we always had fun, and he blended in. Unless you asked him directly, he didn't say much about his life as a musician. We were so happy to see him there, just one of the members of the family.

CASCIO: Stevie and Jimmie both were always real generous whenever they were playing in town. Martha would get the head count of who wanted to go, and they'd provide tickets and passes and sometimes a limo that would drive us right to the backstage entrance.

SUBLETT: I did three California shows with Stevie and B. B. King on the *In Step* tour [August 25–27, 1989]. The first night at Concord Pavilion, Stevie said, "I want to show you something." We went into his dressing room, and he opened up this briefcase filled with herbs and showed me this spirulina that he drank every night for energy. He said, "Come back five minutes before we play," and we drank it. He transferred the obsessive gene into being a healthy guy. He still had a ritual before he played, but now it was all about being a clean machine.

BRAMHALL II: After he stopped doing drugs, I said to him, "You're playing on .011s now. What happened to the big strings?" And he said, "I stopped doing cocaine, so I can't do that anymore—I can actually feel my fingers now!"

LUCKETT: When Stevie got clean, he still had the hunger for adventure. My company bought him a motorized skateboard, which he loved to zip around on. As soon as sound check was over, he'd grab me, and we'd jump on and go all over the place. He'd have his hat on, and we'd ride through the filling parking lots, and people were just amazed to see him. "Look, it's Stevie Ray Vaughan!"

RICKERT: Stevie got more and more interested in doing stuff on the road, and usually much of the band and road crew would come along. So we went salmon fishing on the Kenai Peninsula in Alaska and out to the easternmost part of North America when we were in Halifax, Nova Scotia.

But one of the most memorable nights was one of the simplest. We were playing close to Gettysburg, Pennsylvania, staying in a motel where the doors faced the parking lot. We dragged our chairs out, and eight or ten of us sat there in a line and talked about the

Stevie with his motorized skateboard, July 4, 1990, Lake Compounce, Bristol, CT.
(Donna Johnston)

world for hours. We were so close to the battlefields where so many people had lost their lives and contemplating that spurred a great discussion. The flow was organic and easy, and we all enjoyed each other's company.

Throughout 1988 and 1989, the Fabulous Thunderbirds and Stevie and Double Trouble toured together extensively as legitimate co-bills, with neither band dominating the other commercially. It was the most time Jimmie and Stevie had spent together since they were very young, and they began to reestablish a closer relationship.

"They were constantly together on the bus and began to develop the relationship they really had not had time to develop," says Mark Proct, at the time the Fabulous Thunderbirds' manager. "Their relationship absolutely improved and deepened. It had been difficult for Jimmie to deal with his little brother who had started out idolizing him becoming a huge star. The success of 'Tuff Enuff' made it easier, because it put them on a closer level of success—and no one was happier about that success than Stevie."

Double Trouble with Skip Rickert (far right), visiting the furthest point east in North America, outside of St. John's, Newfoundland. *(Courtesy Skip Rickert)*

Says Wynans, "Stevie talked about Jimmie all the time. He was Jimmie's biggest fan, and we wanted the Thunderbirds to play with us as often as possible."

"There was normal sibling rivalry between Stevie and Jimmie," says Denny Freeman. "Stevie worshipped his big brother, who gave him a rough time trying to guide him in a normal way. But that all just disappeared as they toured together. Jimmie was just so proud of Stevie and loved him better than anything in the world. The truth is, there were no two people that Stevie and Jimmie loved more than each other."

On September 2 and 3, 1989, Stevie and Double Trouble and Jimmie and the T-Birds opened for the Who at the Houston Astrodome and Dallas's Cotton Bowl, performing in front of over sixty thousand people at each show. Before the Astrodome gig, they also performed in the afternoon in the parking lot, with singer/songwriter Joe Ely opening.

"I was playing with Joe, and it had to be at 110 degrees onstage," says David Grissom. "I thought Stevie would be looking to save energy and not

"Texas Flood" outside the Houston Astrodome,
9/20/89. *(Tracy Anne Hart)*

sweat out a gallon of water, but he gave it everything he had. The parking
lot was just solid bodies as far as you could see. I stood right next to his
amp, a single two hundred–watt Marshall Major into a Dumble 4×12 cabinet, and the best way to describe the sound is, 'Oh my God!' "

Jimmie and Stevie were also both part of an *Austin City Limits* fifti-
eth birthday tribute to W. C. Clark filmed on October 10, 1989, along with
Angela Strehli, Lou Ann Barton, Denny Freeman, Kim Wilson, and Clark's
young protégé Will Sexton. Afterward, Stevie and Double Trouble performed a twelve-song set, marking their second appearance on the vener-
able show. Vaughan delivered a breathtaking performance, resulting in a
show that Terry Lickona has often called his most memorable in over forty
years of producing *Austin City Limits*.

LICKONA: This was Stevie Ray completely clean and sober and at the very top of his game. He was blowing everyone else away, and with ease. It was like a higher power channeling through him and his guitar, and to see him play up close during that time was overwhelming. And it was such a contrast to the first time he appeared on the show. For all those reasons, it's the show I cite as my favorite whenever I'm asked after forty-three seasons.

I certainly knew that he had cleaned up and was a much different person to deal with; you could actually sit down and talk to him. Still, it's only natural to be skeptical when you hear these things about an artist who has had abuse issues. You wonder if they really changed for more than a week or two. That day, he was having really bad allergies and struggling with his voice because of congestion, and I offered him allergy medicine, which he kindly accepted. I gave him the little white pill, and he looked at it very carefully, asking, "You're sure this is allergy medicine, right?" He was very mindful about avoiding temptation and any people who might be likely to take him over the edge again. His playing and singing that night were absolutely peak.

Two weeks later, on October 25, 1989, the Fire Meets the Fury tour, featuring Stevie and Jeff Beck, launched in Minneapolis. It would run through December 3 in Oakland, California, twenty-nine cities with Beck and Vaughan alternating opening and closing the shows. The tour was put together by Epic, in part to promote Beck's new album, *Jeff Beck's Guitar Shop*.

HODGES: I got the phone call about the Beck tour and thought it would work musically and maybe present an opportunity to move from civic centers and large theaters to arenas as co-headliners rather than support for a Robert Plant or Moody Blues tour. Stevie was in favor, and we began negotiating who would open and close which shows. I wanted Stevie as the headliner in Dallas and New York, because Madison Square Garden is simply a special place. We sold it out, and it was a fabulous night. The whole tour was special all the way through, and most nights Stevie and Jeff did "I'm Going Down" together at the end.

With Jeff Beck during the Fire Meets the Fury tour, at the Centrum, Worcester, MA 11/8/89. *(Donna Johnston)*

LAYTON: We were playing big sold-out arenas and selling records, and everyone was going, "The only place we can go from here is up." For the first times in our lives, all of us really had our shit together on every level.

GLAUB: I hung out with them in the locker room at the sports arena in LA when they played with Jeff Beck [December 1, 1989]. This was the first time I'd seen him since that night in London before he got sober. He seemed like a completely different person. He was with his girlfriend, and it was clear he was in a much better place. He seemed real calm.

SHANNON: When we got sober, it was our first introduction to "life." Bank accounts, insurance, taxes, payments on this and that, investments— the realities of life that most people deal with. We escaped that for so long, living in this musicians' dream world all of the time with somebody else doing everything for us. Stevie started to mature in many ways, and he became more comfortable with who and what he was.

LEEDS: During the Jeff Beck tour, we did a radio giveaway where Stevie and Jeff signed twenty-four Fender Stratocasters. I brought them to their hotel in Minneapolis at 1:00 a.m. after the first show and laid them out on the lobby floor. It was a hotel with big tube elevators that you can see descending. I have twenty-four new Strats in open cases and a handful of Sharpies, and I hear the elevator and look up, and there's Stevie descending with his arms full of dirty laundry. The guy just played an amazing show and could have had someone take care of this, but part of being in recovery is taking care of your own shit. He walked by and said he'd be right back and went over to the front desk to fill out the paperwork. Then he came back, got down on his knees, and happily signed all twenty-four guitars. I can still hear the Sharpies squeaking.

SRV: I feel like I've gotten more in touch with [the blues]. It's usually when I go and see somebody play who's playing clubs and isn't used to running around in a fancy tour bus and playing arenas. There's a difference there. On one side of the coin, it's like, "The guy sounds that way so we can't sell him," but on the other side of the coin is, "I've been sold, so I can't sound like that." Every time I get to hear somebody sound real, once again I get the chance to come home, inside. That makes me want to play that way even that much more and still snicker when someone says, "Hey, the record sold!"

SHANNON: I never got used to playing with Stevie or took it for granted. It only got more and more exciting.

PAUL SHAFFER: Every time Stevie was on our show, I was struck by how great he was but also how easy he was to work with and how willing he was to try anything, to follow us right out of his comfort zone on songs like "Walk on the Wild Side" and "Baker Street." His easygoing nature was unusual for a star lead guitarist. If you are going to be that great, there's got to be something that makes everyone follow you, whether it's confidence or bravura. He certainly had that leadership quality, and everyone did follow him, but he didn't have a superstar ego at all.

Vaughan's lack of rock star attitude extended toward his personal and musical relationship with the band. "He never told us what to play," says Shannon. "He just played and we followed."

He also treated his crew and anyone else he came in contact with as equals. "I would drive the merch truck all night to the next gig, then sleep in the cab in the parking lot," recalls Luckett. "Stevie always told catering to bring me plates of food, and I would be very touched just that he knew I was there and thought about me."

HODGES: Stevie was unique in his sensitivity towards his bandmates and his awareness of their emotional issues—even if he was the cause of them. I don't think he ever lost sight of his skills at motivating people and being aware of who they were. No one was just a something or somebody. Any person at any job at any level was a person of interest to be respected. If someone said, "I'm just the bus driver," he'd say, "You're not just anything."

LAYTON: That was one of the things most precious about Stevie. One time at Madison Square Garden, [publicist] Charles Comer was looking for Stevie, who was riding his motorized skateboard through the bowels of the hall. He saw an old janitor sweeping and stopped to chat with him as the guy leaned on his broom. Charles said, "We've got very important people waiting for you in the dressing room, and you have to get up there." Stevie said, "I'm talking to this gentleman, and when I'm done, I'll go on up."

LUCKETT: I was ready to accept an exciting offer to go on the road with someone else and I was trying to figure out how I could tell Stevie, who I loved. He came walking off the stage, and I was right behind the curtain, thinking I might talk to him, and as soon as he exited the spotlight, he saw me and said, "Your gold record for *In Step* is in the mail!" I almost cried. Who gives the merch guy a gold record? I realized right then that I could never leave him and felt ashamed I had even considered it.

HODGES: I think Stevie had an awareness of underpaying, overpaying, paying right. He was smart and generous and had a real balanced constitution about being fair that was unique and refreshing. He was keenly aware of the importance of the band—but also of whose picture was on the cover of every album.

24

FAMILY STYLE

When the Fabulous Thunderbirds and Double Trouble toured together, the brothers would often play duets on a single instrument, a one-of-a-kind doubleneck guitar made for Stevie by Robin Guitars. Stevie would sit while Jimmie stood behind him, reaching his arms around his little brother's back as they played the Ventures' surf instrumental hit "Pipeline," an early Vaughan brothers favorite.

"That whole idea came from something we saw the rockabilly kids, the Collins Kids, do in the '50s," says Jimmie Vaughan. "Joe Maphis [country guitarist] would come up behind Larry Collins, and they'd play his Mosrite double-neck at the same time."

All that playing together got them talking with more frequency and seriousness about something they had kicked around for years: recording an album together. "I want to make a record with Stevie—just me and him," Jimmie Vaughan said in 1989. "I don't want a 'guitar battle' record; I want to see what kind of parts we can both come up with."

Less than year later, in early 1990, the time had come to make the "brothers" album.

"Jimmie and Stevie had been talking about doing that album for a long time, but even once they were committed, it was slow going because of their scheduling," says Denny Freeman. "Finally, they both just decided they were going to do it."

A *Family Style* outtake. *(Lee Crum/ Courtesy Sony Music Entertainment)*

With a simple commitment, they carved out a small window of time, and Mark Proct took the lead on making arrangements.

"Stevie wanted to record with his brother, and after *In Step*, the timing of this just felt right," says Hodges. "We surrendered some control of the environment to get it done, because Stevie wanted the atmosphere to be as harmonious as possible, which can be difficult in a situation with two leaders, two managers, new musicians, and a new producer."

"The short list of producers was Don Was, Billy Gibbons, and Nile Rodgers," says Proct. "Don was booked through the year, and it became clear that [ZZ Top manager] Bill Ham wasn't going to let Billy produce. Nile jumped up enthusiastically. Jimmie was intrigued by him, and Stevie liked him a lot from the *Let's Dance* sessions."

Rodgers was not an obvious choice; the Chic guitarist was fresh off work-
ing with Duran Duran, Diana Ross, Depeche Mode, Eddie Murphy, and the
B-52s and best known for his production of *Let's Dance,* Madonna's *Like a
Virgin,* and Sister Sledge's *We Are Family.* He was a pop funk hit-maker.

PROCT: It was a very spontaneous decision. It all seems to make sense now,
but Jimmie really wanted to think outside the box and do things no
one thought he would do. Nobody would have ever suggested the guy
known for Madonna, Duran Duran, and Bowie, and that helped make
Jimmie a huge advocate.

FREEMAN: One thing about Jimmie that's always been true is if you think you
can predict what he's gonna do, you'll be wrong. Nile Rodgers was obviously a very successful guitarist, producer, bandleader, and innovator,
but most people wouldn't think that the Vaughan brothers would work
with him, and I'm certain that made him more attractive to Jimmie.

PROCT: We had a meeting, and they all really liked each other, and Nile
was available in our window. Then he went, "What do you have? Play
me some material." Um . . . we really had no completed songs, though
Stevie and Jimmie both had sketches. We had a short time before we'd
start recording, and Jimmie took his idea for "Tick Tock" to Tulsa to
finish it with Jerry Williams, and Stevie got together with Doyle to finish a few songs.

BRAMHALL: At the end of our *In Step* writing sessions, I had ideas for "Hard
to Be" and "Long Way from Home" and Stevie had an idea for "Telephone Song." If we had finished them, they'd have been on there, but we
didn't, so we put them aside. Things have a way of working themselves
out, and it's interesting that when we got back together to write for *Family
Style,* it was like, "Well, we do have those three songs we can work on."

FREEMAN: Jimmie had a great riff for "Baboom / Mama Said" and needed
help making it a song. He asked to meet up, saying they had to show
the record company something and didn't really have finished songs. I
got to the Sound Lab in Dallas first and was smoking a cigarette when
they pulled up in Stevie's big red Caprice convertible. Stevie was driving, and they both looked great. It's a visual I'll always remember.

I sat down at a Hammond organ, Jimmie played his riff, and we started jamming, and I said, "It needs a middle eight," as John Lennon called a bridge. It had a James Brown funk feel, so I suggested holding one chord, then just going up or down a step, as he did on his great jams. Jimmie went from B, briefly up a half step to C, back to the riff, and when Stevie's improvised solo comes in, it goes up a whole step to C♯. Then Stevie took out a primitive drum machine and programmed a funky drumbeat, and we recorded with Jimmie playing bass. I was impressed that he knew how to program it so well, because we weren't drum machine kind of guys.

Jimmie took half credit and gave me and Stevie a quarter, which seemed more than fair. My contribution was simple, but going to another key was that missing ingredient.

LAPIDUS: The songwriting for *Family Style* was a completely different process than *In Step* because he was sharing the record with his brother, but he was also writing on his own and with Doyle. What came out of them there was something that was pure in a different way.

PROCT: Nile's next question was, "Who's the band?" And again, I had to say that we didn't have one. Jimmie and Stevie didn't want to use Double Trouble or people from the T-Birds. They wanted to do something different.

JIMMIE VAUGHAN: We didn't have to go by anything we've done in the past. It was a new beginning.

RODGERS: The situation didn't even feel a little daunting. That's what I do. I loved them and had nothing but their best interests at heart.

PROCT: Nile called back and said, "I think I have the guys for this project."

On February 13, *In Step* was certified gold, and on February 22, it won the Grammy Award for Best Contemporary Blues Album, a great honor but one which annoyed Hodges a bit; he didn't think Stevie should be pigeonholed in the genre category. A couple of weeks later, Jimmie and Stevie convened at Ardent Studios in Memphis with Rodgers and his handpicked band to begin recording *Family Style*.

PROCT: Nile was there with Al Berry [bass] and Larry Aberman [drums]. The guys all introduced themselves and started cutting basic tracks.

AL BERRY, *bassist on* Family Style: Larry and I had done quite a few things with Nile but were still quite young, and we were thrilled when he asked us to do this record.

RODGERS: Al, Larry, and Rich [Hilton, engineer, keyboards] were some of the finest musicians I knew. They were my band on my VH1 TV show *New Visions*. I knew they could easily cut the gig, and I believed that they'd become the Vaughan Brothers Band.

BERRY: Honestly, I had no idea of the depth of Stevie's talents. I knew, but I didn't know. I loved his playing, but having a close-up view of his passion and drive and his command of the instrument as well as the way he could come up with ideas off-the-cuff was heavy, humbling, and very inspiring. Once I grasped how serious both Stevie and Jimmie were, working with them became a life-changing experience.

PROCT: Stevie and Jimmie were as close as they ever were when we made the record, and these sessions were the opportunity for them to come together and really get to know each other. We did everything together.

BERRY: The true beauty was the relationship between the brothers and how they brought us all in. They trusted us enough to sit down and have meals and spend all this time together, which really built our confidence and the vibe. We sat and listened as they spoke about their journey and their separation, about Jimmie running away from home to be a musician and how Stevie was alone then but also got the confidence to do this thing. All these years having this dream of playing together, and here they were. It was an honor to be a part of. We took in so many stories and so many great times. It was a bunch of guys being in the moment.

LARRY ABERMAN, *drummer on* Family Style: Jimmie was more vocal, but Stevie had a powerful nature and vibe. It felt very balanced between them, and there was a lot of give-and-take. It was very collaborative, which I was too young and naïve to fully appreciate. I've since been in a lot of situations where the band is treated as "the help."

BERRY: I never felt for a second that they thought we were below them, and their attitude towards us translated into the music.

Jimmie and Stevie songwriting with Nile Rodgers, Memphis, TN, 1990, during the
Family Style sessions. *(Mark Proct)*

PROCT: There was a genuine acceptance and camaraderie, and it impacted the way the whole thing proceeded, and that's how it had to be. The songs were barely arranged, so everyone was working on them together. Everyone was throwing ideas off of each other. Nile was writing words for "Tick Tock" as they were starting to record it.

ABERMAN: Jimmie took out his acoustic guitar and said, "I've got this song I've been working on, but it's not quite done. I'd like to know what you guys think." He starts playing the hook: "Tick tock, tick tock, tick tock, people/ Time's slipping away," and goes, "What do you think?" We were all like, "It's a fucking smash!" It wasn't done, but the theme was there, and it was so good.

RODGERS: I'd always loved Kool and the Gang's music, and the intro to their song "Who's Gonna Take the Weight," starts with the phrase "People, the world today is in a very difficult situation." I vibed off that and wrote the start of a song: "People of the World," which Jimmie and I retooled into "Tick Tock."

PROCT: Stevie and Jimmie really connected in the studio with no one telling them what to do. Nile was so creative, a great conduit who was somehow very freeing.

BERRY: Nile has a rare gift of allowing you to be your authentic self in a nonjudgmental way, which creates magic. And he has an amazing way of then manipulating what you did into being even more magical.

JIMMIE VAUGHAN: You can imagine how special making this record was for us as brothers. We wanted to do a record that showed everything that we could do on the guitar. It's got Albert King, B. B. King, Johnny Watson, T-Bone Walker, Lonnie Mack, Hubert Sumlin, Freddie King. It's like a short history of who we listened to.

ABERMAN: They had a record player in the lounge and their favorite records—all the influences that ended up being on that album, notably James Brown and Albert King. Jimmie just kept saying, "Check this out." He wasn't giving us instructions about how something should sound. They were creating a vibe, filling the space with the music they loved and wanted us to understand. Having all their guitars there—most of which they didn't use—did the same type of thing.

Playing video games with guitar tech René Martinez, Memphis, TN, 1990, during the *Family Style* sessions. *(Mark Proct)*

JIMMIE VAUGHAN: We got to spend all that time together, and the whole project was just fun.

BRAMHALL: *Family Style* was really loose, no pressure whatsoever.

ABERMAN: Nile maintains a loose environment, encouraging people to bring friends by and for everyone to make suggestions, and that was right in line with what Stevie and Jimmie wanted. "Long Way from Home" had a train beat on the demo, and we did a take like that, then I started playing a more pop beat that I just felt. Jimmie and Stevie sat back and were like, "Eh." It felt wrong to them, and Jimmie said, "I'm not sure I'm down with this," but Nile was raving about it and was adamant, and Jimmie and Stevie were really leaning on having an open mind, and that's what we used. They didn't want to do what they normally did with their own bands.

JIMMIE VAUGHAN: We didn't have anything to compare this project to. We [were] a "new artist." The Vaughan Brothers was something new. We wanted to say all the shit that we always wanted to say but couldn't for one reason or another, and I think we did that. I love it! There were a lot of times where I was thinking of something to do, and Stevie would already be doing it. I guess it comes from having the same blood, growing up together, and having a lot of the same influences.

ABERMAN: Sometimes the two of them would sit in the control room and play together, unplugged, and the thing that really impressed me was the way they tapped along with the time. The heel goes up and comes down on the beat, and they were in unison, doing exactly the same thing; it looked like the same leg. And the power of that groove was immense. It was like watching a great conductor of an orchestra emitting total control of the music with his body. Their time was unerring, and their playing was so physical and seemingly effortless. Both of them had these big strong hands and just owned the guitar; they exhibited total command, like the guitar was part of their body.

PROCT: Stevie and Doyle were finishing songs, which were not near complete the day we stepped into the studio. Some of them didn't even exist.

BERRY: Larry and I assumed that we were just there to get sounds and help them get the songs together for power guys like Nathan East and Steve Jordan. We were only booked for five days, but we were really clicking, and on the third day, Mark Proct pulled us into a room and said both guys were really happy with how things were going and asked if we could stick around a while longer. *The answer would be yes!*

RODGERS: Bringing other people in was never even a thought in my mind. It's funny how differently people experience the same situation. Maybe Al felt that way, because I didn't speak about it. I just called musicians to make a gig as I've done my entire professional life.

PROCT: There was no plan B! Nile had faith in those guys, and Stevie and Jimmie had totally open minds and were willing to trust him and see what happened. The connection was complete. From the first day those guys walked into the studio, it worked. After a couple of tracks, it was pretty obvious that this was the band.

BERRY: We were hitting a song a day with the most incredible ease and freedom. Stevie would come over and play a riff, and I'd start playing something or Jimmie would play something to Larry, who would hit a beat. It all went down in the most organic, beautiful way. For me, it felt like having the endorsement of the gods.

ABERMAN: The very first song we cut was "D/FW," and the feeling in the control room listening to the playback was like electricity, something I've only felt a couple of times. It was like you could see electricity in the room. It was the feeling of pure jubilation.

RODGERS: Stevie and Jimmie loved each other greatly. I couldn't for the life of me figure out why they hadn't recorded an album yet. So my approach was to get them over whatever invisible barrier existed that had kept that from happening until *Family Style*.

BERRY: Stevie talked about how bad of shape he had been in chemically, and as someone who didn't know him then, it was hard to believe, because he was the most loving, gentle, encouraging, inspiring spirit I've ever encountered. Whatever turned in him turned into the most beautiful thing. It was like working with someone who had discovered their angelic power.

ABERMAN: He was at the top of his game. His playing and singing were incredible, and he had this really lovely girlfriend that he loved. He seemed so peaceful. We'd go out and have these great dinners and talks, and then me and Al and Jimmie would go to hang out and have some drinks and René and Stevie would go their own way. One night, I urged Stevie to come with us, and he said, "No, man. I'm going back to my room to call my girl and to pray." I was blown away. This guy is at the top of his game. He can do whatever he wants, and that's what he wanted. He said a few times, "I don't know why I'm here. Hendrix is gone, and I almost died. I'm here for a reason." It took a couple of years, but his experience inspired me to get sober. Through his example, I could see what was possible.

On March 14, 1990, Stevie Ray Vaughan was named Musician of the Year and Decade at the Austin Music Awards, where he also collected several other awards. He flew in from Memphis to accept the honors and thanked the audience, saying, "I just want to thank God that I'm alive, and I want to thank all the people that loved me back to life so that I could be here with you today."

David Grissom was awarded Best Electric Guitarist at the same awards show and vividly recalls his interaction with Stevie that night. "He was so sweet and humble, with a gleam in his eye and a huge smile on his face the entire time, full of life and joy," says Grissom. "He was so gracious and welcoming to me, offering me a big congratulations. He still had a child-ishness about him in a healthy way, brimming with enthusiasm."

The "Brothers" sessions broke for about a month, and Stevie went back on the road. They reconvened at Dallas Sound Lab to record two more tracks, which would get them up to the minimum needed of ten, and to cut all the lead vocals. Some songs remained incomplete; they had essentially sung scratch lyrics with their scratch vocals in Memphis.

"We were still writing 'Long Way from Home' when they came down to Dallas, so we would write over at Stevie's house, then he'd invite me to the studio," recalled Bramhall. "I had a little room off to the side where I would keep working. He'd just stick his head in and talk, and we finished the song up like that, two or three words here and there over a two-day period."

Bramhall was in the studio for more than just songwriting; he played drums on the two new songs they recorded during the Dallas sessions, with the Fabulous Thunderbirds' Preston Hubbard on acoustic bass. They had always planned to cut "Hillbillies from Outer Space" there, and "Brothers" was an off-the-cuff instrumental, for which they wanted Bramhall's Texas shuffle swing. Jimmie and Stevie cut the song live, swapping the same Stratocaster back and forth.

PROCT: "Hillbillies" was something Jimmie definitely wanted to do with upright bass and a real Texas shuffle, which is why we cut it with Doyle and Preston. "Brothers" was a little bit of an afterthought. It was just a whimsical thing where Stevie was playing and Jimmie came and took the guitar from him and they swapped it back and forth.

RODGERS: I have no memory of who suggested swapping one guitar originally, but I'd seen them do it live and was more than game for trying it.

SRV: We were taking it away from each other. It was one guitar and one amp.

JIMMIE VAUGHAN: We pulled it out of each other's hands. People are always asking us questions about what it was like when we were kids, and they probably think that it was just like that, us fighting over the same guitar. It was just for fun. And even though it's the same guitar and rig, the tones sound different, because we learned how to get different tones from the same setup and the same tones from different rigs. It was a little-bitty Princeton or Deluxe.

SRV: We don't know what it is because it was skinned! It had been an old tweed, but there's nothin' left on it but knobs and a handle!

JIMMIE VAUGHAN: When we switched, I'd turn down a little, switch to another pickup, whatever. We could have manufactured the whole thing: gotten really good tones and played really clean, but what we liked about it was that it was so *real*.

SRV: Doyle played drums on it, and Preston played bass. It was funny, because we started off with a click track. We were gonna try to play to this click, so that if we wanted to change something, we could. But it was like the click was here [*snaps fingers in time*], and we were completely off of it! It had nothin' to do with anything!

JIMMIE VAUGHAN: You've never seen four guys ignore a click so good! Total disregard for the click! We said, "Hey, take that shit off!"

SRV: Nobody even heard it!

BRAMHALL: It was very obvious how happy Jimmie and Stevie were to be doing this album together. The atmosphere was just great. This was the first time I was around both of them for a considerable amount of time in twenty years, since they were kids. They really hadn't been hanging together a lot for a long time. There was a lot of hugging around, and everyone was really happy.

SHANNON: Stevie said cutting that album and spending so much time with his brother was like coming home.

DR. JOHN: You know what's interesting? Jimmie Vaughan was the least affected by Stevie of all the blues guitarists. How many guys you know whose little brothers are excelling in their own field?

BERRY: They really kind of submitted to each other. Their tremendous respect for one another was incredibly humbling, and it maintained an almost spiritual vibe. It was like being invited to a master class of how to express yourself. You could see how much Jimmie respected Stevie, but you could see so much more how much Stevie respected Jimmie. It wasn't an easy path for either of them, but they had arrived in this great spot.

DR. JOHN: Stevie started out early doing a lot of Jimmie's thing. But Jimmie went one way while his brother went as far the other way as you could go, while still playing blues. Then you put a real funk cat like Nile Rodgers into the picture. Add his funk contribution on top of these two different schools of blues guitar, and you've got something real, real special.

BERRY: Jimmie is a very funky dude, and a lot of people underestimate him. He's got groove and melody and that bluesy, funky dirt. When he showed me the idea for "Mama Said," I was like, "Oh my God," and started playing this Bootsy Collins / James Brown–inspired bass line, and he loved it.

FREEMAN: I love that record, and one reason is it's really not what we do. The album popped and cracked. It was a fun album with great songs.

ABERMAN: After Nile came back to New York from Dallas, me and Al hung out with him, and he played us a cassette of rough mixes in his Toyota 4Runner. He was so excited and kept saying, "This is a hit!" We all felt really good about what we had done, and Al and I were of the understanding that we would be going on the road as the rhythm section for the Vaughan Brothers Band.

After completing the album, Jimmie joined Stevie and Double Trouble for a set at the New Orleans Jazz & Heritage Festival on May 6, 1990.

GLAUB: Every time I saw Stevie, he was warm and gracious and played incredibly, but the '90 Jazz Fest was one of the best sets I ever saw him do. It had almost the same impact on me as the very first time I saw him at Montreux.

RODNEY CRAIG: I saw him for the first time in a few years at the Jazz Fest, and I was so happy to see him play such a terrific concert. He had beaten drugs and alcohol and was feeling great. He was so excited about being clean and had a whole new outlook on his career. We had a wonderful visit.

GLAUB: I went into their trailer to say hi and told him about Eddie's, a nearby restaurant that I loved, and he said, "Oh, I'll be there tonight!" I go in there, and he's entertaining a table of fifteen, with his manager, crew, and friends. I also told him that I spent a few days traveling the bayou and had picked up some amps and guitars he might want to see. At 1:00 in the morning, he was knocking on my hotel door with Alex Hodges wanting to see the stuff. We sat on my bed and played some blues for a while.

In June 1990, months after finishing *Family Style,* Jimmie left the Fabulous Thunderbirds after fifteen years. His last show was June 16, 1990.

"Stevie loved the road and the whole idea of going from clubs to theaters to arenas. He wanted the legacy of stepping onto the Madison Square Garden stage, but Jimmie just didn't care about that," says Proct. "Jimmie loved the playing but wished he could beam himself to the gig, then go home. After all those years of being on the bus, he had lost his love of the road. Leaving the T-Birds wasn't even a thought before 'Tuff Enuff' hit, then we were so busy promoting it for eighteen months. When that finally slowed down, he wanted to stay home and work on his hot rods and write and play music."

25

THE SKY IS CRYING

After Jazz Fest, Double Trouble took about a month's break, during which Stevie and Janna rented an apartment in New York, partly to make it easier for her to pursue a modeling career. They planned to split their time between Dallas and Manhattan. On June 8, Stevie Ray Vaughan and Double Trouble kicked off the co-headlining Power and the Passion tour with Joe Cocker at California's Shoreline Amphitheatre. It ran until July 25 in Fairbanks, Alaska.

Stevie met Jimmie at Skyway Studios in New York on July 29 to do a video interview as part of preparing a press kit for *Family Style*. While there, Rodgers played them some mixes, and everyone was thrilled for the progress and excited for a fall release.

The next day, Double Trouble played in Saint Paul, Minnesota, then took a twenty-four-day break, during which Stevie and Janna vacationed in Hawaii and visited her family in New Zealand.

The band reconvened August 24 in Kalamazoo, Michigan, for a single warm-up show before two nights that they had all been looking forward to: opening for Eric Clapton, along with the Robert Cray Band at Alpine Valley, the giant amphitheater in East Troy, Wisconsin. Both shows were sold out, and Stevie made sure that Jimmie could fly up to join them for a closing jam on the second night, August 26, which would also feature Buddy Guy. Everyone involved was excited for the music and reunion of old friends and kindred spirits.

Stevie and Janna on vacation in Maui, HI, 1990. *(Courtesy Janna Lapidus)*

WYNANS: We were looking forward to these shows for weeks. I felt like we had hit our absolute peak, that we were playing as great as we ever played and that Stevie was absolutely in his prime. It felt like we had found who we were as a band. When you get to a big day, sometimes people can clam up and it doesn't come across as wonderful as you want it to be. This was just the opposite; it felt like everything was extra terrific.

RAITT: The first night at Alpine Valley, I was there just to watch, and it was great to see everyone. I really think that Stevie was perhaps the greatest guitarist ever, and he showed it that night. He was more magical than I'd ever seen him.

"I play hard with both hands." *(Tracy Anne Hart)*

LAYTON: The entire air of those two days was very inspired. The shows were big, and we had all of those great people who had tremendous respect for one another together. It was just a great happening. Beyond that, it really felt like things with Double Trouble were finally opening up again, that we were at the beginning of the next, really inspired phase of our career. As a band and an organization, we had never been as together as right then.

BERT HOLMAN, *Allman Brothers Band manager:* Alpine Valley is a great venue that bands really enjoy playing, but getting out of there is a nightmare and everyone knows it, because there's only one two-lane road in and out. You roll in easily in the afternoon, but after the show, the acts are stuck with the departing crowd, so the ninety-mile drive to Chicago can take five hours. Some bands would do a runner, jump offstage, and, with a police escort, fight through the traffic immediately. Some acts chose to use helicopters to avoid that. My guys, especially Gregg [Allman] and Dickey [Betts], refused to fly in helicopters, so we always turned that option down. We waited about ninety minutes and just kept driving west or north instead of trying to spend the night in Chicago.

RICKERT: When you have thirty-five thousand people there and a one-lane access road, getting out after the show is brutal. You might get to Chicago at 6:00 in the morning. I contacted Omni Flights, who informed me that Eric had already contracted them, but I could use two copters if it didn't impact Eric. I would have to get Stevie up to Alpine Valley early enough for the helicopters to return to Chicago and get the Eric Clapton entourage. After the show, I had to wait for the helicopters to return after taking the Clapton camp back to Chicago. I got a quote that was agreeable to Stevie, and it turned out that the promoter graciously offered to pay for that. Perfect! It felt like a sweet deal. We don't have to take buses or dip into our money. The first night was no issue. Stevie didn't jam, and we all left after he played, and the copters came back for Eric and his group.

HODGES: I represented Otis Redding and was deeply impacted by his death in a plane crash, so I had a rule of staying on the ground. I've always felt that musicians travel so much that it's a constant danger we should do everything to lessen. Flying commercial is safe, and if you can't do that, stay on the ground. A Learjet when absolutely necessary is one thing, but helicopters are dangerous, and private planes can be as well. I met up with them at Alpine Valley and showed them the *Family Style* promo video and they were both excited. We had meetings about the next run of dates, about taking time off, and about doing some shows with his brother.

CRAY: What I remember most about these shows is sitting around a table with Jimmie, Stevie, and Eric, talking about life and our careers and laughing about where we had been and where we were. It was just fun. Eric presented a great opportunity for all of us to be together. Jimmie and Stevie were excited about what they called the "brothers" album—*Family Style*. Stevie was saying how good it was to be clean and sober and how happy he now was.

SHANNON: This felt like the culmination of all the good times we'd been having for the last year or two. And as good as we had been playing, those two shows were just unreal.

BUDDY GUY: Eric called and invited me up for the second show and to jam at the end. I don't think I'd ever flown in a chopper before, but I got on and flew up.

CONNIE VAUGHAN: I had never been in a helicopter before, and I was terrified on the way up to the show. Stevie held my hand and told me it was fine and was pointing out things down below, just to distract and comfort me.

HODGES: I flew up there with Stevie, Jimmie, and Connie on the second day. Getting off the helicopter, Stevie said, "Maybe we should think about going back on the ground." I wish I had an explanation for why we violated the rule.

JIMMIE VAUGHAN: On the second show, Stevie was unreal. He just *smoked*—he was on another plane, and we all knew it. It was one of those gigs where you can't believe what you're hearing from a performer. They were all just wailing and happy, making it happen, raising it another notch.

CONNIE VAUGHAN: Stevie was onstage playing, and I saw a rainbow-like aura around him and thought, "How weird." I went to the other side of the stage to see if it was just how the lights were, and it was the same. Then I went to the audience and saw it. I thought, "Damn, what is going on?" He played better than I probably ever heard him play that night. It was like he was plugged into something. He was just so on. I had never seen anything like that, and I'm not the kind of person who talks like this!

LAYTON: People have said things like they saw a huge halo around Stevie when he was playing that night, that he was surrounded with an orange-blue aura. Like it was some sort of a premonition.

GUY: Man, first of all, Stevie was one of the best ever. Period. But those nights, he was just something else. And I remember standing with him and Robert Cray on the side of the stage while Eric was playing, and we were talking and he was sort of playing air guitar, fingering along with what Eric played. Him standing there playing phantom notes is something I've never stopped thinking about.

LAYTON: After the show, Stevie and I sat and talked for about a half hour about how good these two shows had been and about his excitement for the future. He said that the record with Jimmie was something that he'd wanted to do for years and considered a necessary part of his life's progression. He said, "I needed to make that record with my brother, and we'll play a bunch of shows, but I can't wait to get to our next record. I've got some ideas, and I hope they don't sound weird: strings, big horn sections . . . We're gonna bust it wide open." I said, "Hell, that sounds exciting." *In Step* was the fledgling step of putting some twists on our roots, and he was looking forward to taking things to a whole new place on the next record.

At the end of Clapton's set the second night, he stepped to the microphone and said, "I'd like to bring out to join me, in truth, the best guitar players in the entire world: Buddy Guy, Stevie Ray Vaughan, Robert Cray, Jimmie Vaughan." All four walked out to a wash of cheers from the crowd of forty thousand and set off on an extended jam of "Sweet Home Chicago," trading off vocals, red-hot guitar licks, and smiles.

LAYTON: I was standing on the stage when they came out, and Stevie played this one note that sounded so big . . .

SHANNON: God, yeah! That one note was bigger than the whole place! People went nuts when Stevie hit that note.

LAYTON: I'd been with the guy for thirteen years, and I still thought, "That sounds huge!" Not just loud, but big. The same kind of "tone" thing as the first time I ever saw him at the Soap Creek.

WYNANS: I went out front to watch the jam, and it was beautiful. Stevie's playing was just soaring through the air. He was in his element, playing as good as I had ever heard him.

CRAY: Stevie and Eric were both blistering. We finished with this great "Sweet Home Chicago" jam, and everyone walked off the stage very happy. We were all going our own ways. Eric and Stevie were walking back to Eric's dressing room, and I was trailing them and could hear them both saying to each other, "You were great." Everyone was so happy.

CONNIE VAUGHAN: After the show, the fog started coming in. I went up to the pilots and said, "This looks really bad," and three of them said, "Oh, honey, don't worry. We were in Vietnam; we can get you out of anything." But one pilot was standing off to the side with his arms crossed and didn't say anything. He didn't look very happy, and he was not talking to the other pilots.

RICKERT: I'm in the settlement room, taking care of the finances, getting cash, and a note comes letting me know that there is a seat open in one of Eric's helicopters, a total surprise. Holy crap, there is a seat open, and Stevie wanted to get back to Chicago. Alex was there as well as Jimmie and Connie and [financial planner] Bill V., and everyone says, "Stevie can have the seat."

CONNIE VAUGHAN: Stevie felt bad to go first and leave us all. He said, "Connie, there's only one seat. Do you mind if I take it?" The pilot was the quiet one who didn't seem confident.

HODGES: That seat became available, and Stevie was getting on. It all just happened very fast. Why we didn't act on that impulse to stay on the ground, I just don't know. There are so many decisions that could have been made differently, and I don't think we ever get over those questions or doubts.

RICKERT: So he went off and climbed onto the helicopter, and away they go. It was foggy, but it wasn't pea soup, and it wasn't that different from what we had experienced up there before. We were on top of a mountain, and all the helicopter has to do is go straight up about 150 feet, and then you can see the Sears Tower in downtown Chicago. The helicopters take off, no one hears anything or thinks anything is amiss, and we're waiting for two of them to come back and get us.

GUY: The fog had come in, and me and Eric got on the chopper with one of the guys in his band, and the pilot took his T-shirt off to wipe the windshield, and I said, "Man, what the hell is this? How is this guy gonna see a thing?"

LAPIDUS: I was on the phone with Stevie when he got the offer. He said, "I just got a chance to go back now, and I think I'll take it. I'll call you back later."

Stevie's companions in the helicopter piloted by Jeffrey Brown were all members of Clapton's team: longtime booking agent Bobby Brooks; bodyguard Nigel Browne; and assistant tour manager Colin Smythe. The Bell 260B Jet Ranger flew about 3,000 feet, lifting about 100 feet off the ground before slamming into the side of a 150-foot ski hill at approximately 12:50 a.m. CDT. Everyone on board died on impact.

The other helicopters were on their way back to Chicago with no sense of danger or problems afoot. No one at the venue heard anything or was otherwise aware of what had happened. Stevie Ray Vaughan died on August 27, 1990, four years to the day after his father, Big Jim, passed away. He was thirty-five years old.

CONNIE VAUGHAN: It was so foggy we didn't even hear the crash, which was right behind the stage.

RICKERT: We were waiting for the helicopters to come back and get us, and we started getting calls that they didn't think the copters would be able to land back at Alpine due to the increasingly foggy conditions. We were going to have to do something else, like use the production vans for the three- or four-hour drive, which would get us back to Chicago around 6:00 a.m. Then our promoter rep, Brad Warva, suggested we consider the closed Playboy Club, which was at higher elevation about thirty minutes from Alpine Valley in the opposite direction, with a runway and lights. By now, it's 1:30 in the morning, so we might as well try that, and sure enough, we take off: me, Alex, Tommy, Chris, Reese, Connie, and Jimmie. I had the headphones on and heard discussion about a missing vehicle and people asking if it had been seen, and the answer is no, nothing, zip, but it didn't occur to me that this had anything to do with a missing helicopter, much less *our* missing helicopter.

HODGES: I heard them talking on the radio, asking, "Has anybody heard from . . . ," but I didn't recognize it as our issue because there was no description. They could have been talking about anything.

CONNIE VAUGHAN: We flew in to Chicago and I was looking down, and no planes were moving. Something felt eerie.

RICKERT: When we landed at Midway airport, I saw a couple of helicopters, and we're in two, so all four seem to be accounted for. They said that there's a vehicle waiting for us. It was a limousine, and the driver said he had been told to wait for us.

LAYTON: We all piled into the car, and the driver said, "It's about time you got here. I was wondering what happened to you all." It was the same limo that had been waiting for the helicopter carrying Stevie that had never arrived. It had been sitting there waiting for hours.

CONNIE VAUGHAN: Stevie was supposed to call and leave a message, and he didn't, which I thought was weird. We had just gotten to sleep, and Alex called and said Stevie's helicopter hadn't gotten back. So we jumped out of bed, and I started freaking out.

RICKERT: Two hours after going to bed, Alex called and said, "Stevie was killed in a helicopter crash." I said, "This is the worst joke ever." And he said, "I'm sorry, but it's not. Let's get the band together." And we all gathered in one room and had to have this awful conversation.

SHANNON: I got woken up by a phone call from Skip at 6:30 saying that we had to have a meeting right away. I said, "This is no time for a meeting. What the hell is going on?" And he said, "It's very important." I started feeling very uneasy, and a few minutes later, I got a call from Alex, saying that one of the helicopters had gone down, Stevie was on it, and there were no survivors. In the blink of an eye, my life was taken away from me. I was sitting on the bed crying, and Chris came into my room, asking what was going on. I said, "Stevie's dead," and he just lost it, too.

LAYTON: I was in denial, so I called security and forced them to let me into Stevie's room. I really thought he'd be laying there sleeping, but when they opened the door, the bed was still made, the pillow turned down, and I realized, "My God, it's true."

SHANNON: Stevie's coat was laid out on the bed, and oddly, the clock radio was playing that Eagles song, "Peaceful Easy Feeling," with the line, "I may never see you again." It was playing real softly, but it might as well have been a bullhorn into my ear. Then we all went back to my room, and Jimmie was there, and we were all a wreck, sobbing and dazed. It was the most horrible moment. I'll never have anything hurt that bad again, ever.

LAYTON: I felt like a car had fallen on me, just completely helpless. Then we realized that the news reports said that Stevie *and his band* were killed, and I had to get ahold of my family and tell them that I was alive. We spent a bunch of time calling our families, just sort of going onto autopilot. If I started thinking about it, I couldn't function.

CRAY: I got woken up by a phone call from Andrew Love of the Memphis Horns, who were touring with us. He wanted to make sure I was in my room because he originally heard I was in the tragedy. He said, "You better call your mom," so I did. Reporters had been calling her, and she was very relieved to hear from me.

GUY: I was gonna make a big Louisiana gumbo for all the guys at my club. I got up early to go get the crabs and stuff, and on my way out the door, the phone rang. I went back to answer it, and they say, "Have you heard about Stevie?" I'm like, "What he do, get drunk or something?" They say, "No, he's dead." And I went, "What do you mean? I'm on my way to buy crabs for the gumbo I'm making him." It didn't add up.

Wreckage was found scattered across a wide area early in the morning of August 27.

Jimmie and Connie Vaughan, accompanied by Hodges, drove in a limousine to the crash site and from there to Lakeland Hospital about ten miles away to identify Stevie's body.

CONNIE VAUGHAN: At the site, the FAA guy said, "If you see anything of Stevie's, you can just pick it up, because we know what happened here." I picked up a briefcase, which ended up belonging to Clapton's road manager—the guy whose seat Stevie had taken—and he teared up when we gave it back to him. We got back into the limousine and were driving away when they radioed us to stop. This guy ran down and said, "Wasn't this his?" and held Stevie's Coptic cross out to give Jimmie. I said, "Jimmie, don't you know what that means? He's okay. He's telling us he's okay." That's what it meant to me anyhow.

We drove to some building to identify the bodies. I didn't want to go in there, so Jimmie had to go in and do it by himself. It was unbelievable. Decades later, I still feel like it's a nightmare that's not true.

JOE PERRY: I have to wonder why they didn't cancel those flights. I've been in and out of that venue by helicopter many times. I know guys that won't fly at night, especially in bad weather. That accident didn't have to happen.

LEWIS: He survived the substances, and what got him was a fucking helicopter. I know that helicopter. We've played that gig a million times, and they always offer you the ride, and I always say, "No, thanks. I'll drive." It's a tedious bus ride, but I just do it. When I heard the awful news, I thought, "Oh, that fucking helicopter!"

BRAD WHITFORD: Getting in and out of these places where we have to work can be chaotic and dangerous. At Alpine Valley, you can look in almost any direction and there's a clear path, other than this one little hill. If he'd been over a little to one side or the other, they would have been fine. We were in Bologna, Italy, when my road manager came into my room and told me the news. I was just devastated.

HAYNES: I was in the middle of an Allman Brothers tour, and my manager called me at 8:00 a.m. and told me about the crash. There was still speculation that perhaps some of the other musicians might have been on the same helicopter. We had played Alpine Valley eight days before [August 18, 1990]. The Allman Brothers refused to fly in helicopters; that was a deal-breaker for us, so we bussed it in and out.

A two-year probe by the National Transportation Safety Board found that "improper planning/decision" by the pilot was the main probable cause of the crash. An NTSB spokesman said that "darkness, fog, haze and rising terrain were contributing factors." It could all be summed up rather simply as a flight that never should have happened.

26

LIFE WITHOUT YOU

Epic Records sent a jet to fly Stevie's body to Dallas, while the rest of the band and crew made their way home in a daze. "We were running through the airport to catch our flight, and I just stopped in my tracks," says Shannon. "I couldn't find one reason to move."

When Chris and Tommy landed in Austin, Cutter Brandenburg was waiting at the gate. They had not seen him since he quit and left them at Kennedy International Airport in 1983. "It was nice to see him standing there," says Layton. "It felt right."

"Stevie guided me through that horrible day because I did not know what to do," Brandenburg said. "I was walking around in a daze, and having Stevie in my heart and soul is why I went to get them. He somehow sent me to pick them up."

The town of Austin and indeed the whole state of Texas seemed to be in mourning, along with fans all around the world.

"Stevie's death was obviously devastating to those of us close to him, but the fans also felt like they knew him," says Doyle Bramhall II. "He was such a vibrant spirit that even from afar you could feel that this was a light shining brighter than most. He was really tapped into something much, much bigger, the way the great ones in any field always are."

On Monday, August 27, as word of Stevie's death filtered through a shocked city, thousands gathered for a vigil in Austin's Zilker Park, sponsored by KLBJ, which carried Stevie's music over the air to the teary, candle-holding mourners. In Dallas, a vigil was held in Kiest Park, just a few blocks from Stevie's boyhood home, where his mother, Martha, still lived.

Austin musicians gathered at Antone's to console each other and pay tribute to their friend and leader. W. C. Clark was the night's scheduled performer.

FREEMAN: I was driving to Dallas when I heard the news on the radio that Stevie had died in a helicopter crash. I immediately turned the car around and headed to Clifford Antone's office and record store across the street from his club. That spot became ground zero. The phone never stopped ringing.

PRIESNITZ: My assistant called and asked if something had happened to Stevie, because they had been playing his music nonstop on the radio. I immediately made a few calls and was stunned when I heard the news.

SHANNON: Several of us got together at Antone's that night to comfort each other, to console one another, and help each other in our tremendous grief. It's almost impossible to remember—it seemed like it was all a bad dream.

FREEMAN: I believe that the gathering that night at Antone's was born out of an instinctual reaction from everyone in Austin. When something that shocking happens, people just want to gather to support each other. No one knew what to do or say, but they wanted to be together. Everyone was in shock, whether they knew Stevie personally or not. Hearing of his sudden death like that, you don't know how to deal with it or process it. It's too much.

BRANDENBURG: All of Austin was trying to get into Antone's, and I was in line. Lou Ann Barton walked up with Connie Vaughan and grabbed me and hugged me and took me in with them. Walking in, I felt tears well up, looked around and saw that everyone was crying.

LAYTON: I was mostly sitting home, in such a daze that I have no idea what I did. You'd have to ask someone else if I was at Antone's because those days are a black hole in my memory. [He was not there.]

GRISSOM: Two days after Stevie died, Eric Johnson played at Steamboat, and I think I got up and played with him, but it's hard to remember because it was such an emotional time. A lot of people were there,

"He was such a vibrant spirit that even from afar you could feel that this was a light shining brighter than most."—Doyle Bramhall II (Tracy Anne Hart)

showing emotional support for each other, and Eric made some really nice remarks about Stevie. There was a feeling of tremendous sadness and also the need to be together.

PRIESNITZ: I called Eric and asked him if he still wanted to play his scheduled date at Steamboat, giving him the option to cancel if it was too emotional for him. And Eric said, "Do you think Stevie would want us to cancel?" and I said, "No."

GRISSOM: The entire town came together: there were signs in the windows of just about every store or business, saying "Rest in Peace, Stevie" and "We Will Miss You." He was a big part of the city's soul, and his passing was a real demarcation point of the Austin scene. It was the end of an era.

Four days after the crash, on Thursday, August 30, Stevie was buried in Dallas. After a private chapel service at the Laurel Land Funeral Home with family and close friends, the coffin was carried outside for a public graveside service, which was the family's wish. Thousands of people stood behind yellow police tape and jammed a grassy hillside in hundred-degree-plus heat. Given Stevie's deep roots in Dallas and Austin, many of the mourners had some direct connection. A picture of Stevie sat on an easel, his hat resting atop it at an angle.

Stevie Wonder, Bonnie Raitt, and Jackson Browne sang "Amazing Grace" a cappella. Nile Rodgers delivered a eulogy, calling Stevie "someone who was touched by God with the gift of music." Struggling to speak without breaking down, he added, "I learned a lot about family from Stevie and Jimmie. They made me a member of their family. They made me an honorary brother. Thank you for helping me to remember how important family is. Thank you for making me remember music." His words were followed by a playing of "Tick Tock" from the still-unreleased *Family Style*. The members of Double Trouble were pallbearers. None of them delivered eulogies. "We couldn't speak," Shannon says simply.

LAYTON: Stevie Wonder sang "The Lord's Prayer" a cappella. I was crying so hard.

WYNANS: Stevie Wonder's singing was the most beautiful thing you could ever hear in your life. During the service, this woman was playing sort of nondescript church music on the organ. Then Dr. John got back there and started playing beautiful stuff. It was the way it was supposed to be.

DR. JOHN: It was really gut-wrenching. I played every hymn I knew, then Stevie Wonder came up and said, "Ave Maria in G," but I didn't know it. So I stopped and let him sing. Once I wasn't playing, I got really aware, "Man, I'm with his coffin," and went into that zone, where it was all hitting me like gangbusters. Being in that little church and re-alizing that Stevie's feet were just a few feet away from me was so damn heavy I could hardly breathe. And his family is such sweet people, they was supporting me, when it should have been the other way around.

BRAMHALL II: At the memorial, I was wearing a Holter monitor for my heart because I was suffering panic attacks.

SHANNON: I was so numbed out from emotion that there are a lot of blank spaces in my memory.

WYNANS: I felt that I was there to help support the family.

SHANNON: I couldn't support anybody. Stevie was my best friend. There was nothing I was ashamed of around him, so the first thing I thought when I realized he was really dead was, "I was supposed to be with him." His death changed my whole view of the world. I feel now that if you don't have a faith strong enough to face death, it's not faith. You look around at the things you love and realize that someday, it's all going to be gone. But that's not necessarily bad, because freedom comes when you're not attached to anything.

BRAMHALL II: I put Stevie on a pedestal, and when he died, I lost it. I be-came an atheist. I didn't believe there could be a God who could take away the life of someone who had come from such depths of despair, hopelessness, and near death from drug and alcohol addiction, only to then be sober and starting to help so many people and enjoy his life on every level for the first time. It just felt so cruel and meaningless, I didn't see the point. I spiraled into a very dark place of my own. Making a person your higher power is dangerous. I'm sure Stevie would've agreed that your higher power shouldn't be a person. He inspired me so much and still guides me today.

BRANDENBURG: The morning after the funeral, I went back to Laurel Land, and many people were laying flowers and notes to Stevie, and his music was playing from all around. Everyone was trying to console each other, but it just felt like this sadness and heartache was never gonna heal.

SUBLETT: The only comfort I could take was that he didn't go out in the state he had been in back in '86. He was a clean and sober guy preaching that gospel to everyone who came to see him. I'm certain that he changed a lot of lives in those four years.

HUBBARD: His musical legacy is giant and would have been enough, but his true legacy is so much bigger that. He's left a path for others to follow, people that get down in that hole so deep you can't see the top, to help other people recover from a hopeless state of mind and body.

FREEMAN: Fortunately, Stevie got to feel Jimmie's unconditional love and support for a good while there. Jimmie just loved him so much, and that was real obvious, as was the fact that Stevie worshipped Jimmie.

CONNIE VAUGHAN: Recording *Family Style* brought them back together. That's what's so sad, but what's so good, too. Stevie was so grateful for every day he lived, and he got to help so many people. He was on a roll.

BENSON: After he died, it struck me that somewhere deep in his genes he knew he wasn't going to be around forever, and that's why he played the way he did.

BRAMHALL II: Some people have the DNA of destiny, and everything about Stevie indicated that. He worked harder, he burned brighter, he was more kind. He wanted to touch as many lives as he could. It was like it was written in his fate that he would do all these great things, and I think he knew that on some level.

LAYTON: I had never realized how much of an impact he had on the world, though one would think it would have been obvious to me. Coming home the day after Stevie died, I saw his picture everywhere and the tremendous outpouring of emotion from the world. It had never really dawned on me how big it had all become, because I was so wrapped up in it.

LAPIDUS: I was sitting in the funeral home and it suddenly dawned on me that Stevie was going to be a legend. He never thought of himself in that way.

ALBERT KING: Stevie was one of our best players. I was sure hurt when we lost him.

Family Style was released almost exactly a month after Stevie's death, on September 25, 1990. The first single was "Tick Tock," sung primarily by Stevie, with Jimmie delivering a spoken introduction. The chorus suddenly seemed eerily prophetic: *"Tick tock, tick tock, tick tock, people/Time's tickin' away."*

PROCT: The album had been mixed and was ready to go, but Sony was very sympathetic following Stevie's death and asked Jimmie if he was okay releasing it. He was, because he was so proud of it and knew that Stevie had also been very happy with it.

RODGERS: An immense sadness washed over me like a wave when I tried to listen to the album to check quality control. I cried like a baby.

PROCT: It was all hard to deal with, but "Tick Tock" was particularly difficult. We agreed to make a video, and it was really just so, so challenging to complete. I couldn't stop crying. Jimmie was standing up there alone at a microphone instead of with Stevie and the emotions were immense.

Family Style was the highest-charting album of Stevie Ray's career, a Top 10 hit. Though they had not finalized plans or hired a band, Jimmie and Stevie had planned on touring together.

PROCT: Jimmie and Stevie would have gone on the road to promote *Family Style,* likely by January, after Stevie completed other obligations. They had not picked a band yet, but it would probably have been new people. Specifics never got to the table, but it was going to be a serious tour.

ABERMAN: At a listening party for *Family Style* prior to Stevie's passing, [Sony executive] Tony Martell shook my hand and let me know that he was excited for a Vaughan Brothers tour. The label was very excited and was envisioning all kinds of possibilities.

HODGES: The next album was going to be Stevie Ray Vaughan and Double Trouble and then maybe another Brothers album.

SHANNON: Stevie totally lived in the moment. His playing was so immersed in what he was feeling, they became one and the same. If he was in pain, he'd play that pain; if he was happy, he'd play that happiness. He couldn't separate his playing from his own inner being. Playing music for him was a transmission of something deep inside. He reached as far down into his heart, his soul, and his life as he could reach.

RICKERT: To use a current term, Stevie was always present. The guy wasn't a phony in any regard. I've worked with people who are all show; they are entertainers. Stevie was a guitar player, and everything he did had his heart, guts, and soul in it. That's what made it so powerful. He was very attuned to every song being like a snowflake, always different and reflecting the moment.

SHANNON: There are a lot of very technically advanced musicians who are not inspired enough to live as if there is no other time. Stevie always played as if there was no tomorrow. He was always right in the moment. And he went real deep into the moment.

LAYTON: People could identify with Stevie's connection between his feelings and his means of expression. They heard his music, and they *knew* him. Most people would love to be able to express their innermost feelings, but it's a hard thing to do. Stevie epitomized someone that was able to do that.

RUSS KUNKEL: He had a perfect balance of confidence and vulnerability. The sound he was making and the commitment in his singing was powerful and confident. But when you looked at him, you saw that he was vulnerable. There was a softness underneath the power, and that combination was very appealing.

RICKERT: When he was playing, he was like an open door, and emotion came through him and out his fingers. It was just absolutely breathtaking to be around every day.

LAYTON: He touched people in such a way that it was irrelevant that he played the guitar, that he played a Stratocaster, that he played the blues.

It had nothing to do with any of that. Stevie was able to grab on to something that people struggle to express in their own lives and do it for them. That connection was there, even if they couldn't identify what it was about it that moved them so much.

SHANNON: Playing music afforded Stevie the opportunity to communicate on a deep spiritual level. When I was living with Stevie and Lenny out in Volente, we'd been up all night and were sitting out on the back patio as the sun came up. We were looking out over the lake and the hills, and the birds were singing and there were flowers all around. We had been talking about spiritual things all night, and he was in a real deep state of gratification, feeling grateful to God for everything in his life.

He was playing an acoustic guitar, drifting off into the moment; his eyes were like a child's, looking around at the beauty of nature around him, and he wasn't thinking at all about what he was playing. For about thirty seconds, he played the most beautiful thing I'd ever heard. It was unearthly. I said, "Stevie, what was that?" He went, "Huh? Which part?" "What you just played!" And he had no idea; he just went on playing. I'd give anything in the world to have heard that again, because it was so profound. It felt like the sky opened up and this light shined down on him. It was incredible.

LAYTON: Stevie's yardstick was his emotional relationship to music: where he was, spiritually and emotionally, in regard to his playing. He kept very close tabs on his emotional connection, minute by minute. That didn't include yesterday or the day before; that meant right now.

SHANNON: When you tap into that, it's like something is playing *through* you. You are just watching it, and it's going through your hands and out of the instrument. You find yourself doing things that you'd never come up with in your own imagination. But you have to be totally immersed in the moment for that to happen. It's like that moment is infinite. It's about tapping into a universal energy.

LAYTON: That's what *made* it music. It's an intangible thing, but it's the most important thing of all. The best playing experiences are when I feel like I'm right there in that very minute, and I don't have one single thought, consciously or subconsciously, about anything else. When you feel that you are right there, the whole thing gets deep, and it just opens up this feeling of being totally locked into the music. It's all about going past the ego.

SHANNON: Stevie used to describe that feeling by saying, "It's like going home." It's wonderful.

DR. JOHN: Whatever he gave to the world is something that will live on forever, but most people know the music but they don't know the musician. And that's the part that I miss—knowing the person.

SHANNON: Stevie came into my life from out of left field, and though I was a lot older than he was, he opened me up to so many things. I'm blessed to have had that.

BRAMHALL: We were always taking writing breaks and going to a store close to his house to get these frozen fruit bars, and within a minute, people would be surrounding Stevie. I would kind of back off and watch, and he'd look over at me with a big wonderful smile on his face. He loved that he could touch someone in a positive way, and he loved the interactions.

RICKERT: He embraced everyone, and when they invariably told him how great his music was, he'd respond, "Thank you so much. I'm doing my best." His fans hugged and kissed him and took photographs. Everyone would be asleep on the bus, and we're all waiting for Stevie because he would sign every autograph. Every single one! Always.

BRAMHALL: He'd be the last one at a festival, standing there signing autographs, and had to be dragged away so the bus could leave. I've never met anyone who met Stevie who wasn't touched in a positive way. They didn't have to understand or even like the music that much. He loved life, he cared about people and art, and he was just a very compassionate person.

RICKERT: He and Doyle were both naturally kind. When we went fishing in Alaska, I caught a fifty-three-pound salmon, and he was so excited for me. His joy was the same as if he had caught the fish. Being on the road with bands, you see the good and bad, and I never saw Stevie be mean or angry. In five years of touring together, a lot of things go wrong—buses are late, flights are delayed—and he always rolled with the punches. Once our bus broke down driving from Rome to Naples on a two-lane highway with no shoulders. We were blocking travel to Rome, with long lines of blaring horns, Stevie was smiling. We lined up eight cabs to get us to the gig.

LAYTON: A flower that dies on the vine just falls off and is dead. This was a dying flower that came back to life and had blossomed into something more beautiful than ever. Then suddenly . . . *pow!* It's just gone, and all that we had together, an active, living thing, is not there. We had been through so much together, and we were all in acknowledgment of how good we felt about playing together and creating music together in the future. We were ready to turn the next corner, which was going to be a great big superhighway. That made his passing even more poignant.

WYNANS: One of the things I had to deal with after Stevie's death is I didn't feel like playing music anymore.

LICKONA: For many years, I couldn't watch his last appearance on *Austin City Limits*. For him to come back and give such an incredible performance, then die so soon after, was way beyond poignant. He was really Austin's hometown pride and joy; to this day, no one's impact compares to Stevie Ray. His death was a shock wave to the city.

In 1994 a bronze statue of Stevie was erected in downtown Austin on the bank of Lady Bird Lake, next to Auditorium Shores, where he had performed many memorable shows, including his final Austin performance on May 4, 1990.

LAYTON: Stevie's tragic death only punctuates his greatness and puts a mark on his legacy, akin to Buddy Holly, Otis Redding, Jimi Hendrix, Janis Joplin, and Duane Allman. It's like something has been stolen and you can only wonder what might have come next.

HODGES: The fact that he had been sober for four years made it a different level of shock. He was in such good shape, and it felt like he would be around and creative and healthy for decades to come. His career, his life, his spirituality, and his happiness were becoming so whole.

Stevie's last Austin show, 5/4/90. *(Tracy Anne Hart)*

BENSON: A lot of people loved Stevie because he was a genius on the guitar, but if you knew him as a person, he was the sweetest guy.

LAYTON: Since Stevie's death, some people have come to think of him as a pristine, Christ-type figure, and anybody that ever had a rub with him as evil.

SHANNON: That's just not true.

LAYTON: There were times when Stevie was no picnic. Everyone is like that. He was not a saint. He was a human being.

FREEMAN: Since Stevie died, he's been elevated to sainthood. It's strange, and I actually think it diminishes him, because Stevie was a person, and he had faults. But he was sweet and funny and a wonderful guy to hang with, in addition to being an exceptional talent. And I just miss him.

SHANNON: Stevie gave himself to the world, which was something beautiful.

LAYTON: "Good luck to everybody." That's what Stevie used to say all of the time. Good luck to everybody, everywhere, all of the time.

JIMMIE VAUGHAN: The world misses his music, but I miss my brother.

EPILOGUE

Jimmie Vaughan Reflects on His Brother

Stevie's story is about growing up in Texas and the South—America—a place that is not perfect, but it's one that gives you the freedom to discover what you like, what you think is cool, and to connect with it and become a part of it. It's about finding yourself and expressing who you are. It's about the love of music—Slim Harpo, Muddy Waters, Lightnin' Hopkins, Jimmy Reed, and Jimi Hendrix. It's about falling in love with music and discovering the way to express your true nature through music.

People express themselves through painting or writing or music because they *have* to. Many of the people we grew up with in Oak Cliff are dead or in jail, and I'm not sure Stevie or I would have been any different if we hadn't found the guitar.

The guitar was Stevie's instrument of liberation, his magic sword. I can't even fathom Stevie without a guitar. It meant everything to him. It took Stevie around the world. It introduced him to his heroes. It allowed him to express himself so he could speak, so he could have an identity. So he could find out who he was. When Stevie played, his guitar talked and told his story. If you listen, you can hear it. You can hear *him* speaking through his guitar. I know I can.

When he was playing his best, it was like a religious experience, almost. I know what he's going through, because I've been there. I know what it feels like to get hooked up to the "direct link" to whatever it is. I know it sounds deep, but for guitar players, it *is* deep. When you are inspired

Brothers *(Courtesy Jimmie Vaughan)*

like that—when the temperature is right or whatever it is—everybody knows. When other people hear somebody on that wavelength, they get it, too. Because it's *real*. And if it ain't real, you know it, too. You can't fool the audience.

Stevie's personality comes through in his playing, and that's what drew people to him. It's just straight feeling; it's all from the heart. If you could take your emotions and put them on the table, and let everybody come and pick them up, that's what it would be.

Stevie worked very hard at what he did, but his main thing was that he just loved to play the guitar, and it showed. It was a *completely* natural thing. He got the chance to express who he was through his instrument, and he took it. And that's why Stevie got over with so many people.

I'm still amazed at the impact Stevie had and is still having to this day. I believe it's because of the purity and simplicity of his message: find out what you love, and *do it*. That's the message he was sending out into the world.

AFTERWORD

It is so hard to capture in words what my relationship with Stevie Ray Vaughan means to me. He came into my life twice, both at times when I needed him most, though it wasn't so obvious to me the first time.

That was in the spring of 1970, just after I left Johnny Winter. As I was walking into a club in Dallas, I heard this guitar playing, and I knew from those very first few notes that I was hearing something truly great. The spirit Stevie poured into it shined right through—that distinct, one-of-a-kind inner dynamic. I soon discovered that along with his incredible playing ability, he was also a very humble and sweet person.

Our friendship grew as we began playing together in Blackbird and Krackerjack, but when the latter split up, we went our separate ways. My addiction to drugs destroyed my life. For five years, I was completely lost. As I was finally making my way back to playing music, I happened to see Stevie at a Houston club and I had an epiphany. I knew I belonged onstage with him, which I told him that night. By the first week of January 1981, we were back together, and over the next ten years, Stevie became the closest friend I've ever had.

Playing with Stevie night after night was such an inspiration. He always played like he was pouring his life out, finding that one spot inside himself to draw the energy from every show. There is a timeless quality to all of the best music, which I think is undeniable in Stevie's playing. Every time we walked onstage to play, everyone was expected to give it everything they had. We always let the music be our guide; you listen, and you follow where it's taking you. We knew that if we did that, we could do no wrong. So often, Stevie showed us the way, and we followed.

Playing with Stevie in Double Trouble was the height of my musical life. The chemistry we had as a band made it feel like one plus one equals five. It was all about the underlying attitude and the feeling that drove all of that, which was the love for the music, the love for each other, and the common goal that we shared. We were all reaching for the same level of musical fulfillment. Playing music is a spiritual experience, which should be approached with reverence. It validates my very existence. And very often, we got to that place, which was the most beautiful feeling I ever could have imagined.

Stevie approached sobriety with the same intensity, passion, and dedication. He struggled for so long, but when he finally made a change, he changed completely, with every ounce of energy and unerring dedication. By working so hard to pull himself up—to give himself the love and attention he needed to heal himself—he also was able to turn that love toward so many others that were in need. He set an example for living a sober life on the highest level, just as he did for playing music, and for being a compassionate, caring human being toward his fellow man.

Stevie showed all of us what it was to reach down into one's heart and soul—into one's life—and communicate the feeling of love through the guitar on a deep, spiritual level. Reaching people and sending them blessings was really what he was after, and he was successful in his goal. He spoke to and inspired millions of people with his music and continues to do so today. Everything Stevie did turned to gold. I thank God every day for sending me Stevie Ray Vaughan.

—*Tommy Shannon, Double Trouble bassist*
Austin, Texas

ACKNOWLEDGMENTS

We are humbled and honored to tell the story of Stevie Ray Vaughan and did our very best to capture the man and the musician. In doing so, we were helped beyond description by hundreds of people, including those who knew Stevie the best and cared about him the most. Thank you for trusting us to try and uncover and illuminate the real person.

It isn't easy for Jimmie Vaughan to talk about his brother and there are no words to suitably say thank you for his desire to help us tell the story as accurately as possible. Anyone who's seen Jimmie over the years in the Fabulous Thunderbirds, or fronting his Tilt-a-Whirl band or organ trio knows that he always plays the perfect note and never anything extra. The way he plays guitar is a true reflection of his personality, which makes him such an insightful commentator.

The stories of Chris Layton, Tommy Shannon, and Reese Wynans—Double Trouble—form the beating heart of this book. They are the people who knew Stevie best. Chris and Tommy followed the road from broken down vans to stardom, from the edge of death to the height of clean living and the depth of despair in Alpine Valley. We are forever grateful to all three of them for opening up to us so completely, over so many years, and for so many countless hours of talking both on and off the record.

Thank you to everyone who spoke to us and whose words were used in this book: Larry Aberman, Gregg Allman, Carlos Alomar, Susan Antone,

Cidney Cook Ayotte, Lou Ann Barton, Marc Benno, Ray Benson, Bill Bentley, Al Berry, Lindi Bethel, Doyle Bramhall, Doyle Bramhall II, Cutter Brandenburg, Denny Bruce, Bill Carter, Linda Cascio, Eric Clapton, W. C. Clark, Roddy Colonna, Bob Clearmountain, Rodney Craig, J. Marshall Craig, Robert Cray, Tim Duckworth, Ronnie Earl, James Elwell, Denny Freeman, Jim Gaines, Greg Geller, Billy F. Gibbons, Mindy Giles, Bob Glaub, David Grissom, Warren Haynes, Alex Hodges, Bert Holman, Ray Wylie Hubbard, Bruce Iglauer, Dr. John, Edi Johnson, Eric Johnson, Steve Jordan, Mike Kindred, Albert King, B. B. King, Russ Kunkel, Janna Lapidus LeBlanc, Chris Layton, Huey Lewis, Terry Lickona, Barbara Logan, Andrew Long, Mark Loughney, Richard Luckett, René Martinez, Tom Mazzolini, John McEnroe, "Pappy" Middleton, Steve Miller, Richard Mullen, Jackie Newhouse, Derek O'Brien, Donnie Opperman, Joe Perry, Scott Phares, Shawn Phares, Joe Priesnitz, Mark Proct, Bonnie Raitt, Diana Ray, Mike Reames, Skip Rickert, Nile Rodgers, James Rowen, Daniel Schaefer, Paul Shaffer, Lee Sklar, Al Staehaley, John Staehaley, Tommy Shannon, Mike Steele, Jimmy Stratton, Angela Strehli, Joe Sublett, Carmine Rojas, Gus Thornton, Jim Trimmier, Rick Vito, Don Was, Mark Weber, Pat Whitefield, Brad Whitford, Ann Wiley, Gary Wiley, Reese Wynans, and Connie Vaughan.

Jimmie's team of Cory L. Moore and Sean McCarthy were of huge help along the way and much of what we were able to accomplish would not have been possible without them.

We aimed for the book's art to be as thorough and dynamic as the words and our quest to do so was greatly aided by the people who allowed us to use their photos, snapshots, booking calendars, tour itineraries, postcards, etc., including the Vaughan and Cook families, Donna Johnston, Joe Priesnitz, Robert Brandenburg III, Janna Lapidus, Gary Oliver, Skip Rickert, Barbara Logan, Chris Layton, and Tommy Shannon.

An incredible array of pro photographers worked with us to make the impossible possible. Deep thanks to Jay Blakesberg, J. Watt Casey, John Durfur on behalf of his late wife Mary Beth Greenwood, Tracy Anne Hart, Ken Hoge, Andrew Long, Jonnie Miles, Kathy Murray, Mark Proct, Agapito Sanchez, Jimmy Stratton, and Kirk West.

Others who were helpful in ways big and small, oftentimes pointing us toward amazing art or introducing us to crucial people include: the fine folks at the Austin History Center, Steve Berkowitz, John Bionelli, Michael Caplan, Joan Cohen, Roger "One Knite" Collins, Mural Cook, David Cotton, John Cruz, Adam DePollo, Sam Enriquez, Buddy Gill, David Gomberg, Anand Giridhardas, Dayton Hare, Alan Haynes, Craig Hopkins, Beverly Howell, John Jackson, Zana Bailey-King, Robbie Kondor, Lance Keltner, Eric Krasno, Betty Layton, Larry Lange, Steve Leeds, Marc Lipkin, Greg Martin, Vicky Moerbe, Mark Murray, Wayne Nagle, Rob Patterson, Priya Parker, Jack Pearson, Tom Reynolds, Art Rummler, Joe Satriani, Will Schwalbe, Chris Scianni, Kumi Shannon, Ken Shepherd, Jim Suhler, Morgan Turner, Rick Turnpaugh, Jimmy Vivino, Kirby Warnock, Steve Wilson, and Woudie Wu.

Deepest thanks to Robert Brandenburg III for allowing us to quote and adapt from his father Cutter's memoir, *You Can't Stop a Comet*. The inside story of Stevie Ray Vaughan could not be properly told without Cutter's input.

Our agent David Dunton is the best in the business and he shepherded this from idea to completion. Marc Resnick at St. Martin's is always a pleasure to work with, an editor who sees the big picture, offering encouragement, support, and enthusiasm. Thank you also to Hannah O'Grady, Kathryn Hough, Paul Hochman, Martin Quinn, and everyone at St. Martin's for believing in this book and doing so much to bring it to life and get it out to people.

Thank you to Damian Fanelli, Jeff Kitts, and everyone at *Guitar World*, home to both of us in many ways for many, many years. Before all of them, there was our good friend and mentor Brad Tolinski, who assigned both of us so many great Stevie Ray stories and helped us edit and formulate them. He also gave an earlier version of this book an incisive read which helped to make it much better.

We give thanks to each other—we were good friends before this project and that friendship has only grown. Our occasional butting of heads only resulted in a better book.

Both of our families had to share us not only with Stevie Ray Vaughan for many years, but with music forever. Thank you to our wider families and especially to Rebecca Blumenstein, Jacob, Eli, and Anna Paul and to Tracey, Rory, and Wyatt Aledort. We're nothing without you. Our parents nurtured us and encouraged us to pursue our artistic dreams. Thanks always to Robert and Marilyn Aledort and Dixie and Suzi Paul.

Thank you to everyone who's come out to see our bands and to our bandmates in all of them: Andy Aledort's Groove Kings, Alan Paul's Big in China, and our joint project Friends of the Brothers. Support live music!

APPENDIX

Stevie's Gear

Stevie's guitars, November 1985. *(Donna Johnston)*

EARLY GUITARS

MASONITE GUITAR
Given to Stevie for his birthday in 1961, a very inexpensive guitar made of Masonite with gut strings featuring stencils of cowboys, cows, and rope.

1957 GIBSON ES-125T
Inherited from Jimmie.

1951 FENDER BROADCASTER
Inherited from Jimmie.

1963 STRATOCASTER WITH MAPLE NECK
Acquired in 1969.

1963 EPIPHONE RIVIERA
Acquired in a trade for the Broadcaster.

1954 GIBSON LES PAUL JUNIOR TV MODEL

1952 GIBSON LES PAUL GOLDTOP

GIBSON BARNEY KESSEL

1959 GIBSON 335 DOT-NECK
A gift from Roddy Howard, owner of the Continental Club.

TOKAI SPRINGY SOUND STRATOCASTER COPY
A gift from guitar tech Donnie Opperman in 1982.

RICKENBACKER PROTOTYPE STEREO SEMI-HOLLOW GUITAR

PRIMARY GUITARS

1962/3 SUNBURST FENDER STRATOCASTER "PARTS" GUITAR, AKA NUMBER ONE
Known as Number One and First Wife, acquired in 1974 from Ray Hennig's Heart of Texas Music in Austin. Assembled parts from different years: the neck is stamped December '62 and features a "veneer board" rosewood fretboard; the body is stamped '63. *1959* is written on one of the pickups (the reason Stevie often referred to the guitar as a '59).

1962 RED STRATOCASTER WITH THE "SLAB-BOARD" ROSEWOOD NECK, AKA RED

Acquired from Charley Wirz at Charley's Guitar Shop in Dallas in 1984. In 1986, Red was refitted with a knockoff Fender lefty neck, and in July 1990, a new Fender neck was installed after this neck was broken in a preshow accident at the Garden State Arts Center in Holmdel, New Jersey.

CUSTOMIZED YELLOW STRAT, AKA YELLOW

This guitar was sold to Charley Wirz by Vince Martell of Vanilla Fudge; Wirz painted it yellow and fitted it with a single neck pickup before giving it to Stevie in the early '80s. The pickup cavity had been routed out, so the guitar was virtually hollow inside. This guitar was stolen in 1987 and has never been recovered.

1963/64 NATURAL FINISH STRATOCASTER, AKA LENNY

A gift from his wife, Lenny, in the early '80s. It was stripped down to the natural wood and features a brown stain as well as a butterfly tortoiseshell inlay in the body. The guitar originally had a neck with a rosewood fretboard, but it was soon replaced with a maple neck that was a gift from his brother, Jimmie. This was Stevie's only maple-neck Strat.

1961 WHITE STRATOCASTER WITH ROSEWOOD NECK, AKA BUTTER OR SCOTCH

Acquired in the fall of 1985 during an in-store appearance. The non-original wood-grain pickguard was made specifically for the guitar by Stevie's tech René Martinez.

HAMILTONE CUSTOM STRATOCASTER, AKA MAIN

Billy Gibbons of ZZ Top gave this guitar to Stevie as a gift in 1984. Built by James Hamilton, the guitar features a two-piece maple body with a neck-through-body design. It originally included EMG pickups that were replaced with vintage Fender Strat pickups. The fingerboard is ebony with Stevie's name inlaid in abalone, designed by the artist Bill Narum.

WIRZ STRATOCASTER, AKA CHARLEY

This white Strat "parts" guitar with Danelectro "lipstick tube" pickups was made by Charley Wirz and René Martinez in 1983 and given to Stevie as a gift, with the inscription "More in '84" on the neck plate. It features an alder body and an ebony fingerboard and is a hardtail (non-tremolo) guitar with single tone and volume controls.

1928/29 NATIONAL STEEL
A gift from roadie Byron Barr, who bought it from Charley's Guitar Shop in 1981. Stevie poses with this guitar on the cover of *In Step*.

GUILD JF65-12 TWELVE-STRING ACOUSTIC
Stevie used this guitar, owned by his friend Timothy Duckworth, for his *MTV Unplugged* appearance on January 30, 1990.

GIBSON JOHNNY SMITH
Stevie used this guitar to record "Stang's Swang," and possibly "Chitlins Con Carne" and "Gone Home."

GIBSON CHARLIE CHRISTIAN ES-150
Stevie used this guitar to record "Boot Hill," released on the posthumous disc *The Sky Is Crying*.

FENDER PROTOTYPE 1980 HENDRIX WOODSTOCK STRATOCASTER
This guitar features an upside-down large headstock with two string trees but otherwise was set up like a normal Stratocaster. Stevie allegedly bought the guitar in the summer of 1985 prior to performing at the Riverplace Festival in Saint Paul, Minnesota.

AMPLIFIERS

MARSHALL 1980 4140 2×12 CLUB AND COUNTRY 100-WATT COMBO
Used in the early 1980s, either alone or in conjunction with other amplifiers. Refitted with JBL speakers in the early eighties.

FENDER 1964 BLACKFACE VIBROVERBS
Stevie often used two Vibroverbs at once; this type of amp remained in his arsenal for his entire career.

FENDER 1964 BLACKFACE SUPER REVERBS
Stevie usually used two of these amps along with many others for live performances. Refitted with EV speakers.

DUMBLE 150-WATT STEEL STRING SINGER WITH MATCHING 4×12 BOTTOM
Fitted with 6550 power tubes and four 100-watt EVs. For the recording of *Texas Flood*, Stevie used a single Dumble that was owned by Jackson Browne. Shortly thereafter, Stevie acquired a Dumble of his own.

MARSHALL MAJOR 200-WATT HEAD WITH 4×12 DUMBLE BOTTOM
Fitted with 6550 power tubes and four 100-watt EVs.

FENDER LATE '60S VIBRATONE
This amp is essentially an equivalent of a Leslie 16 and features a spinning baffle inside that creates a vibrato effect. This cabinet can be heard clearly on songs like "Cold Shot" and "The Things (That) I Used to Do." This speaker cabinet was driven by one of the Vibroverbs.

PEDALS

IBANEZ TUBE SCREAMER
Stevie started with the original TS808 but, according to guitar tech René Martinez, he used just about every type of Tube Screamer at one point or another, including the TS9 and TS10 Classic.

VOX WAH
Stevie preferred original '60s Vox wahs.

VINTAGE DALLAS-ARBITER FUZZ FACE
Later modded by César Diaz.

TYCOBRAHE OCTAVIA

ROGER MAYER OCTAVIA

UNIVIBE UNIVOX FM-NO 49.5
Used briefly.

CUSTOM-MADE SPLITTER BOX
Featured one input and six outputs to send his guitar signal to six different amplifiers simultaneously.

MXR LOOP SELECTOR
Stevie used this pedal when playing live in order to take his Tube Screamer in and out of his signal chain.

ROLAND DIMENSION D
Used in the studio during *Texas Flood* and other releases for a subtle chorus-type effect, this can be heard clearly on "Mary Had a Little Lamb," "Texas Flood," and "Pride and Joy." "One effect that Stevie liked to use when we mixed *Texas Flood* was this really obscure Roland delay/chorus that gave a little bit of a *growl* sound," says engineer/producer Richard Mullen. "It was a stereo device that created phas-

ing effects, which you can hear on the solo to 'Mary Had a Little Lamb' and the end solo on 'Pride and Joy.' During the mixdown, Stevie sat at the board and brought that effect in and out as the song progressed. He used the same effect on *Couldn't Stand the Weather*, too."

FENDER MEDIUM PICKS

Stevie preferred using the back, or "fat" end of the pick.

EARTH III MUSIC NOTE STRAPS

Made by the Music Note Strap Co., started in the late '70s by Richard Oliveri in Staten Island, New York.

STRINGS

GHS Nickel Rockers gauged .013, .015, .019, .028, .038, .058—tuned down one half step (low to high: Eb, Ab, Db, Gb, Bb, Eb), akin to Jimi Hendrix. In his last few years, he switched to .011, .015, .019, .028, .038, .054.

INDEX